| Hole | | | | Hole | | | |
|---|---|---|---|---|---|---|---|
| 1 | 252 | 4 | 3 | 10 | 157 | 3 | 3 |
| 2 | 418 | 5 | 4 | 11 | 394 | 5 | 4 |
| 3 | 359 | 4 | 4 | 12 | 436 | 5 | 4 |
| 4 | 329 | 4 | 4 | 13 | 333 | 4 | 5 |
| 5 | 435 | 5 | 5 | 14 | 388 | 4 | 5 |
| 6 | 364 | 4 | 4 | 15 | 150 | 3 | 3 |
| 7 | 413 | 5 | 4 | 16 | 421 | 5 | 4 |
| 8 | 125 | 3 | 3 | 17 | 436 | 5 | 5 |
| 9 | 410 | 5 | 4 | 18 | 422 | 5 | 6 |
| Total | 3,105 | 39 | 35 | Total | 3,155 | 39 | 39 |

X Holes Won  
O „ Halved  
— „ Lost  

Total 18 Holes : 74  
Deduct Full Handicap  
Result ... Nett Score „  

Signed *C. B. Hocy.* (Scorer)

*Aerial view, 1930, with amateur course record*

# North Hants Golf Club Centenary History 1904–2004

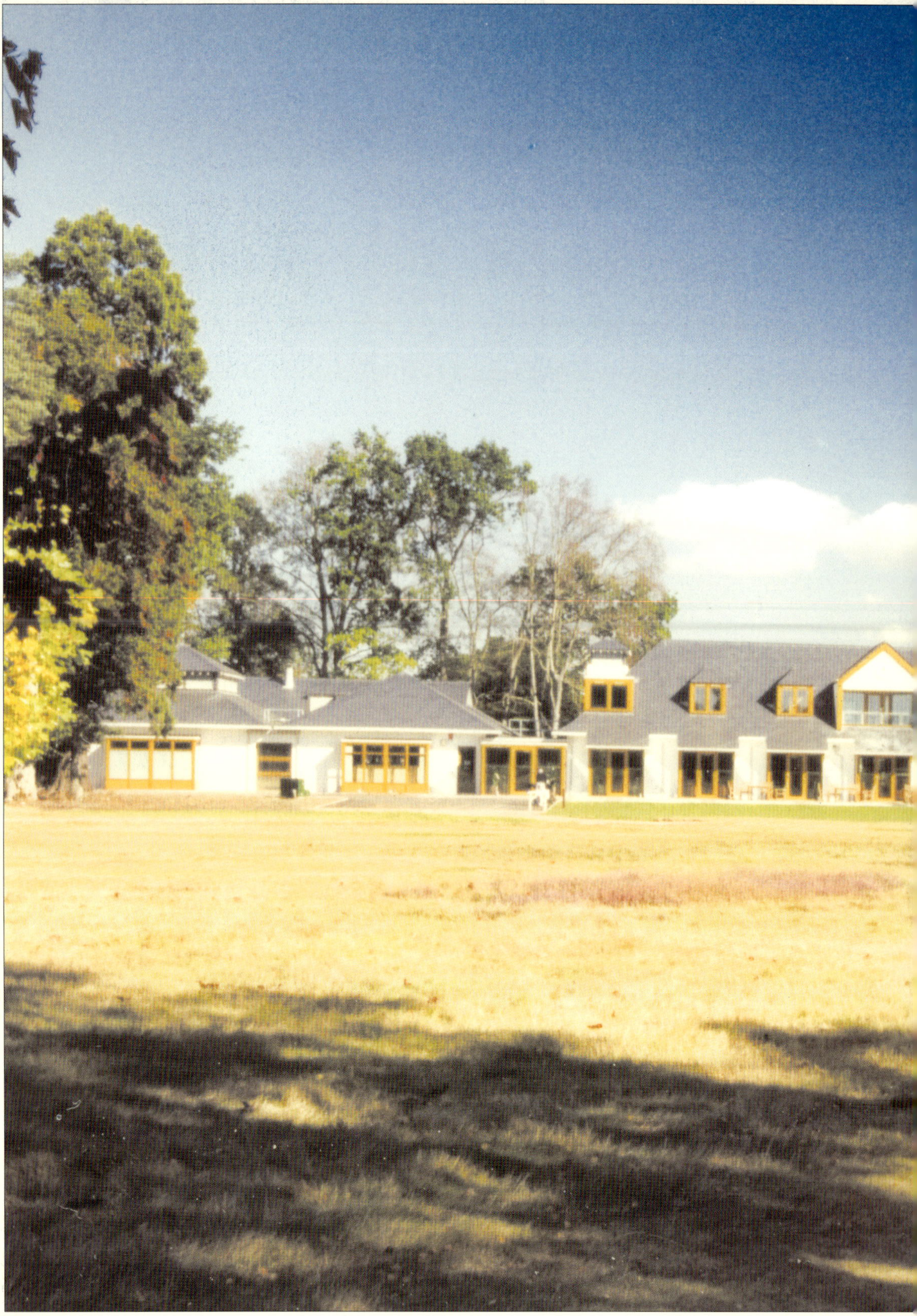

# North Hants Golf Club
# Centenary History
# 1904–2004

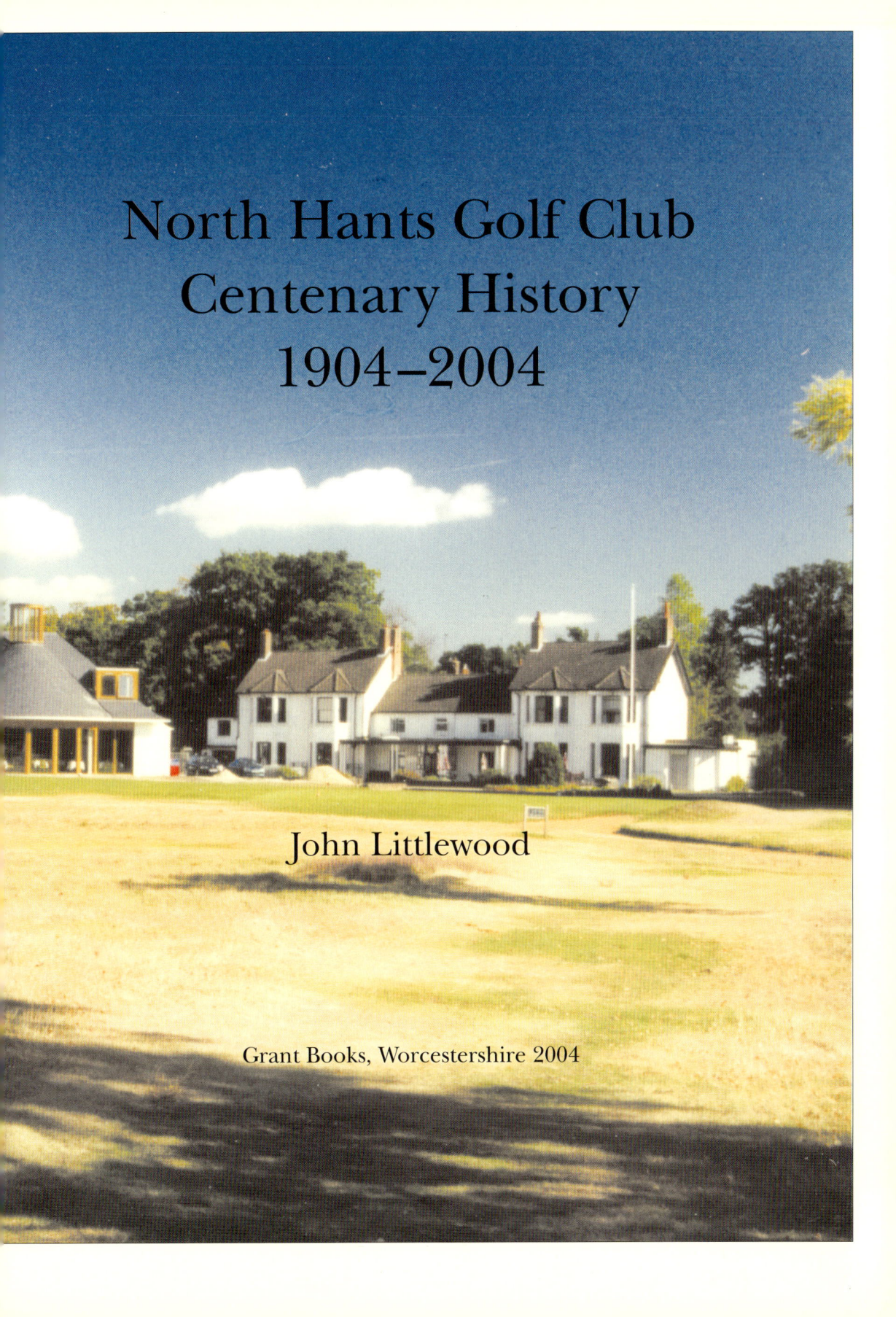

John Littlewood

Grant Books, Worcestershire 2004

First published 2004

Copyright © North Hants Golf Club

ISBN 0 907186 51 3

All rights reserved.

No part of this publication may be
reproduced, stored in a retrieval system or transmitted
by any means, electronic, mechanical, photocopying, recording
or otherwise without the prior permission
of the publishers.

*Other books by the author:*
The Stock Market: 50 Years of Capitalism at Work
Labour and the Stock Market
The President's Putter – 75 Putters: A Statistical Analysis
Oxford & Cambridge Golfing Society 2002

*Contributor:*
The Amateur
The O&CGS: 100 Years of Serious Fun

Typeset in 11 on 13 point New Baskerville
and printed in Great Britain by
**Hughes & Company**
Kempsey, Worcestershire, England

Published by
**Grant Books**
The Coach House, Cutnall Grteen,
Droitwich, Worcestershire WR9 0PQ
www.grantbooks.co.uk

# North Hants Golf Club
# Centenary History
# 1904–2004

Published in a limited edition of 1000 copies
of which the first 45 copies are the President's Edition

## John Littlewood

Grant Books, Worcestershire 2004

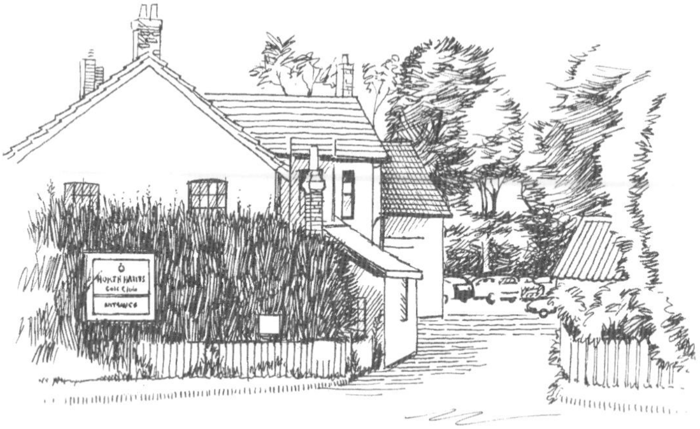

# Contents

| | | |
|---|---|---|
| Foreword by Major General Pat Kay | | ix |
| Acknowledgements | | xi |
| *One* | The Formation of the Club and the Early Years | 1 |
| *Two* | The Golf Course and the Early Golfers | 16 |
| *Three* | Between the Wars 1918–1939 | 26 |
| *Four* | War and Peace 1939–1950 | 58 |
| *Five* | The Prime of Reginald Pearce 1950–1960 | 71 |
| *Six* | Golfing Peaks 1960–1970 | 87 |
| *Seven* | Special General Meetings 1970–1979 | 98 |
| *Eight* | Railroad Heath 1980–1995 | 117 |
| *Nine* | Justin Rose | 140 |
| *Ten* | The Hampshire Hog 1957–2003 | 153 |
| *Eleven* | New Holes, New Clubhouse 1995–2004 | 162 |
| Appendices | | 183 |

NORTH HANTS GOLF CLUB
1904 — 2004
CENTENARY

# Foreword

by Major General Pat Kay

IT IS A great privilege to write the Foreword to John Littlewood's history of the North Hants Golf Club. I first became acquainted with the Club in 1935 when I played on the course in the school holidays as a junior member.

The Executive Committee did well to invite John to write the history. A golfer of proven ability the game runs in his veins. He has a vast knowledge of the Club and of its people, having joined as a junior member in 1951. He has been the Gold Medalist twice and when the Captain's Prize was a knockout, he contested the final on eight occasions, winning four times. He was a Blue at Oxford in 1958 and 1959, being captain in the second year and thereafter played for several years for the Berks, Bucks and Oxon county team. He is also an accomplished author, having published in 1998 a history of the post-war London stock market. He has drawn together all the various aspects of the Club's first hundred years and has written a fascinating book, rich in information, which will surely be of absorbing interest to everyone who reads it.

He describes how the Club has evolved from its earliest days when it aspired to provide the ethos of a gentleman's club and to attract members not only from the vicinity of Fleet, but also from many living in London. As well as golf the Club provided tennis and croquet on lawns of the highest standard. Dinner was served in the clubhouse on most nights of the week and a number of bedrooms were available for members to stay overnight. This concept of a somewhat exclusive club lasted through the 1920s and 1930s when the membership also began to include a strong army presence which was to remain for three or four decades. In the aftermath of the Second World War the Club began to change direction and to open its doors to a wider membership. Tennis and croquet were discontinued and the practice ground established where the lawns had been.

The history describes the ongoing development of the course since it was first laid out by James Braid in 1904 and substantially altered by H.S. Colt in 1913. It contains much information about the members who have reached a particularly high golfing standard or who have brought distinction to the Club by their achievements. It records the feats of Miss Doreen Fowler who won the English Women's Amateur Championship in 1925 and was an English International from 1923–1929, and of Miss Molly Wallis, as she then was, who won the same Championship in 1947 and was captain of the England team in the Home Internationals. Recorded also are the home victories in the Hampshire Hog of Tony Duncan, Tim Koch de Gooreynd, David Blair and Justin Rose and in the Hampshire Rose of Heather Clifford and Jenny Pool, as are the successes of Tique Lock, Stuart Murray, Tim Koch de Gooreynd, Richard Johnson, Gwen Morrison and Heather Clifford in the Hampshire County Championships.

Throughout its existence the Club has been closely linked with the Elvetham Estate and the Anstruther-Gough-Calthorpe family. The various lease negotiations with the Estate and the goodwill and generosity extended to the Club over many years by Sir Fitzroy and Dame Rachel are recounted. The false rumour that the Executive Committee turned down an offer to buy the Club for £8,000 in 1958 and the fateful rejection of the offer from Sir Richard Anstruther-Gough-Calthorpe to sell the freehold for £160,000 in 1979 are comprehensively covered. Also included are the successful negotiations with the Estate from 1990–1998 over the Railroad Heath development which ensured the long term future of the Club.

Separate chapters are devoted to the Hampshire Hog, started by Reg Pearce in 1957, and to Justin Rose, undoubtedly the most outstanding golfer to have emerged from North Hants. How splendid it would be if the Centenary year were to be marked by Justin's inclusion in the European side for the 2004 Ryder Cup.

Many anecdotes are included about personalities, some a trifle eccentric, whose reputations were bywords in their day, and also about incidents and events which have taken place. The names of the many people, both members and staff, who have contributed to the well-being of North Hants over its one hundred years, making it a Club of distinction and excellence are deservedly included.

A feature of the Club has been the readiness of members to offer themselves for election to the Executive Committee with a view to becoming office bearers in due course. Other members have readily placed their professional expertise at its disposal. It is strongly to be hoped that as the Club enters its second century, the desire of members to give something in return for the privilege and pleasure of membership will in no way diminish.

When you have read this excellent book you will, I am sure, feel a deep sense of gratitude to John Littlewood for the great skill, industry and care which he has devoted to it.

# Acknowledgements

I FIRST THANK Brian Gallagher, captain in 1998, and Eric Carpenter, chairman of the Centenary Committee, for inviting me to write this Club history. I was both honoured and delighted to be given this opportunity because North Hants Golf Club has played such a dominant role in my golfing life since I first joined the Club in 1951 as a junior member.

The Club has relatively good written records. Annual accounts and Club leases are complete from the beginning. Executive Committee minutes run from 1923 onwards. There are some wonderfully detailed competition and match records which begin in 1904 and run until 1967, whereupon there is an inexplicable and unwelcome gap for twenty years before they start again in 1987. The one particular disappointment is the absence of any plans of the course laid down by James Braid in 1904 and the extensive alterations made to it by Harry Colt in 1913.

I am especially grateful to Pat Kay for his diligence in gathering together and sorting so much of the research material into the early years of the history of the Club and for his help and encouragement throughout. His early work was an invaluable source for me when I began to write the Club history.

I would like to thank Eric Carpenter for the various sketches that add variety to the pages of the book and in particular his representation of the inter-war tennis courts and croquet lawns. Pat Kay and the late Peter Breedon have been most helpful in guiding me through the workings of the Environment Committee and similarly Derek Skillin has helped me with the Development Committee. I thank H.G. Frew, the archivist of Prestwick Golf Club, for his background information on the Whigham brothers who featured in the opening decade of the Club's history. I thank the magazine, *Golf Weekly*, for providing photographs of front covers of *Golf Illustrated* for inclusion in the history.

Many members, former members and friends have helped with background information, memories, comments and photographs. In particular,

I thank Robert Alexander, Michael Armstrong, Alison Birkenhead, Charles Churchill, Olga Colthurst, Frank Deighton, Charles Donovan, Geoffrey Glynn-Jones, Roy Goodliffe, Nick Green, Hunter Greig, Archie Hunter, David Hunter, John Lidstone, Bill Maclay, Robin Mallinson, James G. McCormick, Philip Mitchell, Mary Morrison, Michael Mounce, Ann Murch, Ronnie Nightingale, Freddie Parsons, Geoffrey Pearce, Peter Pimm, Graham Pool, George Porter, Steve Porter, Justin Rose, Sandy Sellors, Ashley Sharpe, Lionel Smith, Nigel Stainer, Peter Stanbrook, Jess Stiles, Di Stock, Molly Thompson, Kevin Williams, Len Woods and Bob Wyatt. I particularly thank Geoff Jennings and Paul Seivers for the many photographs that they have contributed. Finally, I thank Bob Grant of Grant Books for his invaluable advice and guidance along the path leading to the publication of this book.

I have set many of the changes that have taken place during the history of this remarkable Golf Club against the background of changes taking place in golf itself. The Club has mirrored those changes and I hope this aspect adds interest to a history which for me has been both a pleasure and a privilege to write.

*John Littlewood*

*Chapter One*

# The Formation of the Club and the Early Years

IN DECEMBER 1903, a circular was issued to selected residents of Fleet and its neighbouring villages. Distributed on the initiative of a group of founding members, it announced the intention to form North Hants Golf Club and invited applications for membership.

There was an overwhelming response from some 200 applicants and the decision to proceed was taken in the first week of January 1904. The timing of the proposal was impeccable. Golf in England in 1904 was in its infancy, golf courses were few in number and whilst access was still largely dependent upon the railway it was about to give way to the motor car.

Fleet was then a relatively new residential community with a population of some 2,500 and centred round large Victorian houses set in ample grounds occupied by prosperous families and by senior officers from the nearby Aldershot Garrison. It also offered excellent rail access to London and the proposed clubhouse would be no more than a five minute walk from Fleet Station.

There was a captive potential for membership of the Golf Club not only from what would today be described as the upper middle classes, who in England were just beginning to discover golf, but also from serving officers in the huge Aldershot Garrison. They had already developed an interest in golf. The mobility of army life had brought to Aldershot the powerful golfing influence of the Scottish regiments, which had led to the formation in 1883 of what is known today as the Army Golf Club, first built near Wellington's statue before moving close to its present location in 1900.

It was first known as the Aldershot Divisional Golf Club and an early example of the Scottish influence was in 1894 when the famous amateur golfer, F.G. Tait, an officer in the Black Watch, entered from that club to win the very first Hampshire County Championship. Freddie Tait, who won the Amateur Championship in 1896 and 1898, remains to this day Hampshire's most distinguished county champion and his death in action in the Boer War at the age of thirty robbed golf of one of its finest talents.

THE CLUB HOUSE.

# North Hants Golf Club.

THIS CLUB, consisting of a First-Class Golf Links has been formed, and will be opened for Members on 2nd May next. A nine-hole course will then be completed. The 18-hole course will be ready for use early in 1905, and will be equal to any inland course in the country; being, according to Mr. Braid and other first-rate opinions, "most sporting and interesting."

Experience in preparing the Links has proved that the ground—the whole of which has, for years past, been drained and cultivated—possesses the finest natural qualities for the purposes of a Golf Course; the subsoil being Bagshot sand, and the course, even in the wettest seasons, will be fit for play.

In addition to the Golf Links, but quite away from them, in another part of the Property, are first-rate Lawn Tennis Courts and Croquet Grounds, surrounded by well-laid-out Gardens and Pleasure Grounds, with fine trees and abundance of shade.

*The original prospectus published in 1904*

*The Clubhouse – an early postcard*

To serving officers the attraction of North Hants Golf Club was an eighteen hole course on better golfing land than the wet and boggy terrain of the nine hole Aldershot course. The attraction to other local residents was the limited choice and the inconvenience of reaching the few golf clubs then in existence. Within a radius of fifteen miles there were nine hole courses at Hartley Wintney (established in 1891), Farnham (1896) and Hankley Common (1896), but all with small memberships and relatively remote. East Berks, at Crowthorne, had just opened in 1903 and along the railway line, with easy access from London, was a thriving Woking Golf Club (1893), its success mirrored on another railway line from London by Sunningdale Golf Club (1901).

That was the extent of the choice available to aspiring golfers at the time, and these were exceedingly prosperous times in that Edwardian era for the leisured, moneyed and professional classes from which golfers in England would largely be drawn for the next forty years. The membership and style of North Hants Golf Club at the time of its formation mirrored the early history of golf.

The location of the new course was well known to local residents. In 1888, William Bloore of Bond Street, Vauxhall, a successful timber merchant, leased from the Elvetham Estate a farm of some 130 acres, known as Brooke Farm. It included a main dwelling house, two cottages, outbuildings, gardens

*Lord Calthorpe, president 1904-10*

and a pleasure ground. He obtained permission to change the name to The Beeches and as described in the circular "The old Residence, which is large and roomy, is admirably adapted for a Club House; having a long frontage, with fine rooms opening into a verandah". It is photographed in the circular with its many ornate metalled, glazed and timbered Victorian features and it became the subject of a local Fleet postcard.

William Bloore had three cricketing sons and the pleasure ground, which is today the half of the practice ground closest to the Minley Road, was regularly used for cricket. Since the mid-1890s it had been the home ground of Fleet Cricket Club but in 1903 Bloore left the district and the lease of the farm became available. This created a problem for the cricket club, but an opportunity quickly seized by a number of residents of Fleet to develop The Beeches into a golf club. Twelve of them formed a Committee to enter in discussions with Lord Calthorpe with a view to obtaining a lease for the purposes of constructing a golf course.

The Committee included eleven local residents and one from Winchfield. This was an era when the name of the houses was sufficient for a postal address and some of their addresses will be familiar today to residents of Fleet:

| | |
|---|---|
| Charles J. Lacy | *Basingbourne House, Crookham, chairman* |
| Major W.F. Anstey | *Lismoyne, Fleet* |
| Dr. W. Balgarnie | *The Dutch House, Winchfield* |
| Colonel J.L. Bradshaw | *Tullamore, Fleet* |
| Captain J.S. Bridges | *Woodcote, Fleet* |
| The Honorable Ivo Fiennes | *Concordia, Fleet* |
| W.M. Kenrick | *Broome, Fleet* |
| A.J.F. Nugent | *Gally Hill, Crookham* |
| Major H.G.C. Phillips | *Velmead, Crookham* |
| Baron Pontenani | *Lostwithiel, Fleet* |
| S.L. Simeon | *Little Bounds, Fleet* |
| A.B. Watson | *Woodlands, Fleet* |

Captain Bridges and Major Phillips were to be joint honorary secretaries.

## THE FORMATION OF THE CLUB AND THE EARLY YEARS

The names of the founding members are marked today on a plaque on the monolith standing on the site of the old clubhouse. Charles Lacy was a retired banker and five of the members were either retired or serving army officers. Algernon Nugent was a thirty-eight year old wine merchant who later succeeded to the title of Baron Nugent and donated the Nugent Cup for annual competition. Stephen Simeon was Clerk to the House of Commons. Four of the members lived in consecutive houses in Fleet Road, extending from the junction with Church Road towards the station and these included Alexander Watson and the Honorable Ivo Fiennes.

There is a link with Fleet Cricket Club which explains why the Committee was able to move ahead so quickly with the golf club project. The minutes of the Annual General Meeting of the cricket club in January 1904 refer to an offer communicated to the Club by the Honorable Ivo Fiennes that Alexander Watson was willing to make available "the splendid stretch of turf in front of his house for matches during the coming season". This offer "relieves Fleet cricketers of the anxiety caused by the departure from the district of Mr. Bloore". Their early awareness of the dilemma facing the cricket club alerted them to the opportunity to create a golf course.

Ten members of the original Committee (excluding Dr. Balgarnie and Baron Pontenani) made a Declaration of Trust on 18th February 1904. They became lessees of the lease negotiated with Lord Calthorpe, owner of the estate and resident of Elvetham Hall. He had already built a golfing facility for his estate workers which would later become Hartley Wintney Golf Club and was sympathetic to this new project. He became the first president of the Club, a role that was to continue through family succession until 1981.

The ten lessees became guarantors of the payment of the rent and observance of the other terms of the lease which was to run for twenty-one years from 25th March 1904 at an annual rent of £250. They also became ex-officio members of the Committee and during the tenure of the twenty-one year lease they held the "right to veto or alter any resolution passed at a General Meeting or by the Committee".

The financing of the Club was successfully completed by the issue of twenty debentures of £100 paying an interest rate of four per cent. These were taken up by some of the founding members and by others, who all became life members paying no subscription. They were transferable, but only to a person who was suitable for membership of the Club. Allowing for inflation of roughly fifty times, each £100 debenture would be equivalent today to around £5,000 and the total raised some £100,000.

The farm land of The Beeches on which the course was to be built was divided by a belt of trees running along a line roughly visible today, starting from the greenkeeping sheds, passing between the first green and second tee, along the left of the fifth fairway, behind the ninth tee, and across to the seventeenth tee. The part of the farm between this belt of trees and the Minley Road (1st, 9th–13th, 17th and 18th holes today) was parkland used as open pasture, whilst the land to the other side was partly wooded, with open pasture converted in places to strip farming, possibly for growing hops. Its remnants are still evident today from the ripples and ridges in the carry to the second fairway.

Contemporary accounts suggest that the estate was handed over to the Club in fine condition, and there is many a reference to the beauty and attraction of the shrub and vegetable gardens which stood in the triangle formed from the right of the first hole, across to the greenkeeping sheds and along the track back to the clubhouse. Indeed, so well established were these gardens that the leases through to 1946 required their proper maintenance and the regular pruning and replanting of trees.

The founding Committee had previously arranged for the land to be surveyed by the then youthful James Braid, aged thirty-three, and recent winner of the first of his five Open Championships in 1901. He reported that it was "admirably adapted for playing golf" and the area in pasture "would take a very short time to be fit for playing, as the grass which is very fine, requires only cutting and rolling". He marked out nine holes on this part of the land and remarkably promised they would be ready for play in the spring of 1904, with the remaining nine holes to follow by the end of the year.

The circular to prospective members claimed that the course will be "equal to any inland course in the country" and that the ground "possesses the finest natural qualities for the purposes of a Golf Course, the subsoil being Bagshot sand, and the course, even in the wettest seasons will be fit for play".

The grass must have been fescue of the finest quality, because the area previously used for cricket was quickly to become an extensive area of lawn tennis courts and croquet lawns. A report in the *Aldershot News* refers to a total of nine courts being formally opened for play on 1st May 1905, probably eight for tennis, two of which were already in the garden area, and one for croquet.

There are later references to as many as twenty lawn tennis courts made up of three blocks of six and the two in the garden. The accounts of 1912 refer to the relaying of three new croquet courts at a cost of £40. Members today strolling across to the tees on the practice ground might pause and reflect that at other times they would have heard the different sounds of cricket bat, tennis racquet and croquet mallet.

The original prospectus and application form added further temptations to attract potential members. "There is a romantically situated and picturesque lake, upon which it is intended to place boats for the use of

Members" and "It is also proposed to reserve a sufficient plot of ground for Archery".

The construction of the golf course proceeded apace. Within four months of agreeing to form the Golf Club at the January meeting, the first nine holes marked out by James Braid were ready for play and the course was formally opened at 3.30 p.m. on Friday 6th May 1904 by Her Royal Highness Princess Alexander of Teck. She was one of many granddaughters of Queen Victoria and had recently married Prince Alexander of Teck. He was the brother of Mary of Teck, then the Princess of Wales and later to become Queen Mary to King George V. Prince Alexander had just moved into residence at the Royal Pavilion in Aldershot where he had joined the Garrison as an orderly to General Sir John French. Princess Alexander was aged twenty-one at the time of the opening and was later known as Princess Alice, Countess of Athlone, who died in 1981 at the age of ninety-seven.

The opening ceremony was reported in the golf magazines of the day and at length in the *Aldershot News*. It was previewed in the edition on 6th May and fully reported on Saturday 14th May, with two full-length columns and three photographs. The sense of the occasion can be readily appreciated from original prints of these photographs hanging in the clubhouse today.

The preview article referred to the setting of the new Club:

The estate, which the club has acquired, is looking in the best condition. The nine-hole course which the Princess is to open is in the meadow land, which lies nearest the road. The bunkers, which have been erected, are of quite a temporary character. To complete the 18-hole course the ground on the far side of the belt of trees which runs down from the gardens to the railway is being prepared; as it is not of such a uniform contour as the course which is now ready, it will yield much more sport. The gardens, in which are situated several tennis courts, are most picturesque, and the splendid crease in the adjoining meadow, on which the Fleet Cricket Club used to play their matches, has been converted into tennis and croquet lawns. The club will benefit by the care and attention given to the estate in the matter of draining and cultivation by its last tenant, for good play will be possible even in the wettest weather, so far as golf is concerned.

The later report described the day in great detail. The Princess was accompanied by her "handsome and gallant" husband, Prince Alexander, as they drove in horse and carriage from Crookham House, owned by the Honorable Richard Moreton, who was His Majesty's Marshal of the Ceremonies and a member of the Golf Club. Their procession "raised cheers from the many schoolchildren lining both sides of Fleet Road to celebrate a royal visit".

One of the photographs shows the moment of arrival:

The club grounds were looking charming in their fresh spring garb, notwithstanding the lack of sunshine.... the scene was one of colour and brightness. There were many charming dresses and the Princess herself was most becomingly dressed in a dainty costume of heliotrope.

*The arrival of Princess Alexander of Teck for the opening ceremony on 6th May 1904*

*The opening drive*

## THE FORMATION OF THE CLUB AND THE EARLY YEARS

*The croquet lawns – early 1900s*

After a formal welcome, the Princess was the first to sign the pages of an elegant visitors' book "Alice, 6.V.1904", followed by "Alexander George of Teck". There followed a conducted tour of the converted clubhouse, including the ground floor to the right of the hall which was "set apart entirely for the use of male members and includes a comfortable smoking room".

The Princess then proceeded to the first tee to open the links. She was presented by Lord Calthorpe with a driver bearing a gold plate inscribed "N.H.G.C. May 6th, 1904". It was one of a complete set made by J.W. Moore, the first professional to be appointed to the Club, in an era when the prime requirement of a good professional was to be a skilled club maker. The photograph of the Princess addressing her drive does not suggest one entirely at ease with a golf club but as reported in the *Aldershot News* "Mr. Moore placed the ball in position and with the driver the Princess hit off with a good stroke, and was heartily applauded. She then pronounced the links open".

She was next conducted through the winding paths of the gardens to see the tennis courts and croquet lawns, but she then asked to see the links:

The Royal party first went to the road which runs by the side of the belt of trees dividing the nine hole course, which is all that has been completed at present, from the wilder and more interesting land which is being prepared for the full course. They walked nearly the whole length of this to the railway, and then returned across the turf to which, for the present, play will be confined.

After tea in the clubhouse, the Princess departed, having displayed an obvious enthusiasm and interest that must have made it a memorable day, and an especially rewarding occasion for that small group of people whose venture had come to fruition.

Over the following twelve months the final nine holes were completed. No attempt was made to compete with the majesty of the opening ceremony, and on Saturday 3rd June 1905, the occasion of the completion of eighteen holes was modestly marked with a six-a-side match against members of the Caledonian Club.

The Club is fortunate to have in its possession the original 1905 edition of the rules and regulations and membership list sent annually to members. There is also a copy of the 1913 handbook, an almost complete set of annual accounts from 1905 onwards and remarkably detailed competition results dating back to 1905. The minutes of the Executive Committee meetings have only survived from 1923 onwards, but nevertheless a reasonably clear picture emerges of the membership and the running of the Club from its earliest days.

The annual subscription for gentlemen was £4. 4s. 0d. and shortly thereafter increased to £5. 5s. 0d. This was the normal pre-First World War subscription for a decent golf club with eighteen holes, and allowing for inflation is roughly equivalent to £250 today. Initially the rules limited the number of ordinary gentleman members to 300 and ladies to 60, but within a few years these limits had been raised to 500 and 100 respectively.

The handbook sets out entrance fees and subscriptions and lists the names and addresses of individual members in 1905. Membership was made up as follows:

| Category | Number | Entrance Fee | Subscription |
|---|---|---|---|
| Golfing – | | | |
| Gentlemen | 153 | £4  4s. 0d. | £4  4s. 0d. |
| Ladies | 62 | £3  3s. 0d. | £3  3s. 0d. |
| Non-golfing – | | | |
| Gentlemen | 13 | £4  4s. 0d. | £1  11s. 6d. |
| Ladies | 87 | £3  3s. 0d. | £1  11s. 6d. |
| Honorary | 4 | | |
| Total | 319 | | |

The golfing membership was much more widely drawn from the map than today, reflecting the lack of golf courses and the willingness to travel by train to play golf. This diversity is shown by analysis of the addresses of the original 153 gentlemen members:

| | | | |
|---|---|---|---|
| Fleet and Church Crookham | 40 | London | 36 |
| Crondall and local villages | 12 | Caledonian Club | 8 |
| | | Other London Clubs | 10 |
| Basingstoke | 11 | Woking | 4 |
| Winchfield and Hook | 8 | Farnborough | 4 |
| Various | 16 | | |
| Not known | 4 | | |

Access by rail down from London and up from Basingstoke played a key role in attracting members, and was just as significant a factor as living locally. To attract members the Club was able to negotiate with the London and South Western Railway Company for the issue of special cheap tickets to members from a long list of stations. These were set out in detail in the handbook, beginning with 1st, 2nd and 3rd Class returns from Waterloo at 7s.6d., 4s.10d. and 3s.10d. respectively.

For many of the members based in London the new North Hants Golf Club was offering the facilities and lifestyle familiar to those who were already members of a gentleman's club in London and the list above shows several members providing club addresses, in particular the Caledonian Club and the Junior Constitutional Club. This atmosphere of a London club is apparent from some of the rules. The clubhouse was open every day until 11.00 p.m., members entertaining friends to dinner were asked to give notice to the house steward early in the day and eleven bedrooms were available on the first floor for members staying overnight.

There were strict rules about cards. They were allowed only to be played in the Gentlemen's Smoking Room, but not on Sundays. Specific rules included that "No games of chance or hazard shall on any account be ever played, nor shall dice be used in the Club House" and that "The maximum points at bridge shall be Five Shillings per 100 points". The latter suggests a boldness at the bridge table unlikely to be seen at the Club today of playing for £10 or more a 100.

The membership of the ladies more closely resembled that of today. It was largely drawn locally with forty out of sixty-two from Fleet and Church Crookham and in most cases the wives and daughters of gentlemen members. However, ladies were not allowed to play "on Saturday afternoons, or on Sunday unless by special permission of the Committee". The non-golfing members were almost all local residents and presumably tennis

# THE NORTH HANTS GOLF CLUB, FLEET.

**A VIEW OF THE CROQUET LAWNS ATTACHED TO THE NORTH HANTS GOLF CLUB**

THE title of "golf club" seems scarcely comprehensive enough to describe the varied attractions of the delightful resort in North Hampshire which is illustrated in our photographs. An hour's journey on the South-Western Railway plus five minutes' walk brings one to a rural Ranelagh in miniature, a charming reproduction of that type of country club which, though still too rare in England, has become so popular in the United States. The clubhouse is itself a converted private house with bedrooms for the accommodation of members. It is surrounded by the most picturesque of gardens and lawns, and from its windows one looks out towards the south-west over a broad expanse of old park land which now forms the links. Lord Calthorpe is landlord and president of the club.

\* \*

The fine stretch of lawns which adjoins the clubhouse gives ample room for half-a-dozen first-class tennis courts and as many croquet grounds, and the formation of an archery section in the club is already in contemplation. With such exceptional accessories it need hardly be said that the North Hants Golf Club provides for its members an ideal social rendezvous; and to give full scope to this side of the club a limited membership at a reduced subscription admits non-golfing members, ladies or men, to all the club privileges except the use of the links. But while there are means for the enjoyment of so many outdoor pastimes it is the royal and ancient game which constitutes the chief *raison d'être* of the club. And the golf is of the very best.

**THE NORTH HANTS CLUBHOUSE**

The course of eighteen holes lies in the park enclosed on its four sides by woods, to which the eye of even the most concentrated golfer must sometimes wander in admiration Without being hilly the links traverse a pleasantly varied and undulating course whose natural features offer excellent hazards. The trees, happily, concern none but the gravely errant. The turf, though some holes required artificial sowing, is for the most part a sound, well-rooted sod, giving excellent lies and equal to any amount of wear and tear. The subsoil is extremely fine and sandy. After a night's rain the links come up smiling, and "mud golf" is unknown at Fleet. The course was originally laid out by the master hand of James Braid, the Open champion, and under his advice after a return visit some months ago a considerable reconstruction has been carried out.

\* \*

As it stands to-day North Hants is a fine testing course from the first shot to the last. Here accurate hitting will never play second fiddle to mere length. You must often hit far, but you must always hit sure. The long swiper will reap his full reward if he is on the line, but woe betide him if he leave it, for at hole after hole everything depends upon the nice placing of the tee shot. To the player who can pull and slice at will the course is a golfing paradise, but to him who pulls and slices from mere human infirmity it may prove a very inferno. There are four short holes—two full shots and a brace of iron shots. Of the putting one word only—it is your own fault if you miss.

**FOUR WELL-KNOWN PLAYERS WHO ARE MEMBERS OF THE NORTH HANTS GOLF CLUB**
The names, reading from left to right, are : Messrs. W. K. Whigham, O. T. Falk, C. Armytage Moore, and H. Richardson

*Tatler – 7th October 1908*

players in the main. They were dominated by the ladies with rafts of daughters like the five Miss Bullens from Stockton House in Fleet and the three Miss Bonnetts, Miss Edwards, Miss Warburtons and Miss Watsons.

Caddies must have been readily available because the handbook devotes two pages of bye-laws to them, including a prescribed rate of 1s.6d. for eighteen holes or 2s.6d. for thirty-six holes, equal to some £3.75 and £6.25 respectively today. The rules also suggest the nation's love affair with dogs had yet to begin. They were not allowed anywhere on the course, with a breach of this rule incurring a penalty of 2s.6d., and "members bringing dogs with them must have them tied up in places provided for them".

North Hants Golf Club was an ambitious project and perceived by its founders to be rather more than an ordinary golf club. The opening ceremony had been on as grand a scale as could possibly have been arranged. Facilities were offered to attract members from London seeking the ethos of a gentleman's club, including lawn tennis and croquet on grass of the highest quality. The Club is described in another vein in a page from a sporting and country house supplement to the *Tatler* on 7th October 1908 as a "charming reproduction of that type of country club which, though still too rare in England, has become so popular in the United States". In fact North Hants was not a country club in the fullest sense of the word, because it never sought to build a swimming pool. This article continues:

> ... the fine stretch of lawns which adjoins the clubhouse gives ample room for half-a-dozen tennis courts and as many croquet grounds, and the formation of an archery section in the club is already in contemplation. With such exceptional accessories it need hardly be said that the North Hants Golf Club provides for its members an ideal social rendezvous.

The formation of the Club was an expression of the exuberance of that extraordinary Edwardian decade when maps of the world were largely coloured red and anything was thought possible. However, from the very beginning, North Hants Golf Club was beset with a major competitive problem. Little more than a year after the opening ceremony in May 1904, an unwelcome rival appeared on the scene barely a mile away, when Bramshot Golf Club was opened on 24th June 1905. It, too, was an eighteen hole course situated in good golfing country with heather-lined fairways. Its 1st and 18th holes ran alongside the main railway line and the 2nd green nestled in a picturesque setting on the edge of Fleet Pond.

It was designed by the then even more prestigious name of three times Open Champion, J.H. Taylor, and it attracted wide publicity in its early years. It must have been frustrating for North Hants Golf Club to read in the issue of *Golf Illustrated* of 3rd March 1905, before Bramshot had even opened, that "we have great pleasure in saying that it promises to be one of the best in the neighbourhood of London".

Furthermore, Bramshot was uncompromisingly designed only to be a golf club. It moved further into the limelight in 1913 when a new custom-built clubhouse was opened within a few steps of a dedicated request stop on the main railway line to and from Waterloo. Bramshot Halt was one stop nearer to London than Fleet, and being literally on the doorstep of the clubhouse, it created a psychological advantage over the five minute walk to the clubhouse at North Hants. It was a further boost for Bramshot to hold in 1913 the Southern qualifying round of the News of the World Matchplay Tournament, the next most important event in the professional golfing calendar after the Open Championship.

Competition between the two clubs for membership, whether locally or from London, was to be a continuing problem that weakened both clubs and it all too literally became a matter of life or death when Bramshot was closed at the beginning of the Second World War, became overgrown and never re-opened.

The accounts of North Hants Golf Club for the first five years to 1909 report an accumulated shortfall of income over expenditure of £848, or the equivalent of more than £40,000 today. The golfing membership by 1909 had drifted down from 215 to 175, whereas the non-golfing membership had risen from 100 to 142, but the total subscriptions of the latter group came to only £190 compared with £620 from the golfers. In an attempt to attract more golfers the Committee decided in 1910 to suspend the entrance fee.

It is only possible to hazard an interpretation of the bare numbers. It is probable that the lawn tennis and croquet facilities were not paying their way given their much lower subscriptions and the demands they put on the greenstaff to mow and tend the courts and lawns every day. Tensions between the golf and tennis sections often came to the surface in the Executive Committee minutes in the 1920s and 1930s, and they were probably there almost from the start.

However, another problem was becoming apparent. A leading article in *Golf Illustrated* in 1913 began "The multiplication of golf clubs during the last ten years has been phenomenal". It drew attention to the problem of attracting sufficient members at subscriptions which were in any case inadequate to meet the cost of upkeep of a typical "palatial club house and a course constructed by the most famous and up-to-date architect". The very same words could have been written about the recent explosion of new golf courses in the 1990s.

It was a particular problem in the London area and the south-east, where supply was beginning to exceed demand. Much of it had been prompted by an interest in golf arising from a public awareness of the Open Championship deeds of the great golfing triumvirate. Between 1894 and the

## THE FORMATION OF THE CLUB AND THE EARLY YEARS

outbreak of the war in 1914 J.H. Taylor (5), Harry Vardon (6) and James Braid (5) won sixteen out of twenty-one Open Championships, and their influence in a slower moving age was much the same as Tony Jacklin's later influence in the 1970s following his victories in the Open and the US Open.

So many new courses had been built that clubs everywhere were suspending entrance fees and struggling to attract enough members to cover running costs. North Hants faced further competition for membership from several new clubs formed within easy distance by motor car or railway in the years leading up to the First World War. These included Hindhead (1904), Basingstoke (1908), West Hill (1909), Worplesdon (1909), West Surrey (1910), Swinley Forest (1911) and Camberley Heath (1914).

Nevertheless, despite this surfeit of golf courses and tough local competition, North Hants brought its financial position into balance from 1910 to 1914, and by 1913 a surviving handbook shows that the number of golfing members had risen to 239 gentlemen and 113 ladies. Furthermore the Club continued to attract members resident in London, of whom there were now eighty-four. The Club was enjoying success, financial stability and favourable prospects but, as will be seen in a later chapter, everything was about to come tumbling down with the outbreak of the Great War, as it came to be known. The war was to have a devastating effect on the Club's finances over the next five years.

*Chapter Two*

# The Golf Course and the Early Golfers

W<small>E HAVE</small> a reasonable profile of the early membership but little knowledge of the original layout of the golf course. Sadly, there is no plan in existence of the eighteen holes designed by James Braid, but there is a card of the original course in the 1905 edition of the rules and regulations issued to members. The importance of this is that extensive alterations were made to the course in 1913 by another famous golf architect, H.S. Colt, and cards of the course in existence from the 1920s reveal significant differences from the card of the original Braid layout.

What we do know from the annual accounts is that as early as 1908 a further £260 was spent on the "costs of improvements to the Course, as well as structural alterations to the ladies' room and professional's shop" and that this sum was "provided by private subscription amongst the members". The article in the *Tatler* mentioned in the last chapter refers to James Braid and "under his advice after a return visit some months ago a considerable reconstruction has been carried out". The article refers to "four short holes – two full shots and a brace of iron shots", whereas the original card of the course had only three, as did the later card after further alterations in 1913.

Whereas the 1905 card of the course records a total length of 5,500 yards, *Duncan's Golfing Annual* for 1909/1910 states 6,003 yards and the difference probably reflects these changes. The same Annual describes the course "The soil is light, and play is possible immediately after the severest rain. The hazards are heather interspersed with gorse, water, and sand bunkers". The advantage of a sandy sub-soil was much greater then than it would be today, because drainage techniques were primitive and the mud thrown up by worm casts made for appalling winter conditions on courses built on clay and loam soils. The article in the *Tatler* refers to the pleasing absence of "mud golf" at Fleet.

It is unfortunate that no Committee minutes have survived prior to 1923. As a result there is no written record of why the decisions were taken to make improvements to the course in 1908 and to redesign it in 1913. However, there is a likely explanation which carries with it some uncanny echoes today. Although the word would never have been used at the time the problem was that new technology was making a nonsense of the layout of the typical golf course.

The particular development was the American invention in 1902 of the rubber cored golf ball, known as the Haskell ball. Its design was further improved and within a few years it replaced the gutta-percha ball or gutty then in use. Bernard Darwin, the famous golf writer, later wrote that "There was nothing perhaps so fraught with fundamental change to the game as the sudden bursting on the world of the Haskell ball at Hoylake in 1902". Contemporary accounts suggest the advantage in length of the new ball ranged from twenty to forty yards with the driver, gained primarily because the rubber cored ball ran so much further after landing than the more inert gutta-percha. This would have been particularly noticeable on the fast running fescue fairways of courses built on Bagshot sand.

With hindsight the timing of the Club's formation, which seemed impeccable at the time, was unfortunate in that the course was designed almost at the very moment that the new rubber cored ball was about to make it outdated. Golf courses built up to and around this time were sooner or later forced to make expensive alterations. With North Hants Golf Club at 5,500 yards being typical of many already in existence, it is not surprising that James Braid returned in 1908 to lengthen it to 6,000 yards. In 1910, the Club was the venue of the Hampshire Amateur County Championship.

All of which begs the question whether the relatively inexperienced James Braid was slow to realise how golf course design was in the process of changing to accommodate the longer golf ball. Just as Braid was completing the second nine holes at North Hants to a total of 5,500 yards, J.H. Taylor was laying out a course of 6,220 yards just round the corner at Bramshot. In his earlier years Braid must have been something of a celebrity architect with little time to spare, given his extensive golfing commitments both as a leading playing professional and as club professional at Walton Heath Golf Club.

The course was further extended and extensively redesigned in 1913. It remains a matter for speculation why major alterations were made and why a different architect, H.S. Colt, was chosen. It may have been a need to lengthen and improve the course to compete with the acclaim being achieved by Bramshot. It may have arisen from dissatisfaction with the original design. It may have resulted from a moment of grandeur on the part of leading lights in the Club at the time. More likely, it was simply an attempt to keep up with changing technology. With more uncanny echoes for today, the opening paragraph of an editorial in *Golf Illustrated* on 19th December 1913 raises again the effect of the new rubber cored golf ball on golf courses:

…unless some restriction is imposed, both with regard to the size of the present-day rubber-cored ball and the material of which it is composed, a time will surely arrive when even the most modern of golf links will prove all too short for the prodigious distances to which the American introduction can be propelled with both wooden and iron clubs. Immense sums of money have already been spent in extending courses to suit its requirements…

Nobody really knows why, but the alterations undoubtedly happened and at 6,260 yards the course became a whisker longer than Bramshot. The accounts for the year to 30th April 1914 refer to the cost of "alterations to course" of £424.19s. (including Mr. H.S. Colt's fee of £25.4s.) which is a substantial figure when compared with the original cost of the golf course, tennis courts and croquet lawns of £962. The *Fleet News* carried a brief report of the Annual General Meeting of the Club held on 27th June 1914 "Reference was made to the fact that during the year the golf course had been much improved, great alterations having been carried out under the supervision of H. Colt".

Indeed, the scale of the alterations that took place at North Hants and one of the methods used attracted particular publicity, as reported in the *Golfing* magazine of 31st December 1913:

An interesting experiment in the quick clearance of trees from a golf course was carried out last week at Fleet, Hampshire, where the North Hants Golf Club is making extensive alterations, advised by the well-known links architect, Mr. H.S. Colt.

These alterations necessitate the felling of about a hundred large trees between the eighth and ninth holes, and this work is being accomplished by blasting.

The operations are in charge of a couple of experts from Nobel's Explosives Company, and the demonstrations were entirely successful, whilst providing a very interesting spectacle, which was witnessed by a large number of members, land owners and officers from Aldershot.

The episode even made the front page of one of the national newspapers. The edition of the *Daily Mirror* on 27th December 1913 was made up of four photographs reporting an extraordinary story headed "What would Mr. Gladstone have said? Dynamiting trees for golfers". The photographs show a tree being drilled, charges being placed, an explosion and the result. The headline is a reference to Mr. Gladstone's hobby of tree felling.

The significance of these events is that whilst the course is commonly believed to have been designed by James Braid, it almost certainly owes as much to H.S. Colt. A caricature of personalities of the Club published in *Sketch* in September 1928 has a footnote referring to the golf course as being "originally, in 1904, a nine-hole course: but Mr. H.S. Colt made it, seven years later, one of the most sporting of the many courses he has designed". The *Sketch* writer must surely have been briefed by the Club to emphasise the role played in its design by Harry Colt.

## WHAT WOULD MR. GLADSTONE HAVE SAID? DYNAMITING TREES FOR GOLFERS.

Placing charge in the tree

What an explosion looked like. A large number of people watched the demonstration.

Trees after an explosion.

Drilling a hole for the charge.

There are 100 trees between the eighth and ninth holes on the course of the North Hants Golf Club at Fleet, which are being removed in order that the links may be improved. But there are no old-fashioned woodmen with their axes to be seen, the work is being done by dynamite charges under the supervision of the Nobel's Explosives Company, Limited. Ten were accounted for yesterday, when a piece of roof weighing 40lb. was blown over the heads of the crowd for a distance of 150 yards. The late Mr. W. E. Gladstone's favourite hobby was felling trees. What would he have said to this new and quicker method?—(*Daily Mirror* photographs.)

*Front page story* – Daily Mirror, *27th December, 1913*

There is a further clue in an article written about North Hants in *Golf Illustrated* in January 1951 by J.S.F. Morrison, a member of the Club and a personality who will feature in a later chapter. He begins the article by referring to the course "designed by the great golf architect Harry S. Colt" but then incorrectly refers to the year 1904. As a distinguished golf architect himself, best known for the Burma Road at Wentworth, he would be unlikely to have ascribed the course to H.S. Colt without good reason.

A comparison of the cards of the course show the differences between the Braid and Colt layouts and as it is today:

| Hole | 1905 – Braid Yards | Bogey | Post-1913 – Colt Yards | Bogey | 2004 Yards | Par |
|---|---|---|---|---|---|---|
| 1 | 245 | 4 | 252 | 4 | 214 | 3 |
| 2 | 400 | 5 | 418 | 5 | 433 | 4 |
| 3 | 346 | 5 | 359 | 4 | 489 | 5 |
| 4 | 241 | 4 | 329 | 4 | 300 | 4 |
| 5 | 500 | 6 | 435 | 5 | 443 | 4 |
| 6 | 157 | 3 | 364 | 4 | 377 | 4 |
| 7 | 298 | 4 | 413 | 5 | 422 | 4 |
| 8 | 295 | 4 | 125 | 3 | 122 | 3 |
| 9 | 420 | 5 | 410 | 5 | 423 | 4 |
|   | 2902 | 40 | 3105 | 39 | 3223 | 35 |
| 10 | 173 | 3 | 175 | 3 | 189 | 3 |
| 11 | 300 | 4 | 394 | 5 | 374 | 4 |
| 12 | 128 | 3 | 436 | 5 | 450 | 4 |
| 13 | 330 | 5 | 333 | 4 | 334 | 4 |
| 14 | 250 | 4 | 388 | 4 | 392 | 4 |
| 15 | 475 | 6 | 150 | 3 | 161 | 3 |
| 16 | 324 | 4 | 421 | 5 | 425 | 4 |
| 17 | 200 | 4 | 436 | 5 | 500 | 5 |
| 18 | 418 | 5 | 422 | 5 | 424 | 4 |
|   | 2598 | 38 | 3155 | 39 | 3249 | 35 |
|   | 5500 | 78 | 6260 | 78 | 6472 | 70 |

There is common ground between Braid and Colt for the first five holes, the 9th, 10th, 11th and the 18th, but explaining the whereabouts of the other nine holes is a challenge that members may wish to meet. The Braid design was unusual with the inclusion of a bogey 6 and the three short holes bunched together in the middle of the round.

Whilst the length and alignment of individual holes has been changed from time to time, the Colt layout basically remained until 2001 with the exception of the 4th hole which, following visits by golf course architect Tom Simpson, was reshaped with a new tee in 1929 and then shortened to a par 3 in 1931. It was restored to a par 4 and roughly to its original tee by Donald Steel in 2001. Following his visit in 1929, Simpson added his mark to the course by introducing several new bunkers and tees and some further adjustments to the course were made in the 1930s by Captain L.J. Torrie, a golf architect and a low handicap member of the Club. These are described in more detail in the next chapter.

The Club is fortunate to have detailed competition records of the earliest days, and the decade before the outbreak of the First World War provides a revealing picture of the early days of amateur golf. A pattern of annual competitions was quickly established and many of the cups played for today date back to these early years.

The highlights of the year were the Spring and Autumn Meetings in late May and early October which regularly attracted some twenty to thirty entrants. At the Spring Meeting an eighteen hole medal was played in the morning on handicap for the Founders Cup (established in 1906) and scratch for the Currie Cup (1908), and an eighteen hole bogey foursomes was played in the afternoon. At the Autumn Meeting there was an eighteen hole medal played in the morning on handicap for the Calthorpe Cup (1905) and scratch for the Gold Medal (1905), and a separate eighteen hole bogey competition in the afternoon for the Nugent Cup (1906) which was later divided into two handicap sections with the Hood Cup (1910). The Orman Cup (1907) was presented for the best thirty-six hole handicap aggregate medal scores from the two meetings.

The other principal event was the Captain's Prize (1905), initially a running handicap match play competition played in the winter from October to an indeterminate date early in the new year, but from 1924 played over the four days of Easter. There was also the Lloyd Cup (1908), initially a thirty-six hole bogey competition on one day, but quickly reduced two years later to an eighteen hole bogey competition. Regular monthly medals and monthly bogey competitions were held throughout the year with a traditional spoon for the winner. A feature of all these competitions, both for cups and monthly medals, was that any ties were decided by play-offs over eighteen holes. The monthly medals were erratically supported. On many occasions only two or three cards were returned, and from time to time only one card or none at all.

The concept of Spring and Autumn Meetings has now lapsed, but the Founders/Currie and Nugent/Hood combinations still prevail at roughly the same time of the year. The Gold Medal was separated from the Autumn Meeting in 1964 to become a thirty-six hole scratch event. The Captain's Prize lost its distinctive Easter match play character in 1979 when it briefly became a two day aggregate thirty-six hole stableford, before settling down as an eighteen hole stableford on the first day of the Captain's Weekend.

The standard of golf in the early years does not appear to have been very high, but few comparisons are available from other clubs. In all competitions between 1905 and 1914 only twenty rounds of 79 or better were recorded and many a medal competition would list more scores above 100 than below. Scores between 110 and 120 were frequent, with a highest gross score returned in May 1908 of 128 off a handicap of 18.

However, there were a handful of quality golfers whose names appear at different times in the Club records. The 1908 *Tatler* article includes four cigarette card size photographs of "four well-known players who are members of the North Hants Golf Club", W.K. Whigham, O.T. Falk, C. Armytage Moore and H.J. Richardson, and in a "Who's Who" in amateur golf section in *Nisbet's Golf Year Book* for 1914 the names of Whigham and F.V. Hutchings are mentioned as being members of North Hants.

The best golfer of these was Walter Whigham. He twice reached the last eight of the Amateur Championship, first in 1898, entering from Comrie in Scotland at the age of twenty, and again in 1905 entering from Prestwick. He must have been a prize catch for the newly opened North Hants Golf Club, playing off a handicap of plus 3.

He was one of six sons of a Scottish wine merchant and a partner in Robert Fleming, the famous city merchant bank of that name. He and two of his brothers were based in London and members of North Hants Golf Club. One of these was his elder brother, H.J. Whigham, who played off scratch, but only rarely appeared in Club competitions. However, Henry James Whigham could lay claim to having been the most distinguished golfing member in the history of North Hants Golf Club. He won the United States Amateur Championship in 1896 and 1897 and played in the top single for the United States in the inaugural international golf match against Canada in 1898 at the age of twenty-nine. He lived most of his life in the United States where he was a writer and journalist and is distinguished on that side of the Atlantic for having written and published in 1898 the first book on golf instruction, *How to Play Golf.*

Walter Whigham was a regular competitor at North Hants during these early years. He first appeared in the Autumn Meeting in 1905 when, in the inaugural Gold Medal, he was runner-up with a gross 82 to G.M. Archdale who, playing off plus 1, won with a score of 78. This was the first recorded score under 80, presumably setting a new course record. Whigham then returned gross scores of 83, 80, 80 and 80 in successive monthly medals, whilst at the same time winning his way through to the final of the first Captain's Prize in March 1906, when he gained his revenge by crushing Archdale by 7 and 6.

In the July monthly medal Whigham lowered the course record to 77 and went on to win the Gold Medal in October with a score of 83. He continued to return consistently low scores, including a 75 in the Spring Meeting in May 1907, which equalled the course record earlier set up by H.J. Richardson. Nothing further is heard of him after April 1908, except for a sole appearance in 1911 to win the Currie Cup with a gross score of 82. However, the family name was famous in other respects. Another of the six sons, George Hay Whigham, became a wealthy Scottish textiles industrialist and his daughter, Margaret Whigham, became better known as the late Duchess of Argyll.

Of the remaining names mentioned in the well-known categories above, H.J. Richardson played off scratch and golfing annuals show that he held the amateur course record of 74 recorded in November 1907. The same annuals show the professional course record as 66 by James Braid also in November 1907. O.T. Falk was at times scratch or plus 1 and won the Gold medal in 1908 with a score of 84; C.A. Moore won the Captain's Prize in 1910 and shared the Gold Medal in 1913 with 80; and F.V. Hutchings, with the second lowest recorded handicap in the Club of plus 2, won the Gold Medal in 1910 with a 76.

All these well-known golfers lived in London, but there were two other local golfers of note. These were E.J. Dobson, who lived in Cresswell, Fleet and, playing off plus 1, won the Gold Medal in 1911 with 74, and tied for it with C.A. Moore in 1913. In the latter year Dobson also won the Club's scratch lawn tennis singles title. C. Wood was a scratch golfer from Guildford who won the match play Captain's Prize three times in 1908, 1909 and 1911. The appendices will show that the Gold Medal was frequently won with scores between 84 and 86 and in 1907 by a golfer with a handicap of 10.

The ladies' records are complete only from 1905 to 1908. The struggle of the men to break 80 is matched by an equal struggle by the ladies to break 100. In 1906 there were only five cards in the nineties with the lowest at 96, but successive new records were set by Miss B. Partridge of 94, 88 and, in October, 1907, a remarkable 82 off a handicap of 16. At the other extreme the patience of the ladies extended to a return of 150 by Miss G. Chinnock off a handicap of 20 in December 1905.

Miss B. Partridge appears to have been one of several golfing sisters from Kimberley, Fleet, three of whom regularly played in almost every competition. She was clearly the best ladies' player in the early years, becoming the first single figure handicap player, off 9, in 1908. The

*The 3rd green c. 1910*

*The 6th Green c. 1910*

competition book records the result of a long driving competition in the Spring Meeting of 1908 which she won with a drive of 156 yards.

As with the gentlemen, the highlights of the competition year were the Spring and Autumn Meetings, with the Founders Cup played on handicap and the Palmer and Bradshaw Cups played for the best scratch rounds. The Lady Captain's Prize was a running match play event played towards the end of the year and there was a regular monthly medal.

The early records of Club matches are sketchy. Between 1905 and 1908 there are records of matches against Royal Winchester, Twyford & Shawford and Hartley Wintney Golf Clubs and against Winchester College, the House of Commons, Aldershot Army Corps and the Royal Military College, Sandhurst. Matches were six- or eight-a-side over foursomes and singles, with an extra one-quarter of a point for winning the bye. The ladies played matches against Reading, East Berkshire and Guildford Golf Clubs.

The golfing pleasures of these Edwardian years must have seemed timeless to the members of this new burgeoning golf club, but they were about to end abruptly. As the Foreign Secretary, Sir Edward Grey, put it in 1914 "The lamps are going out all over Europe". The competition records show the cancellation of the Autumn Meeting in 1914 but the continuation of monthly medals until April 1915. The next recorded competition is not until April 1919.

*Chapter Three*

# Between the Wars
## 1918–1939

MOBILISATION FOR the First World War denuded the Club of both its membership and its staff and a notice posted in the lobby of the clubhouse in May 1915 listed the names of sixty-four members serving in the forces. Its scale can best be judged by the fall in subscriptions from £1,665 in 1914 to £624 in 1917, and as low as £540 in 1919, suggesting that the membership was reduced by some two-thirds. The same pattern is repeated in the wages paid to the ground staff which fell from £625 in 1914 to £213 in 1917.

The Club struggled to survive and was only able to curb its losses by the generosity of the landlord in foregoing the annual rent of £250 for six successive years. It was also helped by buoyant sales of hay, always a source of some annual revenue, but rising sharply during the war to between £100 and £200 each year from sale to the military authorities. It remains something of a mystery from exactly where the hay was reaped.

The Club was presumably put on little more than a care and maintenance basis during the war and the accounts reveal a picture of serious financial strain. It would have been far worse but for the generosity of the Elvetham Estate in foregoing their rent. This was acknowledged in an introductory paragraph to the 1919 accounts:

The Committee and Members are indebted to Mr. and the Hon. Mrs. Anstruther-Gough-Calthorpe for the great consideration shown to the Club. By their assistance the Club has been placed in a more favourable position than many of the Golf Clubs of the present day.

Elvetham Park was originally enclosed as a 300 acre park in 1403 by licence from Henry IV and in 1535 Elvetham Hall became the home of Jane Seymour, the third wife of Henry VIII. The Estate was later acquired by Sir Henry Gough-Calthorpe in 1759. The original lease with North Hants Golf Club had been agreed in 1904 with Lord Calthorpe, but he died in 1910 and his daughter Rachel Gough-Calthorpe became heir to the Estate. She was married to Fitzroy Lloyd-Anstruther, who upon the death of Lord Calthorpe changed his name to Anstruther-Gough-Calthorpe and became the second president of the Club until his death in 1957. The Honorable Mrs. Rachel Anstruther-Gough-Calthorpe became the landlord and a member of the Club and it was her decision to forego the annual rent during the war years.

From information provided by Brigadier R.A. Nightingale it is believed that the course was used during the war for a purpose that scarcely seems credible today. A long-standing member of the Club since 1957, Ronnie Nightingale will be familiar to many members for his fondness for making eloquent contributions at Annual General Meetings and as founder of the Stoics. He clearly remembers the reminiscences about the First World War of a fellow regimental officer and member in the 1950s, Colonel J.A. Middleton who, in his earlier sporting days, had represented England against Scotland at Twickenham in 1922.

*Sir Fitzroy Anstruther-Gough-Calthorpe, Bt. president 1911-57*

A little known background to that war is the extent to which the huge British Army was still dependent on horses for transport close to the front lines. It is believed that over 600,000 horses were imported from Argentina, Canada and the United States and the majority of these disembarked at Southampton. They were then carried by rail for training and:

> those arriving on the up-line at Fleet were unloaded on the West side of the railway bridge where what remains of an unloading dock can still be seen behind the 17th green. Depot headquarters was located in the clubhouse and in addition to the extensive use of club grounds, animal pickets extended both sides of the B3013 up to Minley Manor.

Another reference is from the diaries deposited in the Imperial War Museum of a Brigadier H.N.G. Watson, who refers to his posting in September 1915 to a unit of 780 mules at Fleet Pond Camp.

There followed the apocryphal but believable story of a newly joined veterinary officer who was seen galloping at speed towards his commanding officer, pulling up, saluting and excitedly reporting that he had discovered some excellent sand pits that would be ideal for jumping practice.

*Alf Hindley with greenstaff, horses and machinery – early 1920s*

Once the war was over the Club quickly recovered its revenue from subscriptions which by 1921 exceeded pre-war levels, but the war had left behind it an aftermath of inflation. Prices and wage rates had roughly doubled over five years, wages for the ground staff of £625 in 1914 rose to £1,077 in 1921. With subscription rates left unchanged, the Club continued to face serious financial pressures and recorded a deficit for ten successive years from 1914 to 1923, at which time the accumulated deficit had reached almost £1,800.

The post-war position became so serious that a Special General Meeting was convened on 4th March 1922 when it was agreed that every effort should be made to ensure that the Club carried on at least until the expiry of the lease in February 1925. The initiative was seized by the captain, Brigadier General O.C. Herbert. Subscriptions were increased to £7.7s.0d. for ordinary members and £5.5s.0d. for lady members and their payment was brought forward from May to January. All members were invited to make donations to help tide the Club over this difficult period and the president, Fitzroy Anstruther-Gough-Calthorpe, continued the generous traditions of the family by opening the donation list, offering to match one-quarter of all other donations and guaranteeing an overdraft up to £250. The appeal was repeated one year later and with further generous help from the president a total of £690 was raised from the members.

Meanwhile, economies were sought in all possible ways. The secretary, Mr. W. Bailey, resigned in early 1923 after fourteen years in office whereupon one of the members, Mr. Fred Dunn, agreed to act as honorary secretary, thus saving an annual salary of £200. In 1924 the Club made a surplus of £324 and with financial health restored there would now follow ten successive years of financial surplus, neatly offsetting the previous ten year sequence of financial deficits.

The shape of the membership of the Club was beginning to change and it was in the late 1920s that the popular image of being an "army" golf club began to take hold. In the years before the First World War the membership was largely civilian, reaching a peak of 227 ordinary men members in 1914 and producing the bulk of the subscription revenue of £1,665. By 1929, subscription income had roughly doubled to £3,284, but the shape of the membership was rather different, with all subscriptions quoted in that unusual currency of the day of guineas, or twenty-one shillings:

|  | *Number* | *Subscription* |
|---|---|---|
| Ordinary Men | 189 | £7. 7s. 0d. |
| Ladies | 150 | £5. 5s. 0d. |
| Military | 55 | £4. 4s. 0d. |
| Juveniles | 35 | £1.11s. 6d. |
| Mess Memberships | 96 | £2.12s. 6d. |
| Non-Playing | 144 | £1. 1s. 0d. |
| Tennis | 41 | £3. 3s. 0d. |
| Croquet | 17 | £3. 3s. 0d. |
| Total | 727 | |

The particular significance of 1929 is that it was the year of the Wall Street crash which was to be followed by a world slump that left its indelible mark on Britain in the 1930s. The famous Wall Street share index, the Dow Jones, rose to a peak in 1929 that would not be reached again for another twenty-five years in 1954. Subscription income at North Hants Golf Club stood at a peak in 1929 that would not be reached again until 1956.

A particular feature in the list is that whereas the Ladies' section had reached its ceiling of 150, the ordinary men membership had declined from its pre-war level to 189. However, if the 151 military and Mess members are added back, a balance is restored and the scale of the army influence is fully revealed. Noticeable also is the generosity of the terms offered to military members, the paucity of the tennis and croquet sections and the extraordinarily high number of non-playing members.

## GOLF CLUBLAND CARICATURES
### PLAYERS ON A COURSE THAT HAS "GROWN UP"! PERSONALITIES OF THE NORTH HANTS GOLF CLUB

Though just outside the Surrey border, this course shares all the well-known attractions for which that county is noted. It was originally, in 1904, a nine-hole course; but Mr. H. S. Colt made it, seven years later, one of the most sporting of the many courses he has designed. It is laid on land leased from Mr. F. H. Anstruther-Gough-Calthorpe, the club president. The club is a boon to officers stationed at Aldershot, who are given special terms as temporary members. It has also nineteen lawn-tennis and four croquet courts.

SPECIALLY DRAWN FOR "THE SKETCH" BY H. F. CROWTHER-SMITH

*Caricatures from the* Sketch *magazine, 12th September 1928*

The new category in the list is the Mess membership. Generous terms were available to the Officers' Mess of regiments stationed locally in Aldershot and nearby. The normal basis was a Mess subscription of £26.5s.0d., or twenty-five guineas, entitling the membership of ten nominated officers, whose names could be changed during the year. In effect, membership of the Club was available to an enthusiastic golfing officer for £2.12s.6d. a year, with all rights of membership except voting at an Annual General Meeting and being allowed only to enter the monthly medal and bogey amongst the Club competitions. It was to meet the latter point that the United Services Cup was presented in 1928 for competition by members who were serving officers. One of the earliest Mess members of the Club in 1927 was a youthful junior officer and dentist who would later become the most senior member of the Royal Army Dental Corps. He was the late Major General Henry Quinlan, Club captain in 1973 and known irreverently in the Club as "top tooth".

In 1929, subscribing regiments nominated a total of ninety-six officers from the Royal Army Medical Corps, Royal Army Service Corps, Royal Corps of Signals, Royal Tank Corps, King's Royal Rifles Corps and Royal Air Force, Farnborough. In other years various regiments would come and go. When these numbers are added to the existing military members it can be seen how widely spread the army influence had become and it was further enhanced by the willingness of the Club to allow regiments to hold their annual meetings at the Club and play matches against other regiments, often on a Saturday or Sunday.

We do not know whether this army influence was deliberately cultivated as a matter of policy or happened out of the need to generate revenues from new sources in the difficult years after the First World War. The only reference to army membership in the 1913 handbook refers to a concessionary green-fee, so the Mess membership must have been created after the conclusion of the war in 1918. It is likely that the large Aldershot Garrison was seen as a captive market offering a steady flow of subscriptions from regimental golfing officers. Other clubs in the area offered special terms to serving officers, but it seems that North Hants Golf Club captured the army membership from Aldershot just as Camberley Heath Golf Club drew membership from Sandhurst.

So began a reputation amongst the golfing public that the membership of North Hants Golf Club was dominated by the Army. It was a reputation still prevalent as recently as the 1970s, long after service privileges had been withdrawn, and even to this day strangers to the Club will occasionally raise the question.

This powerful army presence must have influenced the character of the Club in the inter-war years, introducing an element of exclusiveness and a degree of structured formality. It may also have reinforced a public awareness that North Hants Golf Club was open only to the professional or leisured classes and it was well known that members of a trade should not apply, presumably just as soldiers of the other ranks would not have sought membership.

This observation is no criticism of the Club because the practices of earlier generations should never be judged by the standards of today. There was nothing unusual about the exclusiveness of membership of private golf clubs at the time, particularly in the south of England where golf in the 1920s was an exclusive game played primarily by the public school educated upper middle and professional classes. It was evident even at the highest levels of the amateur game when, for example, in 1926, seven of the ten members of the England international team chosen to play against Scotland were public school educated members of the Oxford & Cambridge Golfing Society.

Whilst membership of the private clubs was exclusive, there were opportunities for the less privileged to play golf at an increasing number of public courses and also from the creation by many private clubs of Artisans' sections. These allowed access with limited playing rights to some famous golf courses in return for a low subscription and an agreed number of hours working on the course, typically filling divots and raking bunkers. At North Hants the question of forming an Artisans' section was discussed by the Executive Committee in May 1931, but it seemed to be influenced mainly by the possibility that a reduction in Land Tax could be obtained and the idea was not pursued.

If it is remembered that the founding members of North Hants Golf Club had in mind to provide the facilities of a London gentlemen's club, then it is not surprising that the early style and membership of the Club would reflect an ethos of rules and conventions that might seem suffocating today. Codes of conduct both on and off the course would have been enforced with a formality that few members today would relish or understand. The Club would have taken pride in its membership in the late 1920s. The founder member, Baron Nugent, had died in 1923 but there were four peers of the realm, Viscount Elibank, Lord Basing, Lord Dorchester and Lord Revelstoke, and a dozen or so Knights.

It was also an ethos in which the army membership would have felt entirely comfortable and the Executive Committee in the 1920s was dominated by army officers, presumably mostly retired after the war. Proceedings were strictly formal and the Committee was made up of the captain and eleven other members, seven of whom were ordinary members, three to represent tennis and one for croquet. A detailed printed agenda for the monthly meeting was circulated to Committee members and, it is assumed, also posted in the clubhouse for information to members.

The minutes of the Executive Committee meeting held on 23rd May 1927 show that it was attended by the captain, F.H. Anstruther-Gough-Calthorpe, by one Lieutenant General, one Brigadier General, four Colonels, one Major, one Captain and a lone civilian. It is likely that sensitivity to rank would have made free and open discussion difficult, but the impression would have been that events were being controlled with military efficiency.

The outcome was often a mixture of the enlightened and the stubborn, particularly with regard to lady members. For example, a Special General Meeting was called for 24th January 1925 to approve various changes to the Rules and to agree the formation of "The North Hants Trust Company Limited" to become the lessee of the new twenty-one year lease negotiated with the Elvetham Estate. This new company would consist of the members of the Executive Committee with a limited liability of £1. This proposal was accompanied by changes to the rules of which the most enlightened, and very unusual for the times, was the decision to allow lady members, and also tennis and croquet members, the right to vote at Annual and Special General Meetings of the Club.

The meeting which approved these changes was chaired by the captain, Sir Herbert Cayzer, who said that this was the only "radical alteration" to the Rules and it would make the Club "very much more democratic". In the event, democracy was not quite fully extended, because another rule stipulated that each member "shall have one vote for every guinea subscribed to the Club". Nevertheless, extending the right to vote to lady members was a radical step in 1925 and the Club was ahead of the suffragettes who first achieved the right for women over the age of twenty-one to vote in the 1929 general election. An interesting detail from the same meeting is that a proposal to change the name of the Club to Fleet Golf Club was rejected.

Two years later, in May 1927, the Executive Committee meeting considered a proposal that its membership should include an ex-officio member of the Ladies' Golf Committee. The outcome was a compromise that a nominee of the Ladies' Golf Committee became an ex-officio member of the House Committee.

However, whilst these really quite far-sighted gestures were being introduced, an Executive Committee meeting in September 1926 carried the proposal that "A notice be put up on the staircase leading out of the Club Hall requesting ladies not to use this staircase" and another meeting in September 1929 obviously wrestled with complexities of a proposal to allow ladies, "accompanied by a man member", to be taken into the Smoking Room, before agreeing to this concession between the hours of 10.30 a.m. and 1.30 p.m.

The influence of the lady members was in some ways stronger in the 1920s than it is today. At the 1926 Annual General Meeting a motion was proposed that the verandah along the front of the clubhouse should be glazed and the smoking room be moved to a smaller room to allow the existing room to be made into a mixed lounge because the "club had 120 lady members, or nearly as many as they had men, and there was no accommodation for joint teas or anything of that sort". The possibility of losing the smoking room produced an apoplectic response from a certain Colonel Harvey who said he was "astounded to hear of such a Bolshevistic motion. This is the best room we have. Don't do away with something which is good for something which is bad".

The fact is that in February 1928 the quota of a maximum of 150 lady golfers was filled and a limited five day membership was introduced. By comparison the quota of a maximum membership of 500 of men golfers was never even remotely approached and their numbers were little higher than the ladies. The membership quotas in the 1920s were more favourable to lady golfers than they are today.

The minutes of the Executive Committee provide many insights into life at North Hants Golf Club in the inter-war years. A coin box telephone was installed in February 1923 and a G.P.O. letter box with a regular collection in May 1930. In December 1929 the gift to the Club of a wireless set was greeted with the same enthusiasm given a few years ago to the installation of a satellite dish to receive Sky television.

The dining room was furnished with the heads of animals brought home from distant lands and the minutes conveyed thanks to one member who lent a tiger's head and a bear's head in 1923 and to another who presented a further three trophy heads in 1926. The attitude towards dogs remained as resolutely hostile as ever. The rule confining them to be tied up in places provided was strengthened in 1927 to ban them altogether and an amendment to increase the penalty from 2s.6d. to 10s. was carried. That is equal to some £20 today.

Events in the social calendar were different. In 1923 the Club regularly held dances jointly with the Polo Club and in 1928 the Garth Hunt held its first meet at the Golf Club, an occasion illustrated in a photograph in the *Sketch* magazine. This shows Lord Dorchester, who was joint-master of the Garth Hunt and captain of the Golf Club in 1927 and 1928, driving off the first tee with his hunting crop. He became captain almost immediately upon election to membership but was an absentee who never attended, let alone chaired, a single Executive Committee meeting throughout his two years of captaincy.

In later years he would write irritable letters of complaint to the Executive Committee and he incurred the wrath of the Club when he wrote a letter to the *Hants & Berks Gazette* in July 1934. In a long letter he criticised the policies of the local Water Board at a time when a serious drought was creating a water shortage, but he concluded with a last paragraph that seemed to have been added as an afterthought:

Finally, let me call your attention to the following. Today, July 9th, I saw an unattended hose vomiting water on to a green at the North Hants Golf Club. Upon inquiry I learnt that the North Hants golf course is given an unlimited supply – this at a time when the Water Company not only impose restrictions upon hosing gardens and allotments, but are seeking powers to pump up an additional half million gallons daily out of the underground springs upon which your wells, brooks and streams depend.

The publication of this letter caused a Special Meeting of the Executive Committee to be convened. As a result a letter was sent to the *Hants & Berks Gazette* stating that hoses are never left unattended, no restrictions on water supply are in force and the Club is complying with a general request from the water company to be sparing in the use of water. Furthermore a letter was sent to Lord Dorchester, enclosing a copy of the reply to the newspaper and concluding:

*Sketch magazine, 22nd February 1928. Lord Dorchester Drives off the 1st tee with a hunting crop on the occasion of a meet of the Garth Hunt held at the club*

I am further instructed to say that the Committee are greatly surprised that you, as a Vice-President and Ex-Captain of the Club, should have thought fit to issue statements to the press tending to bring opprobrium upon the Club, before verifying their accuracy by enquiry of the Secretary or Committee.

Later minutes merely record that a reply was received.

Contract bridge was allowed to be played in the clubhouse in 1932 for a maximum stake of 6d. per 100, and this new found form of bridge immediately led to disputes about the existing right of a member automatically to cut in on a table of four. It was agreed by the Committee that members may make up a table of four without others cutting in, but one table was to be reserved and marked a "cut in" table.

The character of the membership of North Hants Golf Club in the inter-war years was unusual for such a fine golf course. Many of its rivals were golf clubs pure and simple but North Hants had been created and had evolved with a mixture of motives. It must have been difficult to establish the Club's identity as it spread out in different directions. Firstly, there was the separation between the golfing membership and the tennis and croquet membership. Secondly, it was seeking to attract a London membership from those who would regard it as an offshoot of a West End gentleman's club, offering overnight accommodation with dinner and breakfast. Thirdly, there were a large number of mess memberships whose transient officers could not play in cup competitions and probably played mostly together. Fourthly, there was a large lady golfing membership but without any facilities where they could easily congregate with the other members. Finally, there were the ordinary members who form the backbone of most golf clubs, but who at North Hants were barely greater in numbers than the ladies.

There must have been many members whose paths barely crossed with others from the different circles of membership. This unusual ethos might have discouraged many male golfers who simply wanted to join a golf club to play golf with other men, were not interested in meeting tennis and croquet players and did not want to play on a golf course which had become the home course of mess memberships, a rough equivalent to the golfing society of today.

Evidence from the Committee minutes suggests that the course was often crowded. In 1926, a request from the Royal Aircraft Establishment Golfing Society that it be offered the same terms as a military mess was refused "owing to the crowded state of the course". In the 1930s the Committee received several complaints about congestion on the course, particularly at weekends, caused by visiting matches and meetings. However, this complaint was dismissed by the formidable Captain Torrie, who in a letter to the Committee in December 1930, asserted that congestion at weekends was due to the late arrival of members from London who all wanted to play at around 10.30 a.m. which was also the earliest time that visitors and military members were allowed to play. He timed one of several singles playing on a typical Sunday morning which started at 10.05 a.m., reached the turn at 11.10 a.m. and finished at 12.18 p.m.

If tensions existed between the different circles of members, much the most difficult quandary facing the Club was to achieve a fair balance between the income generated and the costs incurred by the golfing and the lawn tennis and croquet memberships. Ordinary and lady members were able to play golf, tennis and croquet for their subscription and we have no knowledge of the extent to which golfers played tennis and croquet. The income generated by membership subscriptions from tennis and croquet amounted only to some five to six per cent of total subscriptions and visitors' fees obtained from tennis and croquet were only a tiny fraction of those obtained from the golf course.

*Scenes on the golf course taken by Anthony Sanders, 1981*

*Scenes on the golf course taken by Anthony Sanders, 1981*

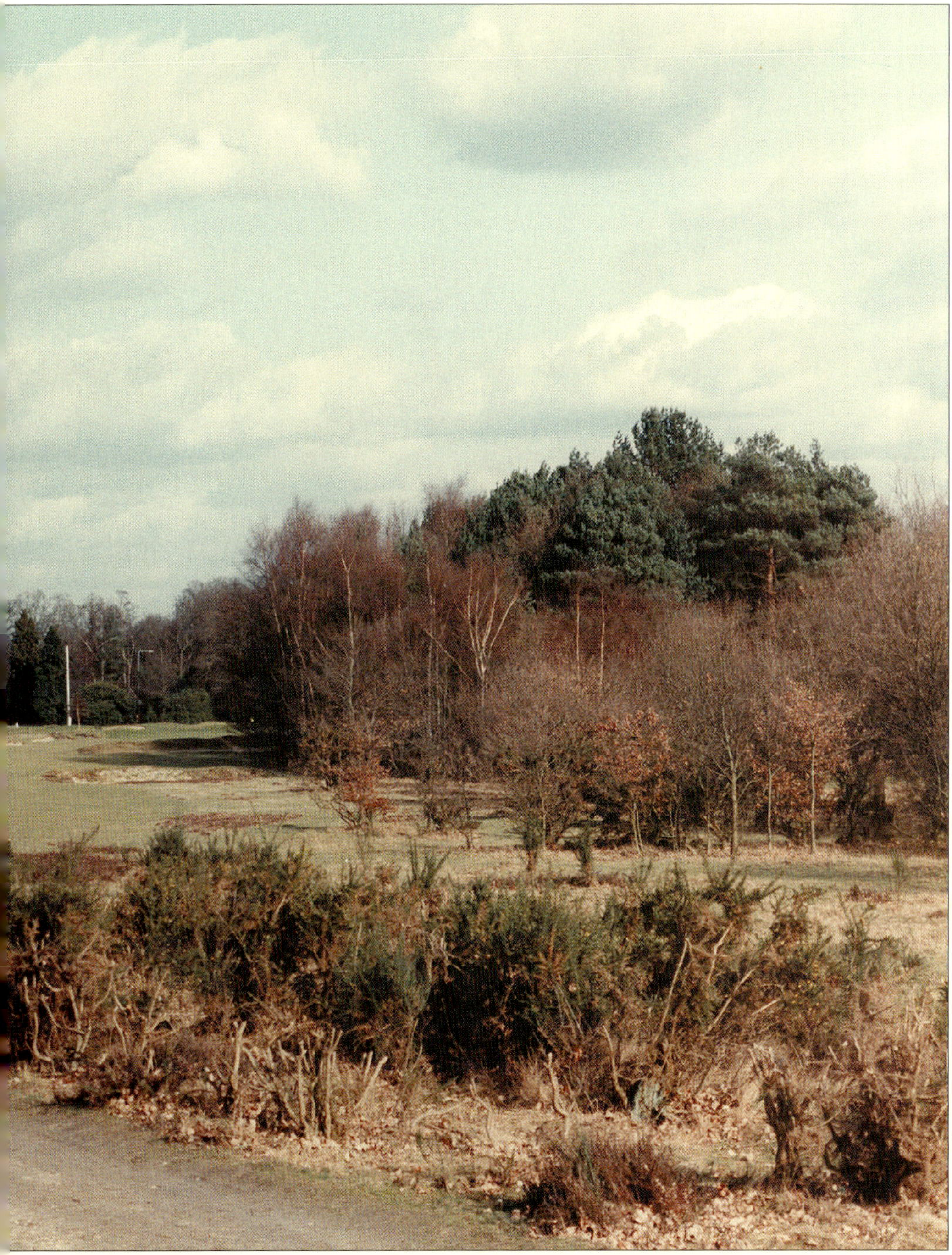

Watercolour painting of 10th green, 1929

The care and maintenance of the tennis courts and croquet lawns took up a significant proportion of the work of the greenkeeping staff. The tennis courts were rodded, mown and marked almost daily and at the end of the season they were harrowed, weeded and re-sown. There were twenty courts in all and four croquet lawns. Two of the courts were in the gardens and the remaining eighteen in three blocks of six, extending across the original practice ground. The four croquet lawns were at the near end adjacent to the former car park. All were maintained to a very high standard and, according to people who remember playing on them before the war, they were in constant use. Nevertheless, frustration came to the surface from time to time, particularly in the late 1920s when the Executive Committee discussed repeated complaints about the state of the golf course because of too great a diversion of work to the tennis courts and croquet lawns.

*Advertisement for the annual LTA Open Tennis Tournament held at North Hants.* Lawn Tennis Association *magazine, 1926*

Frustration was regularly expressed in Committee discussions about the inability of the tennis section to mount its prestigious annual Open Tournament without incurring financial losses. The Open Tournament was officially recognised by the Lawn Tennis Association and included in its programme for the year. *Lawn Tennis and Badminton*, the official journal of the L.T.A., advertised the event as shown in the copy for May 1926. The subsequent report of this tournament in the journal stated that it "seems to have taken a fresh lease of life. Entries were almost twice as many as those of 1925 and it deserves to succeed if only because its courts compare favourably with any others in the country". It was perhaps as well because the Executive Committee had resolved in the previous autumn that if it again showed a considerable financial loss its future would be under question.

The Open Tournament attracted a number of class players. Perhaps the best known was C.R.D. Tuckey, a serving army officer, who won the Men's Singles event in 1933 and 1934. He went on to win the Men's Doubles title at Wimbledon in 1936 and to represent Great Britain in the Davis Cup. The

*Birds-eye view of the tennis courts and croquet lawns in the 1930s drawn by Eric Carpenter*

Open Tournament held pride of place, but in addition there was an Invitation Tournament, an Open Junior Tournament and a Club Tournament. No records of the croquet section have survived, but it is known that Open croquet tournaments were convened.

Concerns about the viability of the tennis were raised again in 1937, when the Committee gave careful consideration to why the tournaments were financially unsuccessful and questioned the advisability of their continuing. It was suggested that the Open Tournament did not carry the support of the membership and was only continued in 1938 because of an earlier commitment. In April 1939 it was resolved that "owing to the general situation and the outlook for the Club finances the Open Tennis Tournament be abandoned". As will be seen in the next chapter it was from this moment that tennis and croquet went into gradual decline and eventual closure.

It is difficult now to imagine what must have been a setting of great beauty nestling beneath a line of majestic beech trees with glimpses through to the shrubs and flowers of the manicured gardens. The sketch by Eric Carpenter captures this beauty. Tennis and croquet players filled the green grass of immaculate tennis courts and croquet lawns. There were separate pavilions for tennis and croquet, the latter with a thatched roof. At one time there was talk of a bowling green, a proposal formally put in 1931, but never pursued.

Whilst the tennis activities may have been under scrutiny from time to time, changes and improvements were taking place on the golf course, primarily under the influence of the famous golf course architect, Tom Simpson, but also with help from Captain L.J. Torrie, a leading member of the Club and a talented enough golfer to play in the Amateur Championship. He was a more or less permanent member of the Green Committee and a golf course architect in his own right.

Occasional changes were made to individual holes during the inter-war years. For example in 1923 the rear of the 6th green was cleared to create the lower tier of the putting surface and the bunker in front of the 15th green was extended along the left hand side. There were many more bunkers on the course than there are today and proposals to change the bunkers were as frequent as proposals to plant trees today.

However, most of the changes were made after the Club commissioned a visit from Simpson who made a series of recommendations in a report dated 25th May 1929 and a follow-up report in March 1931. These changes were significant enough for his contribution to the character of the course to be recognised alongside Braid in 1904 and Colt in 1913. We are fortunate to have the original reports with his hole by hole comments and recommendations.

He followed two themes. The first was that bunkers should be "strategic" rather than "penal" and by this he meant that they should be designed to make the better golfer think strategically rather than punish the bad shot of the less able golfer. He was very critical of many of the shortish wing bunkers on either side of the fairway which penalised already bad tee shots, and of those cross bunkers which presented few problems to the better golfers. Golf courses were typically more heavily bunkered than they are today, partly because labour was cheaper, but also because the excavation of a bunker provided soil to create the feature of a mound or slope.

Simpson recommended that many bunkers should be filled in and a number of strategically placed bunkers be introduced. His report identifies more than twenty to be filled in, but a match report in *The Times* in December 1929 refers to the "scrapping of 38 unnecessary bunkers". For example, wing bunkers on either side of the fairway on the 7th and 9th holes were filled in and replaced by a pot bunker sixty yards short of the 7th green and a new bunker on the angle of the 9th fairway at driving distance. A similar new bunker was built at driving distance on the right of the 5th hole. All survive today.

His second theme was to introduce or enhance a dogleg effect to the par four holes wherever possible in order to add variety and to make the better players think strategically. He moved the tee at the 2nd hole to a new position

*The 8th green – 1930s*

further back and across the other side of the track behind the 1st green. He enhanced the dogleg effect on the 5th and 9th holes with new bunkers and built a new back tee on the 14th hole behind the 13th green. These remain today, but two other proposals have to be left to the imagination. He built a new back tee at the 18th close to the current 17th green and recommended that the par 4, 4th hole, roughly where the new hole is today, should be turned into a dogleg with a new tee behind the 3rd green.

Simpson made one specific recommendation that was immediately accepted. A new green was to be built to lengthen the 10th hole from 175 yards with a strategic bunker in front of the green. For the first two years the length of the hole was increased to 225 yards with an escape fairway to the left, but it was then shortened to a more reasonable 195 yards.

However, much the most significant alteration concerned the 329 yard 4th hole. In his 1929 report Simpson stated that it was "crying out to be played on the dog-leg from a new tee behind and slightly left of the 3rd green" but in his 1931 report he agreed with a proposal from the Green Committee, or more likely, Captain Torrie, that this hole "should be a one-shotter" adding that "At present you only have three one-shot holes ... that is not enough. Normally it is considered advisable to have five one-shot holes on a golf course". Perhaps Simpson regarded this as an alternative to a strong suggestion made in his original report, but not accepted, that the 1st hole was an unsatisfactory distance and would make an excellent short hole of some 175 yards. Here is a debate turning full circle seventy years later.

In the memory of Hunter Greig, a junior member in the 1930s, the 4th hole was a "nondescript 300 yards with the tee beside the pond and a blind drive" and the tee was for a brief time relocated in accordance with the first Simpson report. When it was redesigned as a new short hole the bank on the green was steepened and *The Times* reported in February 1934 that "the new fourth hole, a gem of its kind, excited much admiration".

Simpson was critical of the 16th as a "very bad hole – a frontal attack on a hill" and suggested that the green be shifted to the left to create a slight dogleg effect. His pencilled sketch of the hole does not show the controversial bunker at driving distance in the middle of the fairway and in a list of supplementary notes in 1929, Simpson commented that the hole was "without bunkers of any kind from start to finish". Simpson made a return visit in March 1931 and congratulated the Green Committee and the greenkeeper in particular on the "admirable manner" in which his recommendations had been carried out.

It is clear from this second report that an alternative proposal had been put to him for the 16th hole by Captain Torrie which he largely accepted with greenside bunkers and, more significantly, the controversial fairway bunker which fitted in with Simpson's preference for strategic bunkering. Simpson's sketch shows this bunker to be positioned at 210 yards from the tee and for many years thereafter it would be a memorable feature of the hole, tempting the longer hitter to flirt with the railway line to seek an easier second shot.

Over many decades this bunker in the middle of the fairway at driving distance remained a fascinating talking point, rather similar to the bunker in the middle of the fairway at the 4th hole at Woking, which also combines the reward of an easier second shot with the risk of out of bounds to the right. Both Bernard Darwin, who wrote the hole by hole description of the course in the *Official Handbook* in the 1930s, and J.S.F. Morrison writing in *Golf Illustrated* after the war, refer to the resemblance of the 16th hole to the 16th hole at St Andrews where the Principal's Nose bunker in the middle of the fairway narrows the gap between it and an out of bounds to the right.

The influence of Captain Torrie lay mostly in changes to the greens of the 16th hole in 1932, the 17th in 1933 and the 8th in 1934, all carried out by the existing ground staff under his supervision. The change to the 17th green was extensive. He lengthened the hole by some forty yards with an entirely new green further on and to the left. The original green had been close to the railway line and too visible from the hotel. The new green was designed as a broad imitation of the famous 17th Road Hole at St Andrews with a

*Aerial view of the clubhouse and 18th green – 1930s*

bunker within the neck of a raised green. Nobody knows whether the imitation by Torrie of this 16th and 17th holes at St Andrews was deliberate or happened by chance. This historic link was broken by a controversial decision to fill in the bunker at the 16th in 1993.

A consequence of the redesigned 17th green was that the tee making the 18th into a dogleg was returned to its original and present location. In 1934 he redesigned the green of the 8th hole to create the figure of eight shape with two alternative pin positions. Other minor alterations included a line of cross bunkers at the 2nd hole in 1935, which later reverted to the line of grassy hollows running from the large oak trees. In 1936 alterations were made to the 12th hole and in 1938 a new bridge was constructed over the gully at the 6th hole, presumably later replaced by the causeway used today.

The redoubtable Captain Torrie must have been a persuasive member, ever restless to improve the course, always refusing any fee, but demanding total control over any project once it had been agreed by the Committee. By all reports he was an abrasive character. All these alterations were carried out by the ground staff under his supervision, apart from the major reconstruction of the 4th hole which was personally overseen by Simpson. There is no doubt that the Club was fortunate in having a fine head greenkeeper, Alf Hindley, throughout these inter-war years. There is many a tribute to his skill in the Committee minutes and when he reached twenty-five years service in April 1935, a testimonial fund raised £180 from the members, the equivalent of some £5,000 today.

Hindley received special praise after one of the rare occasions when the course was put to an outside test. On 1st September 1926 the Southern Qualifying section of the News of the World Professional Match Play Tournament was held over eighteen holes at North Hants. Heavy overnight rain changed the character of the course when a distinguished field of 133 professionals set forth in twoballs teeing off at five minute intervals for twenty-six places. The clear winner on the day by a margin of three strokes was Fred Robson of Cooden Beach, with a new professional record of 69 on what was described in the press as a "reconstructed course". A year later he was runner-up to Bobby Jones in the Open Championship in 1927 and he was a member of the first four Ryder Cup teams.

The qualifying score was 76, and as reported in *The Daily Telegraph* on the following day "A pleasing feature of the day's play was the success of T.H. Cotton, the young public schoolboy, now professional at Langley Park". At the age of nineteen, he returned a 73, as did the 1902 Open champion, Alex Herd, at the age of fifty-eight. J.H. Taylor, one of the famous triumvirate and five times Open champion, also played at the age of fifty-five, but failed to qualify. His presence perhaps owed more to his role as correspondent for the *News of the World* and on the following Sunday he wrote that "Cotton is a very stylish player and should be assured of a bright future".

However, of more interest, J.H. Taylor also wrote in the same edition in full praise of North Hants Golf Club in an article entitled "Pleasures of an almost unknown course". The article began "I venture to say that many people have only just discovered one of the most delightful courses in the country". He continued:

> It is one of the most beautifully kept I have played on. If a course is judged by the quality of its greens, then North Hants is in the front rank. Better greens of uniform growth and fineness it is impossible to conceive, and this state of things is the reward of Hindley, the greenkeeper. Their appearance proves that he knows his job.

Such praise is always welcomed by those who receive it, but who would have thought that in the 1920s it would also have led to an immediate pay rise. At the Executive Committee meeting immediately following, Hindley was awarded a wage increase of 10s. a week. It was well deserved. Many reports in *The Times* newspaper of society or Guildford Alliance meetings in the 1930s referred to the outstanding condition of the greens at North Hants and the Club owed much to the greenkeeping skills of Alf Hindley.

The report of the News of the World event in *Golf Illustrated* by Harold Hilton concluded:

> I believe that the executive of the North Hants Golf Club had never previously been through the experience of staging an event of such importance. One can only say that there was no evidence of any such lack of experience. the management was excellent, both inside and out, and, according to those who played upon it, the course was in superb condition.

The Club was not inspired by this success to attract outside interest at the higher levels of golf. A rare exception was a thirty-six hole professional challenge match in February 1932, when A.J. Lacey and J. Donaldson beat A. Perry and G. Faulkner by 3 and 2. They were one down after the first round to a better ball score of 66, but retaliated by playing the sixteen holes in the afternoon in nine under fours. Both Perry and Lacey would later become Ryder Cup golfers and Perry was Open champion in 1935.

The Club was a regular host each year to one of the fortnightly winter meetings of the Guildford Alliance which attracted large entries from leading local amateurs and professionals and it was at these meetings that the course was put to the test by fine golfers and new course records were achieved.

Fred Robson set the new professional course record of 69 in September 1926 and a new amateur record of 74 had been set a year earlier by Major C.O. Hezlet in an exhibition match on 1st November 1925 with T.A. Torrance. They were both members of the Walker Cup team that had played against the United States in the previous year. Hezlet was a serving army officer who played in three Walker Cups and many times for Ireland. Torrance played in five Walker Cups and many times for England, and, amongst several clubs, was a member of nearby Bramshot.

The Guildford Alliance meetings produced new course records. The amateur record of 74 had been equalled by Major C.G.S. Irvine, playing as a service member in the United Services Cup in October 1930, but on 12th November 1931 the three times Walker Cup golfer, W.L. Hope, playing in the Guildford Alliance off a handicap of plus 3 returned a gross score of 72. This record stood until 25th March 1936 when W.H.H. Aitken returned a 68. "Jumbo" Aitken was a fine amateur golfer, later to be Army champion and Durham County champion and on this occasion he entered as a member of North Hants. As an army officer he was presumably a service member and his hole by hole score some sixty years ago reads well to this day:

```
4 4 3 3 5 4 3 3 5   34
3 4 4 4 4 2 5 4 4   34
```

The professional course record of 69 set in 1926 by Fred Robson was lowered to 67 by Alf Perry on 2nd March 1933. He had played the previous year in the challenge match described above and on this occasion entered the Guildford

Alliance from Leatherhead Golf Club. His hole by hole figures show a magnificent back nine and it is a rare course record that includes a 6 on the card:

3 4 4 3 6 4 3 3 5    35
2 4 3 4 4 3 4 4 4    32

The ladies competed for the attention of better players with an annual Open Meeting and it was in April 1934 that a new ladies' course record of 74 was returned by Miss Molly Gourlay, many times an international golfer in the 1930s, and entering from Camberley Heath. Several golfers had shared the previous record of 76.

When these records were being set, the card of the course for the men would seem eccentric today. In 1926 the standard scratch score, or bogey as it was then known, was 78. It was later reduced to 76 and a new standard scratch score of 74 was allotted as part of a national revision in 1933. Bogey remained unchanged at 76 until 1938 when it was reduced to 74. These were the figures used for the monthly bogey competition of holes up or down against the card, a method that has now almost completely given way to the stableford, but then used for some of the Club cup competitions.

However, it was the stroke index that would have confused golfers today. Strokes were given according to a matrix based on the St Andrews Table which was printed on the reverse of the card and widely used by many golf clubs. This table simply distributed strokes across the holes in mathematical proportions, irrespective of the difficulty of the hole. Thus, at North Hants the card instructed the golfer in receipt of one stroke to take it at hole 9, but two strokes were to be taken at holes 6 and 14, six strokes at holes 2, 5, 8, 11, 14 and 17. Nine strokes were simply taken at the nine odd numbered holes. It is doubtful whether the typical fourball of today could actually cope with such a system. A new and conventional stroke index was eventually introduced in 1938.

Whilst the course records may have been impressive, the standard of golf amongst the members was generally poor. This was particularly so in the 1920s when the lowest winning score in the two scratch medals, the Gold Medal and the Currie Cup, was 80 and on several occasions 87 and 88 were good enough to win. Only nine gross scores under 80 were recorded in all medal competitions through the decade and there would only be a handful of gross scores under 90 in the well attended Spring and Autumn Meetings. It would not be until 1934 that a net score of under 70 was first returned in a medal competition. At the other extreme in one year the Lloyd Cup, a bogey competition, was won with a score of ten down and in another year a monthly medal was won with a net score of 130.

*Doreen Fowler wins the English Women's Amateur Championship, 1925*

*Phyllis Lobbett and Doreen Fowler win the Ladies' London Foursomes for the third time, March 1930*

One particular moment of golfing distinction happened on 16th May 1929. There is a framed copy of a notice in the clubhouse which reads "Certified that Lt. Col. W.A. Farquahar, a member of this club, playing in a singles match on May 16th, holed the 8th hole (125 yards) in one stroke. Lt.Col. Farquahar is a one-armed golfer". This was immediately included in the Feats and Interesting Facts section of the *Golfer's Handbook* and at the time his was only the second recorded hole-in-one by a one-armed golfer.

In fact the real golfing merit of this decade belongs to the ladies. In pride of place was Miss Doreen Fowler who, after being runner-up to Joyce Wethered in 1924, won the English Ladies Championship in 1925, entering from North Hants. She was a tall and powerful golfer, who overwhelmed her opponent in the final at Westward Ho! by 9 and 7. In the *Evening Standard* she was described as "a striking figure on the links, a striking personality and one of the most powerful hitters" who "certainly drove the ball as far as any lady player has ever driven". She was an England international from 1923 to 1929.

She brought further distinction to North Hants Golf Club by winning the Club match play foursomes tournament, the Ladies' London Foursomes, in 1924, 1929 and 1930, in partnership each time with Miss Phyllis Lobbett. They both played regularly at North Hants, but their provenance was from

Somerset. Miss Fowler won the Somerset Ladies Championship for five consecutive years from 1921 to 1925, defeating Miss Lobbett in four of the finals. In their first final for North Hants in 1924 they defeated Worplesdon, who were represented by the almost unbeatable Joyce Wethered.

The standard of golf improved in the 1930s. The reason for improved scoring was almost certainly the introduction of steel shafts to replace hickory, as dramatic a change at the time as the recent introduction of the metal wood. Famous golfers like J.H. Taylor and Harry Vardon were unhappy, the latter observing that "It is a shame. The game was going along quite well without these steel shafts".

For many years, L.J. Torrie had probably been the best golfer in the Club and in 1930 he won a medal competition in August with the lowest gross score recorded by a member of 75, followed by winning the Gold Medal for a second time with a gross 79. He was the first regular member of the Club to play from a scratch handicap and later entered the Amateur Championship from North Hants, as did A.E.L. Mackenzie-Grieve, who later played from a scratch handicap, winning the Currie Cup three times but never the Gold Medal.

However, the outstanding golfer in the pre-war years was J.W. Nelson, who joined the Club as a scratch golfer in 1932 after retiring from a career in the Indian Civil Service where he reached the high level of Land Revenue and General Administrator for East Bengal and Assam. John Nelson was good enough to play in the British Amateur on three occasions in the late 1920s, taking summer leave and entering from the Royal Calcutta Golf Club, then the regular home for some of the best golfing expatriates. In his first competitive appearance in the October monthly medal in 1932 he returned a 74 and immediately proceeded to establish what still remains the most remarkable record of any in the history of the Club, by winning the Gold Medal for five consecutive years from 1933 to 1937. He was a marvellously consistent golfer in Club competitions of all kinds, as his winning Gold Medal scores testify: 76, 80 (76 in play-off), 75, 74 and 74.

He joined the Club just before the revision of the standard scratch score from 76 to 74, which caused all handicaps to be raised by two, but by 1936 he had worked his handicap back to scratch. He regularly played in the monthly medals and bogeys and played top in the singles and foursomes in almost every Club match up to the outbreak of war in 1939. These matches were mostly played against Aldershot Command, Blackmoor, Bramshot, Hankley Common, Liphook and the Seniors, occasionally mixed, but normally ten-a-side with singles before lunch and foursomes after. He played once more in the Amateur in 1935, entering from North Hants. In the late 1950s he achieved fame at the age of seventy-five when he featured in one of Henry

Longhurst's weekly articles in *The Sunday Times*, this time on eclectic scores. Nelson's eclectic at North Hants was 40, 22 out and 18 home, and Longhurst highlighted his sequence from the 8th to the 16th which was 1 2 1 2 2 2 2 1 2 – 15.

Another member who made an immediate impression was Douglas Bader, later to become a famous World War Two fighter pilot. After losing both legs in an aircraft crash in 1931, he was persuaded by friends to take up golf. He was introduced to North Hants in 1934 by Dick Ubee, then a young R.A.F. pilot and later to be an Air Vice-Marshal and captain of the Club in 1964 and 1965. Bader was still learning how to swing a golf club without falling over and initially played two or three holes at a time. He was offered a year's subscription at a nominal rate and persevering with that legendary determination he became a full member in 1935 and began to enter Club competitions. In November he won the monthly bogey competition with a score of 4 up playing from a handicap of 18 and *Golf Illustrated* highlighted his win with a brief report "As a result of a plane crash Mr. Bader has two artificial legs. In spite of this he walks and plays unaided by crutches or sticks, and on Saturday last completed the course in under two hours. There's courage for you!" Within four months he had reduced his handicap to 12 and in October 1937 he won the Hood Cup after a play-off and so the name of 'D.R.S. Bader' appears on the Club's honours boards.

This decade closes with the little known achievement of I.P. Garrow in 1938. Peter Garrow was one of three golfing brothers playing just before the war as junior members at North Hants in the school holidays between term times at Winchester. In 1938 he won the Carris Trophy, then recently introduced as an Open Boys 36 holes Strokeplay Championship at Moor Park, with a winning total of 147. He entered the war as Fleet Air Arm pilot and was sadly killed in action, as indeed were a number of other members. The distinction of his achievement may best be judged by the quality of the two names that he follows in the list of winners. They were J.D.A. Langley and R.J. White, both Walker Cup golfers and the latter widely regarded as the finest British amateur golfer of the immediate post-war years. It would be fifty-seven years later that Justin Rose would follow as the second member of the Club to win the Carris Trophy.

At this point in the narrative it may be worth pausing to reflect upon the character of the golf course in the 1920s and 1930s. An aerial photograph taken in 1930 shows no more than a dozen trees in the whole of the wide expanse from the boundaries of the course to the right of the 17th and 18th holes across to the tree lined avenue running from the 1st to the 13th greens. The whole of the 17th and 18th holes were clearly visible from the 12th tee. There was not a tree to be seen between the 3rd and 4th holes.

Nevertheless the trees along the boundaries were sufficient for the course often to be described as a parkland course although large parts were exposed to open windswept heathland. The fairways and greens were thinly grassed with fine fescue, a grass with deep roots which often appears to die in the summer. The very fast greens would have contained far fewer blades of grass than today. In the summer the fairways would become rock hard where the ball would run and run and the cricketing enthusiast will know from *Wisden* that the 1930s was a decade of long hot summers. There was more heather off the fairways and large parts of the 3rd and 11th fairways were mown heather. The belt of heather across the end of the fairway on the 16th was a formidable trap.

The result was that despite inferior golf balls and with steel shafts in their infancy, there were times of the year when the ball travelled long distances. However, these same conditions of fast, hard greens guarded by bunkers often made a direct shot to the flag almost impossible. When Captain Torrie designed the raised green at the 17th hole and its narrowness was challenged, he commented that it was not intended to allow a pitch on to the green, but only to be approached by a pitch and run. "Firm turf for running shot" is written in his own hand on the original design. In similar vein, Bernard Darwin describes in the handbook mentioned earlier how the 4th hole is played with a tee shot that "carries a rough knoll, pitches in the hollow and runs up the bank".

The size and shape of the greens was another difference. Early photographs suggest that the greens tended to be rather square in shape and even in the 1950s they were significantly larger than they are today, fully embracing many of the greenside bunkers. Notes of the planning of the redesigned 10th green in 1929 refer to its area of 2,000 square yards, or forty-five yards square, extending to the edges of the bunkers in front and to the right of the green. The greens were as fast as those on seaside links. The agenda for a meeting of the Green Committee in October 1931 refers to a suggestion from some of the ladies that the greens are "too fast" and steps should be taken to slow them. "God help us!" is written in large capital letters in his own hand by the chairman.

These were the years before sapling trees were allowed to grow unhindered and before automatic watering softened the greens and encouraged meadow grasses to crowd out the fescues. Along with the belt of Surrey courses built on Bagshot sand, North Hants Golf Club played like a seaside links.

The highly praised Hindley would have witnessed many changes during his years as head greenkeeper. The fairways were cut with horse-drawn mowers and the photograph of the greenstaff and their equipment taken in the early 1920s shows four horses in attendance. In July 1926, shortly before the News of the World event the Club faced a major financial decision for which a lengthy questionnaire was sent to each Committee member. The opening question was "Are you in favour of a mechanical tractor being purchased?" It was explained that horse traction for the triple mower was too slow for cutting the rough efficiently and that a tractor could be purchased for £120. One of the horses would be sold for £20 and the stables would be converted into garaging, leaving a loose box for Jasper, obviously a horse of sufficient standing and affection for him to merit a personal mention in the minutes.

The proposal was agreed and implemented in April 1928 with the purchase of a Metropolitan tractor at a cost of £140 plus £35 for a mowing unit. Mechanisation proceeded apace and over the next two years a 30 inch Dennis motor mower was purchased along with five Ransomes Certes 14 inch mowing machines. In January 1928 the installation of a water system was approved taking water in 2 inch pipes to central positions near the 4th and 13th holes, with further distribution in 1 inch pipes to various greens.

The accounts show that this flurry of capital expenditure between 1926 and 1929 amounted almost to £1,000, but these were financially buoyant years for the Club and it was comfortably financed from annual surpluses. However, this changed when the Club entered the 1930s and began to feel the pressures of the economic problems facing the country as a whole arising from the Wall Street crash of 1929 and its aftermath of world-wide slump. The Club's income from subscriptions and green-fees of £4,392 in 1930 fell within two years to around £3,600, a level broadly maintained throughout the rest of the decade.

The sequence of ten successive years of financial surplus came to an abrupt end in 1933 and for sixteen of the next seventeen years the Club would record annual deficits. Personal financial pressures were particularly apparent in unpaid subscriptions, as for example when 173 subscriptions due on 1st January 1932 were reported as unpaid to an Executive Committee meeting held on 20th February, although there was often a remarkable laxity about the payment of subscriptions on time throughout the inter-war years.

The Executive Committee was sensitive to the general situation at an early stage and at a meeting in September 1931 the chairman "in view of the difficult times asked the opinion of the members of the Committee as to the policy that should be followed". It was agreed that all possible economies should be exercised and encouragement be given to meetings and matches to attract visitors to the Club. The state of the country was later brought to the attention of the members in 1934 when the editor of *Golf Illustrated* wrote to all golf clubs to promote a scheme for old clothing left behind in the locker rooms of golf clubs to be collected and given to the unemployed.

## BETWEEN THE WARS 1918–1939

The Club was fortunate that key positions were filled by individuals who gave long service. We have already referred to Alf Hindley who was greenkeeper from 1910 to 1951. There was little permanence amongst the Club's early professionals, J.W. Moore (1904–1906), C. Hope (1906–1907), J. Tickle (1907–1912), J.H. Oke (1912–1915), but this changed with the appointment after a gap through the war of A.B. (Abe) Sibbald in 1919. He remained the Club professional until he retired in 1946. He gained a mention in a *Times* golf report in 1934 "…it was delightful to see again the style and ball-control of the professional of the old school, and some of his shots were a joy to behold".

Another key servant of the Club and a pillar of strength was Lieutenant Colonel W.G. Huskisson, who was secretary from 1927 to 1946. The first paid secretary was W. Bailey, from 1909 to 1923, but after his resignation there followed an unsettled period. Fred Dunn was a member and honorary secretary for two years, followed by two paid appointments, J. Deakin Yates and Captain H.W. Inglis, neither of whom lasted more than a year, the latter resigning because he was refused additional clerical assistance.

Within the clubhouse the key positions of steward and housekeeper were always advertised for a married couple without children and four different couples occupied the position in the space of eleven years. The most intriguing of these were Mr. and Mrs. Burgess. In August 1927, the Club purchased a new Remington cash register for cash receipts, but Mr. Burgess refused to operate it claiming that the Golf Club Stewards Association, of which he was a member, disapproved of the use of such machines. He stood his ground when called before the Executive Committee and was promptly sacked.

The original twenty-one year lease from the Elvetham Estate was renegotiated in 1925 for a further twenty-one years and the annual rental was increased from £250 to £310. From time to time the lease would be discussed by the Executive Committee and it may be a surprise today to learn that on two separate occasions in the 1930s serious proposals were put to the Elvetham Estate asking that a new clubhouse should be built.

The first occasion was in 1931 when the Club was still hopeful of expanding and much emphasis was given to the unsuitability of the clubhouse. The Club approached the Estate about gaining greater security by increasing the term of the lease to fifty years and building a new clubhouse. Concern was also expressed about a particular clause in the lease which preserved for the Estate the right to build a metalled access road next to the railway line along the length of the 16th and 17th holes. As we have seen, plans were in hand to improve these two holes and the Club was much relieved when the Estate agreed that it would not insist on the retention of this right.

However, the discussions for a new lease failed to come to any agreement. The Estate insisted that the existing clubhouse would have to revert to a

> ## The Club Lease.
>
> As Members are aware, the Club's present Lease expires in 1946. For some years its renewal has formed the subject of negotiation with the Landlords. It was desired firstly to obtain an assurance of the would-be position after 1946 and secondly to make immediate improvements to our very ill-equipped premises.
>
> This note explains the proceedings taken since the last Annual Meeting.
>
> In August, 1938, at a meeting with the Estate's local agent, we undertook to make certain alterations to the Club-house in return for a 50-year Lease at a certain rent. In reply the Estate offered an immediate 30-year Lease at a figure slightly higher than ours. The Crisis of September interrupted negotiations. Before re-opening them, we had the premises thoroughly examined by the Club's Architects. The latter gave it as their considered opinion that they were quite unable to recommend the Club to take the present buildings on a repairing Lease for a fresh period of 30 years.
>
> In the Committee's opinion, this report was conclusive; so if the Club was to continue to use the present Golf Course and Lawns, there must be a new Club-house. Accordingly in January of this year we wrote to the Estate asking them to build a new Club-house for us at a cost of about £6,000 and offering to pay a rent of £450 for a 30-years' Lease of the grounds and new Club-house. We further suggested that the building should be started without waiting for the expiry of the existing Lease. No reply to our proposal has yet been received.
>
> The suggested rent is £140 more than the present one. The Committee think that by economies resulting from the occupation of modern premises and by the increased Membership which the greater amenities should create, this rent is not beyond the means of the Club.
>
> W. G. HUSKISSON,
> Secretary.
>
> 7th March, 1939.

*Notice to members, 7th March, 1939*

domestic residence and was reluctant to spend £8,000 to £10,000 on a new clubhouse without a substantial rent increase. The Club was unwilling to pay a higher rent even for a longer lease, particularly as economic conditions were worsening, and the negotiations limped to a halt.

The subject came up again in 1938 with concerns expressed about its unsuitability, its condition and the cost of repairs imposed by a clause in the lease. With fewer years of the lease remaining the Club was unwilling to spend money which could only be justified by the certainty of a longer lease and there were fears about losing members. The Club commissioned a survey of the clubhouse which disclosed enough defects to suggest the "necessity for a new club building" and a proposal was made to the Elvetham Estate in

January 1939 that it should build a new clubhouse at an estimated cost of £6,000 in return for an annual rent of £450. This was curtly rejected by the Estate which offered to spend money on the clubhouse in exchange for a higher rent, but negotiations petered out as the international situation worsened. The notice issued to members about the Club Lease in March 1939 makes interesting reading in the context of a clubhouse that would survive for a further sixty-four years.

This chapter on the inter-war years closes with the outbreak of the Second World War in September 1939. Trouble had been looming for some time. A year earlier in September 1938 a Committee decision was postponed "until the international situation is cleared up" and in May 1939 the Club was notified by the military authorities that a searchlight station might be established near the 13th green.

The Prime Minister, Neville Chamberlain, broadcast to the nation at 11.15 a.m. on Sunday 3rd September 1939 to announce that a state of war now existed with Germany. Quite remarkably at 12.30 p.m., little more than an hour later, a Special Meeting of the Executive Committee was convened. The solemnity of the day is vividly portrayed by the minutes of that meeting, reproduced below in full:

**Declaration of War, Future of Club**

Decided that the Club and Golf Course should be kept open and work continued as feasible. Authority given to Secretary, who should obtain concurrence of members of Committee when possible, to decide any matters of immediate moment to the Club.

**Regarding outside work:**

Golf Course – To be maintained at least possible expense.

Tennis Lawns – With exception of one section and of the garden courts, to be closed.

Croquet Lawns – In consultation with the Hon Sec Croquet, to be closed.

Outside Staff – Men called to colours not to be replaced.

Equipment – All not required for use to be labelled and properly stored.

**Club House:**

To be kept open as far as possible. All means to be taken to reduce expense of upkeep.

Bedrooms – Cannot be held available for members.

Meals – With the exception of teas will not be served.

Bar – A reasonable stock of whisky, gin, vermouth and draft beer to be maintained, as allowed by any regulations that may be made. The stocks of wines, spirits and beer to be exhausted.

Trophies – To be called in and stored.

Gas and telephones – Hirings that can be dispensed with to be terminated.

Few members survive who will remember that day, 3rd September 1939, but they alone will understand what it must have been like to have six years taken out of their lives. It was an intrusion almost unimaginable today.

*Chapter Four*

# War and Peace
## 1939–1950

THIS CHAPTER is the story of the struggle of a golf club to survive six years of war and five years of impoverished peace. Financial deficits were reported in every year, on occasions threatening the viability and future of the Club and accumulating to a level in 1950 that required drastic action.

The effect of the Second World War on the Club was uncannily similar to that of the First World War when mobilisation denuded the Club of membership and staff. Subscriptions and ground staff costs fell by some two-thirds from 1914 to 1919. This time subscriptions fell from £2,555 in 1939 to £900 in 1945 and ground staff costs more than halved.

An early decision was taken in November 1939 to suspend entrance fees and reduce the annual subscription for ordinary members from £7.7s.0d. to £4.4s.0d. and for lady members from £5.5s.0d. to £3.3s.0d. This rather strange decision, when combined with inevitable resignations, had the predictable effect of immediately reducing subscription income for 1940 by more than half and putting the Club under financial strain. It is difficult now to speculate whether there was optimism that the war would not last too long or pessimism that golfing facilities would be greatly diminished. These reductions remained in place through the war until they were reinstated in 1946.

References to the war abound in the minutes. The Club was fortunate to have a course built on barren Bagshot sand because those golf courses built on fertile soil in country surroundings were forced to plough up two holes for arable farming. North Hants was required to accommodate a detachment of No. 537 Searchlight Battery and its two associated hutments. The searchlight was positioned on the brow of the hill of the 6th fairway with the huts tucked in below to the right of the 7th fairway. The 6th hole was reduced to a short hole of 156 yards from which a hole-in-one was recorded in June 1940. For a time the Club agreed that members of the detachment could take baths in the clubhouse at a weekly charge of 6d. per man, but within a few months the facility was withdrawn as usage increased and payment never materialised.

## Views from the 1930s and 1940s

*3rd green*

*Ravine in front of the 6th tee*

## Views from the 1930s and 1940s

*8th hole*

*10th green*

*12th tee*

Normal access to the battery was by footpath from behind the 15th green and common usage led to a trespassing problem in the immediate post-war years. There was a flurry of concern when the war ended and Fleet Urban District Council proposed housing two families in the abandoned hutments. After discussion the Council was persuaded that the idea was impractical and the huts were dismantled.

The reality of the war impinged in other ways. An air raid shelter was built for the staff and the clubhouse windows were protected against the risk of flying glass. In February 1941, the Club was advised that in the event of a national emergency the clubhouse would be closed and made available for the housing of up to thirty-six refugees. It was also designated in the event of emergency as the local rendezvous headquarters and accommodation centre for 120 personnel from the Air Raid Precaution Services and the Home Guard. This only materialised to the extent of occasional rendezvous practices. In 1942, in a national scheme which history now shows to have been little more than a gesture, the ornate iron railings were requisitioned from the clubhouse.

Those facilities taken for granted such as heating the clubhouse and providing food and drink became difficult to maintain. Heating was dependent on open fires but restrictive quotas for the supply of coal and coke were imposed on the Club. Maintaining the stocks of whisky and gin presented the biggest problem behind the bar and the minutes refer to attempts to buy up stock from Bramshot Golf Club, which had closed when the war began. An original notice to members dated October 1942 confining them to one measure of whisky or gin is framed in the clubhouse. This was increased to two measures in 1943, but "drinks ordered by members for their guests are included in the amounts stated above".

Particularly severe was the decision of the Food Control Office in 1941 to cease regarding the Club as a catering establishment, therefore denying access to basic food supplies. Lunches and teas could no longer be served, but in a spirit of self-help members were encouraged to bring their own tea-time provisions into the dining room. On the golf course it became increasingly difficult to obtain supplies of fertiliser for the greens and petrol for machines.

The financial strain began to show. Annual deficits, which peaked at £483 in 1940 and £388 in 1942, were slowly eating away the slender reserves in the balance sheet. The Club was probably torn between meeting financial needs and being seen to be generous in times of war and hardship, which showed itself in the form of reduced subscriptions to members and the honorary memberships given to the officers of regiments posted locally for brief stays. These included officers of the Free French Army based at a camp in Cove after escaping from France in August 1940.

A decision was taken in January 1943 that no further members would be elected until the end of the war and income from subscriptions drifted below £1,000 in 1943, and as low as £900 in 1945, a far cry from the immediate pre-war peak of £3,025 in 1937. However, green-fees remained closer to pre-war levels through most of the war years. Mess memberships and those honorary memberships to regiments passing through were abandoned in favour of concessionary green-fees of 2s.6d. a round. Canadian army personnel stationed nearby played regularly on the course.

At the same time economies were regularly sought. Not a penny of capital expenditure was incurred on the clubhouse or the course. The Elvetham Estate agreed to a twenty-five per cent reduction in rent in the early part of the war and the Club's rateable value was sharply reduced on appeal in 1943.

During the war occasional matches and competitions were held for the likes of the British Sailors Society and the Red Cross, the latter being a weekend of a Saturday medal with the leading four qualifying for match play on Sunday. The result found its way into the *Sunday Express* in April 1940 which reported that "the final was won at the 19th by J.K. Drinkall". Otherwise, regular competitions ceased with the monthly bogey in August 1939 and did not return until the monthly medal in June 1945. Bernard Darwin captured the peculiarity of the time with the opening words of his book *Golf Between Two Wars*, published in 1944 "War-time, in which there is so little golf and none of it serious, is well adapted to looking back at peace-time

*Bob Mounce displays goods from the professional's shop, 1950s*

when there was so much and so desperately solemn, when short putts missed were really tragic".

The fabric of the Club and course was sustained during the war by the hard work and loyalty shown throughout by the secretary, the Club steward and stewardess, the professional and the head greenkeeper. No account of these war years should pass without paying tribute to them.

Lieutenant Colonel W.G. Huskisson, known to many members as "Husky", was secretary from 1927 until he retired in 1946 and with nineteen years remains the longest serving secretary in the history of the Club. The best tribute to pay to his secretarial skills in dealing with a demanding membership is to record that he was preceded by three secretaries in three years and followed by five in five years. The remarkable neatness of his minutes and competition records, all handwritten with carefully pasted press cuttings is a credit to him. He was fondly remembered by the Club's post-war professional, Bob Mounce, who wrote that when he came to play at North Hants in the 1930s as an assistant from Camberley Heath "In those days pros were not allowed in clubhouses, but Colonel Huskisson was years ahead of his time. He would meet us on arrival, allow us to change in the locker room and eat in the dining room".

In December 1939, the Club steward and stewardess resigned after less than a year in place. After an unsuccessful attempt to persuade the professional and his wife to replace them, they were succeeded by Mr. and Mrs. F.B. Goddard, who maintained the clubhouse facilities in some semblance of order throughout the war with limited resources and staff shortages. The custom of the day was that the steward and stewardess were a married couple living in the clubhouse, one looking after the bar and the other responsible for the catering. Young children were not allowed, but the Goddards were helped by their teenage daughters who were frequently and affectionately referred to in the minutes as the two Misses Goddards and whose services the Club fought to keep by resisting demands for their call up.

The professional, Abe Sibbald, joined the Club in 1919 and retired in November 1945. His professional's shop was the upper half of a converted granary with wooden steps and is just visible in the early postcard of the clubhouse. The occasion of his twenty-five years of service fell during the war and a testimonial was postponed until his retirement when he was made an Honorary Member and received a collection from the members of £100, equal today to some £2,000. His succession had its sad and dramatic moment. Jack Sidey, professional of the abandoned Bramshot Golf Club was appointed in October 1945, but he died suddenly within days of accepting the appointment. He was a strongly built man who on occasions wielded an enormous trick shot driver with a meandering shaft some 2 inches thick.

R.E. Mounce, son of the Camberley Heath professional, was then appointed as professional, joining the Club in January 1946 following his demobilisation. Bob Mounce recalled how in those difficult early post-war days the first thing he did was to scour all the local junk shops in a search for discarded golf balls. He collected some 500 many of which he repainted. Golf balls were in desperately short supply for three or four years after the war and repainting used golf balls was a regular task for all club professionals.

Perhaps noblest of all the Club's servants was Alf Hindley, the widely acclaimed head greenkeeper since 1910, who maintained the course throughout the war with a staff of three and in a good enough condition to warrant its selection in 1947 as the venue for the Hampshire County Championship. He was ably assisted by many of the lady members who each adopted a green to keep the bunkers tidy and an eye open for stray weeds. Eight of the tennis courts remained open in the early part of the war, but they were reduced to two by its end. Hindley collapsed and died at the wheel of his tractor in April 1951 after forty-one years service. A moving notice pinned in the clubhouse paid "tribute to the modest skill and unremitting industry which he applied to the work he loved. He gave of his best asking but little in reward". His ashes were scattered on the 8th green in the presence of a large number of members.

The last chapter showed that after the First World War the Club quickly recovered its fortunes in line with the general economic prosperity in the country. The aftermath of the Second World War was altogether different as

64

the cost of the war had brought the country to its knees and for another five years or more rationing and financial crises dominated the headlines. Confidence was slow to return.

The Club restored subscriptions to pre-war levels in 1946, but this did nothing to offset the effect of inflation during the war. Prices had increased by one-third and the cost of employing people by rather more. The embargo on new members was lifted and some thirty were elected across the different categories in the first four months of 1946. We have already seen from earlier chapters that, in a variation of the modern phrase about glass ceilings stopping upward promotion, membership at North Hants and many other private golf clubs, involved glass doors through which not everybody passed. There was an immediate controversy because amongst the new members were three who, in the words of letters of complaint to the Committee, were "engaged in trade in Fleet". The Committee responded that the three members concerned had played regularly during the war and their election was not to be taken as any "change of policy".

As the Club faced a difficult post-war future, it was fortunate that its local rival, Bramshot Golf Club, never opened its doors again after the war. The opinion was later expressed by Reg Pearce, whose name figures strongly in the next chapter, that if Bramshot had re-opened North Hants would not have survived. In the years leading up to the war Bramshot had stolen a long lead over North Hants in building a reputation as one of the best golf courses in the south of England. It was a publicity triumph that in 1936 it was selected as the venue for the celebrated Daily Mail £1,000 Professional Tournament, which was won by Alf Padgham in the same year that he was Open champion.

An early task undertaken after the war was the renegotiation of the lease. The two previous leases had been for twenty-one years, but in 1946 a thirty-five year lease was agreed with the annual rent increased from £250 to £400. More important to the Club was the thankful removal of the clause allowing the Estate to build a road inside the boundary along the railway line by the 16th and 17th holes. In essence, North Hants still faced something of an identity problem about its membership and its role. For some a hankering remained to be the country offshoot of a London club. This surfaced in November 1947, when the petrol ration was withdrawn. Four rooms for visitors upstairs had been reopened and the decision was taken to write to a number of London clubs to draw their attention to the facilities available and the ease of rail access. In keeping with this theme, the Club warmly received the gift of further animal heads from Colonel Watts to be hung in the dining room including a "record Bara Singha", a twelve-horned Indian deer.

The army influence remained as strong as ever and the Club became something of a refuge for many retired officers who had served in the Indian

Army before and during the Second World War. Indeed, David Hunter, then a junior member, recalls that the town of Fleet was known as the "Elephant's Graveyard" because so many who had served in the Indian Army and Indian Civil Service retired to live there "to see each other off". Local regiments were encouraged with Mess memberships available for £3.3s.0d. for a minimum of seven officers and individual service membership at £4.4s.0d., both comparing favourably with the annual subscription of £7.7s.0d. for ordinary members. However, a crucial difference was that in the late 1940s the Executive Committee was largely made up of civilian members including, in particular, Hugh Clifford, Charles Neate, John Nelson, Reg Pearce and Sir Paul Pechell. They took three important decisions that would begin the process of change.

The first was to recommend to the Annual General Meeting in March 1948 that tennis and croquet be discontinued. A half-hearted attempt was made in 1946 to bring one section of the tennis courts back into play, but the facility had always been a luxury that the Club could barely afford and the financial realities of the post-war years made closure inevitable. The decision was taken with little protest and in August three and a half acres of prime quality turf forming the tennis courts and croquet lawns were sold for £195 an acre. This, together with some £350 raised from the sale of tennis equipment, produced a useful cash inflow of £1,100 spread over the years 1948 to 1950.

The second decision followed naturally from the first. In August 1948, Sir Paul Pechell proposed that the area of the tennis courts and croquet lawns from which the turf had been lifted be turned into a practice ground "to relieve congestion on the golf course and to spare the fairways and greens from damage from members practising iron and approach shots". This was agreed but not immediately implemented because of the cost of preparation and sowing. On the advice of Hindley the area was allowed to recover naturally and be cleared of weeds in time for the practice ground to be formally opened for the Hampshire Ladies County Championship held at the Club in April 1950. The practice ground was something of a triumph for the Club. The beauty of the immaculate lawns may have been lost, but a financial liability had been turned into a rare asset of a large practice ground situated in the perfect position next to the car park. It was to remain for many years a competitive advantage for attracting members to the Club.

*The Times*, in reporting how this County Championship was won by a home member, Mrs. J.S.F. Morrison, as lady golfers such as Gwen Morrison were then known, also referred to the new practice ground:

> An interesting new feature of the North Hants Golf Club, which was much appreciated by players, was the practice ground. Here, players could hire balls for a small fee from the professional, hit them, and leave them to be picked up later.

A recent article in the trade magazine, *Golf Range News*, suggested that this facility provided by Bob Mounce was possibly the first of its kind. In fact it lapsed after a few years, becoming too labour intensive to be viable and clashing with members wishing to use their own practice balls.

The third important decision taken by the Committee was to take action to increase subscriptions. Despite an influx of new members at the end of the war and the closure of Bramshot, membership had continued to dwindle and by 1949 had fallen to levels scarcely believable today:

| Ordinary Men | 100 | Military | 27 |
| Ladies | 31 | Juniors | 10 |

In some ways these were idyllic times. Most of the members knew each other. There was little pressure on tee times and for much of the week the course lay fallow in beautiful condition. Miss E.M. "Sandy" Sellors, a distinguished member of the Club, who joined in 1948 and was made a Life member in 1964, remembers how "friendly a club it was with much less of the bustle and hurry of today".

In 1948, the Executive Committee had identified the need to recruit fifty new members by controversially proposing that "membership be thrown open to all residents of the town", but the sale of turf from the tennis courts was cushioning the Club from financial realities. Early in 1950 the captain, E.H. Curling, wrote to all members asking them to introduce new members or face higher subscriptions. A modest increase in the full subscription from £7.7s.0d. to £8.8s.0d. from January 1950 had already been agreed, but he now realised that more was needed. Apart from the temporary reduction during the war, the basic subscription of £7.7s.0d. for ordinary members and £5.5s.0d. for ladies had remained unchanged since 1922.

The seriousness of the financial situation was explained to members at a Special General Meeting held on 25th November 1950. The Club was heading for its largest ever annual deficit of £500 and reserves stood at little more than £1,000. In the event the members willingly endorsed a further increase in subscriptions for ordinary members from £8.8s.0d. to £10.10s.0d., lady members from £5.5s.0d. to £7.7s.0d. and service members from £4.4s.0d. to £6.6s.0d. In money terms today these increases may seem small but in percentage terms increases of 40 to 50 per cent were dramatic. The effect of the proposal was to return the Club to modest and gradually increasing surpluses in the 1950s. The meeting also took the decision to simplify the voting rules to one member one vote from the previous method weighted by the amount of subscription.

These bold decisions were taken by the Executive Committee against a background of chaos in other areas, not least in the secretary's office. Colonel Huskisson had been an outstanding secretary in his long reign from

*Molly Wallis wins the English Ladies Amateur Championship, 1947*

*Gwen Morrison wins the Hampshire County Ladies Championship, 1950*

1927 to 1946 but, after he retired he was followed by five different secretaries in five years. Mr. P. Brailsford (January–November 1946), Commander K.T.J. Southgate (December 1946–June 1947), Colonel E.G. le Patourel (September 1947–October 1949) and Lieutenant Commander H.N. Sheffield (October 1949–May 1951) came and went in quick succession. This series of failed paid appointments led to a sharing of duties amongst Committee members. As a result R.W. Bellamy became honorary secretary for two years, followed by C.W. Neate for nine years. Ron Bellamy and Charles Neate made immense contributions to the Club, but they feature more in the next chapter.

Life in the clubhouse was just as difficult for the steward and stewardess. Post-war rationing made catering difficult, particularly in providing both variety and quantity in lunches at 4s. and dinners for visitors and residents at 5s. Hot shaving water was brought to the rooms upstairs until 1950 when wash-basins with running hot and cold water were provided for the first time.

Events on the golf course struck a happier note with new competitions and some outstanding golfers amongst both ladies and the men. The Stronach Cup was presented by Mrs. Stronach in memory of her late husband, J.L. Stronach, a former captain of the Club. This running mixed foursomes knockout remains today as popular as ever in the Club's fixture list and it was fitting that the

*Molly Wallis captains the England team to victory in the Home Internationals, 1948*

inaugural event in 1947 should have been won by Miss Molly Wallis, playing with her uncle, H.S. Whetham. He had recently introduced his niece to the Club from Basingstoke where she learned to play golf and from where she entered championships, although she now played most of her golf at North Hants.

Her golfing achievements in 1947 and 1948 make Molly Wallis, now Mrs. Molly Thompson and an Honorary Member, the outstanding post-war lady golfer in the history of the Club, matching the pre-war achievements of Doreen Fowler. In 1947, at the age of twenty-four, she won the English Ladies Championship at Ganton where she defeated Elizabeth Price in the final, and in the same year she also won the Hampshire Ladies County Championship. She played for England in the Home Internationals in 1948 and 1949, successfully captaining the team to victory at Royal Lytham St. Annes. In 1948 she represented Great Britain against France in the Vagliano Trophy at Royal Mid-Surrey. In 1949 she married "Tique" Lock and then gave up competitive golf to look after a young growing family. Her relish and enjoyment of match play was mirrored by an equal distaste for medals. Barely known when she won the English Ladies Championship, she went on to the distinction of captaining the England team but, strangely, throughout her golfing career the lowest club handicap she ever achieved was 3.

She attributed much of her success over those two remarkable years to achieving a high level of physical fitness after W.A.A.F. service during the war and to coaching at Wentworth from Archie Compston, a famous Ryder Cup golfer in the 1920s and twice runner-up in the Open. But after appearing in the Vagliano Cup, her long, flowing swing and length off the tee was not to be seen again at championship level. She had been particularly unsettled by the abrupt departure of her coach earlier in the year from Wentworth to exile in Bermuda. It is believed that his idea of coaching one of the more senior lady members at Wentworth had been taken further than the club was prepared to tolerate.

The other outstanding lady member of the time was Gwen Morrison. She won the Hampshire Ladies County Championship three times in 1950, 1951 and 1962, adding to her four Derbyshire county titles won in 1929, 1931, 1932 and 1934 as Miss Gwen Cradock Hartopp, her maiden name before she married the famous J.S.F. Morrison. In 1935, entering from Buxton, she won the Worplesdon Foursomes, playing with her brother Sir John Cradock Hartopp, later to become a distinguished member of North Hants after the war. Gwen Morrison was an England international in 1936. She played regularly for Hampshire from 1949 to 1967 and was County captain in 1964 and 1965.

The men could not match those distinctions but the standard was high in the late 1940s. J.W. Nelson continued where he had left off before the war, still playing off scratch and winning the Currie Cup in 1946 and 1947 and the Gold Medal for the sixth time in 1947. F.H. Hayward won both Gold Medal and Currie Cup in 1948, playing off scratch whilst briefly a member of the Club and R.L. Pearcy won the Gold Medal in 1949. He was also a member of the R.A.E. Golfing Society and winner or runner-up of countless monthly medals and bogeys. The remarkable common factor of these three consecutive winners of the Gold Medal was their age. They all became eligible in 1947 or 1948 to play in the Wilks Plate, a competition open only to those aged fifty-five or more.

This chapter closes with a flurry of decisions in 1950 which reflected changes in the world of golf. The emergence of the golf trolley required one of the barns to be converted into a trolley shed. A fashion for providing more information on the golf course led to the positioning of 200 yard distance posts from the tee at the "long holes" and some direction posts pointing from the green to the next tee. The Club tie was introduced. The English Golf Union rationalised the national system of calculating the standard scratch score and as a result it was lowered at North Hants from 74 to 72 and a newly designed score card was introduced. Lastly, sadly, despite resistance from Hindley, the last remaining horse was put down. Earlier in the year he had drawn the attention of the Committee to the risks involved of having "no second line of defence if the tractor broke down" and the risk of a reduction in the petrol grant, but by September it was agreed that the horse was getting old and lame and should be put down before the winter.

Chapter Five

# The Prime of Reginald Pearce
## 1950–1960

No INDIVIDUAL has played a greater part in the history and development of the Club than R.H.F. Pearce. A well-known local dentist practising in Farnborough, Reg Pearce was a well-built stocky man with strong features, sleek hair, a welcoming smile and ready laughter. Impeccably dressed, he was immensely sociable and in his element in the company of friends exchanging stories in the bar of a busy golf club. He sported a monocle and would endlessly light and relight a large pipe from which he was rarely parted, even in full swing on the tee. But his natural friendliness went further than that. He would extend a welcoming hand to new members, juniors and visitors alike and was altogether a wonderful ambassador for the Club, enjoying the company of a network of friends in the wider golfing community.

He joined the Club in 1945. He immediately made his presence felt and became a member of the Executive Committee in 1948, where he retained a seat for the next thirteen years as member, vice-captain or captain. These were the days when the Executive Committee would of its own choice co-opt its new members and Club members saw no reason why people doing a good job should be required to step down. Reg Pearce also made his presence felt in the car park, which always bore witness to his life long belief that the best value in a motor car was a second-hand Rolls-Royce.

He was a competent golfer with a rather rigid but powerful swing and his lowest club handicap was 5. He suffered from what today might be described as acute noise distraction syndrome, real or imagined, and would often be heard cheerfully explaining how the round had got away from him in the closing holes because of some distraction, such as, on one occasion, the buzz of an electric razor emanating from the open window of a house in Elvetham Road opposite the 17th tee. On far distant parts of the course he would wait for a train to pass before playing his next shot. He loved to recount the story of the hole-in-one he achieved at the 15th in a Sunday morning fourball in the days when railway workers would lean over the fence by the green as they took a break from collecting lost golf balls from the railway line. One of them knowingly informed Reg that "he was the first one to get it in all morning". He was a traditionalist who believed that the rules of good behaviour and golfing etiquette were there to be observed but at the same time he was a no-nonsense individual who applied his talents to leading the Club forward and building its reputation.

He was a Committee member from 1948 to 1961 and captain in 1955, 1956, 1959 and 1960. He was involved in the crucial decision to raise subscriptions described in the last chapter and as captain in 1955 he pushed through further increases to keep the Club on a proper financial footing. He presided over a necessary expansion in the Club membership through the decade, but, above all, it was his inspiration to found the Hampshire Hog in 1957. He presented a magnificent trophy for a thirty-six hole Open Amateur scratch medal competition, adding an important event to the fairly modest amateur circuit of the day. From its inception the "Hog" has attracted fields of international quality and, above all, it was his particular vision which built in the golfing world a reputation for the golf course comparable to that of its local rival Bramshot in the pre-war years. In particular, the course was admired for the quality of what at the time were eight long and testing par fours. The history of the Hampshire Hog and its list of winners is the subject of a later, separate chapter.

Amongst members who played regularly with him was the late Peter Breedon who remembered him well:

A pipe-smoking, snuff-taking, hard-drinking, bemonocled dentist, he was undeniably a character. Possessed of great charm and old-fashioned courtesy, his gracious welcome to me as a new member just returned from abroad in 1967 was genuinely heart-warming. Off the course, Reg was usually the life and soul of the party. A dedicated beer-drinker, he had an additional penchant for Black Bottle Whisky – blended by Graham's of Aberdeen – not entirely coincidentally the home-town of his delightful wife, Peggy. On the golf course, he was a most agreeable, amusing and punctilious companion. Among his wide golfing acquaintances was the legendary Bobby Locke to whom he had administered substantial emergency dental treatment overnight between rounds of a tournament at Wentworth.

Bobby Locke frequently played at North Hants in the 1960s and there hangs in the clubhouse a signed card of a round of 66 played with Reg Pearce and Heather Clifford in June 1967.

It is important to put on record the part played by Reg Pearce in the history of the Club in the 1950s. These were his best years because, as with so many people who take the lead in building something special, he could never really let go. After thirteen successive years on the Executive Committee from 1948 to 1961 and four years as captain, he sought re-election to the Committee in 1963 where he served for another seven years. Thereafter he

| Player A.D. LOCKE | | | | | Player's Sig. Bobby Locke | | | S.S.S. 71 |
|---|---|---|---|---|---|---|---|---|
| H'cap | Date 30-6-67 | | | | Marker's Sig. R. Buller | | | |
| Hole | Marker's Score | Yards | Par | Player's Score | Hole | Yards | Par | Score Player's |
| 1 | | 280 | 4 | 4 | 10 | 200 | 3 | 3 |
| 2 | | 476 | 5 | 4 | 11 | 388 | 4 | 3 |
| 3 | | 366 | 4 | 4 | 12 | 454 | 4 | 4 |
| 4 | | 165 | 3 | 3 | 13 | 337 | 4 | 3 |
| 5 | | 453 | 4 | 4 | 14 | 400 | 4 | 4 |
| 6 | | 396 | 4 | 4 | 15 | 153 | 3 | 3 |
| 7 | | 433 | 4 | 5 | 16 | 428 | 4 | 4 |
| 8 | | 133 | 3 | 3 | 17 | 502 | 5 | 4 |
| 9 | | 434 | 4 | 3 | 18 | 439 | 4 | 4 |
| Out | | 3136 | 35 | 34 | In | 3301 | 35 | 32 |
| | | | | | Out | 3136 | 35 | 34 |
| | | | | | Total | 6437 | 70 | 66 |
| | | | | | HANDICAP | | | |

*Bobby Locke goes round in 66, June 1967*

rather sadly became somewhat disenchanted with matters in the Club. Rightly or wrongly, his influence came to be perceived as rather proprietorial and his closing years at the Club were less happy.

In 1983, he and his wife Peggy emigrated to South Africa to be close to their son, Geoffrey, who had earlier left to work and live in Port Elizabeth. And the Rolls-Royce came too, as the many members who visited them in Port Elizabeth came to discover in the car park of the beautiful Homewood golf course. Reg Pearce died in 1997 at the age of eighty-four. His son Geoffrey was a good golfer in his days at North Hants where he won the Gold Medal in 1972 at the first extra hole after a triple tie with father and son Barry and Michael Armstrong.

However, in the 1950s Reg Pearce had not been alone in caring deeply about the Club. He played a lot of golf with Hugh Clifford and Ron Bellamy, who both served the Club as Committee members soon after the war and later as captains. Hugh Clifford was a successful business man who had such a long pause at the top of his backswing that unsuspecting members would look on with some concern. Ron Bellamy was a tall, distinguished man with a moustache, looking the part of the army officer he had once been. Following a succession of unsatisfactory paid secretaries after the war, he volunteered to become honorary secretary of the Club, a role he carried out from May 1951 to July 1953, despite commuting daily to London to his responsibilities at the offices of Middlesex County Council.

Ron Bellamy was succeeded as honorary secretary by Charles Neate, a member since 1922 and another wonderful servant to the Club. He was manager of the Fleet branch of Lloyds Bank at a time when bank managers stayed long enough in one place to become pillars of the local community. He brought those qualities of diligence and discretion to a long reign of nine years of unpaid service as honorary secretary from 1953 to 1962, often cycling down to the Club to open the post during his break for lunch. He was an enthusiastic golfer who, as the years went by, became possessed of the minutest possible backswing on a short putt.

Another distinctive character was Sir Paul Pechell, a long-standing Committee member and captain in 1957 and 1958. He was a Baronet with a distinguished war record who suffered an injury to an eye and skull damage which required the insertion of metal plates. He held the interests of the Club at heart in so many ways and was one of only two members of the Club to become president of the Hampshire County Golf Union, an office he held from 1951 to 1953. He was a great enthusiast, not least for what he believed to be his driving skills which, returning after one particular evening function at Camberley Golf Club, found him taking his surprised passengers into a darkened Blackbushe Airport and down the runway. Meanwhile, the ladies were equally well served by Sandy Sellors, Ladies' captain in 1950 and 1951, Ladies' secretary from 1956 to 1972 and Hampshire Ladies County captain for five years in the early 1950s.

It was towards the end of the 1950s that the army influence began to wane. Its post-war presence was epitomised by Major General C.H.H. Vulliamy, a redoubtable soldier in the Royal Corps of Signals in the Second World War, a tartar on the golf course and an abrasive personality who firmly believed that civilian members of a golf club were there to be called by their surname. He was only of modest build but those piercing eyes and an abrupt economy of speech were a long way short of friendly to those who did not know him well, although he mellowed in later years. In fact, as we have already seen, the initiative of the running of the Club at this time was firmly in the hands of civilian members. Another small sign of changing times occurred in 1953, when the tiger's head in the dining room was returned with thanks to its owner and replaced by a framed copy of the famous Annigoni portrait of Queen Elizabeth on the occasion of her coronation.

A critical moment in the balance of the membership occurred in November 1955 when a Special General Meeting was convened by Reg Pearce to gain approval for an increase in subscriptions. The Club was generating annual surpluses, but looking ahead, the Committee decided that an extra £800 should be raised from subscriptions to finance continuing improvements. A restructure of subscriptions involved taking a harder line with the previously generous service and mess memberships.

The numbers in the different categories of membership in 1955 make interesting reading today:

| | | | |
|---|---|---|---|
| Ordinary Members | 137 | Country Members | 34 |
| Ladies | 55 | Service Members | 34 |
| 18/25 | 25 | Mess Members | 82 |
| Juniors | 34 | R.A.E. Golfing Society | 38 |

The subscription for ordinary members was increased from £10.10s.0d. to £12.12s.0d. and for ladies from £7.7s.0d. to £9.9s.0d. For officers on the active register who qualified as service members and for the R.A.E. Golfing Society, it was increased from £6.6s.0d. to £9.9s.0d. Mess membership, previously £4.4s.0d. per head, was to be raised to £9.9s.0d. with the intention of phasing it out altogether.

The R.A.E. Golfing Society appeared as a mess membership with some thirty members in 1946, growing to a peak of some sixty by 1950 and had become what might be described today as a loose cannon in the membership of the Club. An earlier chapter mentioned that it was refused a request for mess membership as long ago as 1926 on the grounds of the "crowded state of the course". Mess membership for serving officers had been created to reflect the transient nature of regimental life with a rotating membership and the reason for refusal probably had more to do with a belief that most of the members of the R.A.E. Golfing Society were in effect permanent residents. When mess memberships of all kinds were abandoned in 1962, those members of the R.A.E. Golfing Society wishing to join the Club were, somewhat controversially, offered full membership and fifteen of them accepted.

By the end of the decade the Club was in good financial shape. Membership numbers continued to grow and, in 1959, the Committee felt confident enough to re-introduce entry fees, which had been suspended since the outbreak of the war, and to warn that the ladies' membership was approaching its limit.

In the context of the golfing membership, the decade began with H.P. Lock succeeding John Nelson as the best golfer at North Hants. By one of those quirks of infant sibling pronunciation, Henry Parmiter Lock had been known since childhood as "Tique", and not, as many members supposed, "Teak", because of his ruddy complexion from an outdoor life as a supplier of agricultural lime to the farming community. He joined the Club as a scratch golfer in 1948, shortly after winning the inaugural Men's Open

## The 1950s

*Tique Lock*

*Frank Deighton*

*Sir John Cradock Hartopp*

*J.S.F. Morrison*

Meeting with two rounds of 76. He completed a fine double by winning the inaugural Open Mixed Foursomes in 1949, playing with Molly Wallis whom he would later marry.

Tique Lock was a talented cricketer, good enough in his youth to achieve a trial for Sussex, but golf became his first love. He was one of three golfing brothers playing at Goodwood Golf Club, where he won the Club Championship six times between 1928 and 1947. He was not particularly tall or well-built but he had strong arms and hands. He was a deceptively good golfer, and in those days of fast running fairways he generated length off the tee by drawing the ball in Bobby Locke fashion with a wristy "in to out" swing. He was a fine iron player and used a hickory shafted putter with a silky touch well suited to fast greens. He played county golf for Sussex in the pre-war years and regularly for Hampshire in the post-war years when he and John Cradock Hartopp formed a powerful foursomes combination.

His golfing achievements at North Hants include winning the Gold Medal four times in 1951, 1952, 1953 and 1955 and the Hampshire County Championship in 1954 at the age of fifty-four. In that event he also led North Hants to a rare victory in the associated Club Team Championship, based on the aggregate score of a team of three in the thirty-six hole scratch medal from which sixteen qualifiers emerged for the match play stage. Lock scored 152 as did George Meier, together with 163 from Ken Barker.

His low scoring and consistency round North Hants was legendary, particularly in the monthly medals and bogeys and in August 1951 he returned 7 up in a bogey competition with a gross score of 65. He narrowly failed to achieve his keenest ambition of all, which was to win the inaugural Hampshire Hog, by driving out of bounds at the 35th hole when in close contention. Shortly after that he suffered a heart attack that curbed his golf but not sufficiently to prevent him from recovering to win the Currie Cup in 1960. His was always a refreshing presence in those more formal days and he took a keen interest in the golfing careers of the younger members.

A controversial golfer at the time was B.W. Parmenter, who became holder of the course record in 1950. Bert Parmenter was the Berks, Bucks & Oxon County champion when his name came before the Committee for election to membership in June 1950, one week after he won the Club's 1950 Open Meeting with gross scores of 67 and 72, establishing a new course record in the morning round. Parmenter was a talented golfer and he celebrated his election by winning the 1950 Gold Medal with a 72. His membership was controversial and he left the Club under something of a cloud after being a member for only two years and there was some relief in the Club when the first hole was lengthened in 1954, by converting its original tee into the present practice putting green, so enabling Parmenter's course record of 67 to be put quietly to one side.

Around this time, the Committee elected some distinguished golfers as Honorary Members of the Club. The first was Dr. F.W.G. Deighton in 1951, followed by Lieutenant Colonel A.A. Duncan in 1952, G.H. Micklem in 1958 and Miss Enid Wilson in 1959.

Frank Deighton was a twenty-three year old doctor and Scottish international golfer who was a service member of North Hants whilst doing national service in the R.A.M.C. He was such a pillar of strength in the Army golf team that for two years he was not allowed to escape from Aldershot and he was elected an Honorary Member of the Club to mark his selection for the 1951 Walker Cup team. Tony Duncan, a pillar of Welsh and Army golf, was well known at the Club during his years at the Staff College and was elected in 1952 to mark his selection as captain of the 1953 Walker Cup team. Gerald Micklem, who was a dominant figure in amateur golf as player, selector and administrator, was elected in 1958 to acknowledge the strong support he gave to the Hampshire Hog in its early years. His encouragement to leading amateur golfers to play in it amounted to a three line whip and he ensured a high quality field from its inception.

Enid Wilson was the British Ladies Amateur champion for three consecutive years from 1931, twice England Amateur champion and a frequent international. She became a leading golf correspondent on women's golf for *The Daily Telegraph* and her election was a thank you for bringing to North Hants in 1959 two well-publicised matches between a British girls team against Canada/South Africa and Australia/New Zealand, many of whom were over here for a Commonwealth tournament.

Perhaps the most remarkable member of the Club was J.S.F. Morrison, a towering figure of a man in every sense of the word. John Stanton Fleming Morrison was a man of many talents. At Cambridge he won Blues for cricket, soccer and golf, the first two before the First World War in which he served as an R.A.F. pilot and all three when he returned to Cambridge in 1919. He played left back for the amateur soccer team, the Corinthians, and was famous for taking goal kicks from one end of the pitch to the other with the heavy leather ball of the time. He was captain of the Corinthians team that defeated Blackburn Rovers in the F.A. Cup in 1923 and also played briefly for Sunderland. In the golfing world he won the Belgian Amateur Championship in 1929 and played for England against Ireland in the Home Internationals in 1930. He formed a successful foursomes partnership with Joyce Wethered, the finest lady golfer of her generation, and together they won the Worplesdon Foursomes in 1928 and the Sunningdale Foursomes in 1935 and 1936.

He was captain in 1933 of Sunningdale Golf Club, where his name on the honours board follows the Prince of Wales in 1930 and the Duke of York in 1932. In the pre-war years he became a well-known golf architect and a partner in Colt, Allison & Morrison where he indulged his preference for long par fives, evidenced by his work on the West Course at Wentworth and Princes at Sandwich. He was also a writer and editor of books on golf.

He married Gwen Cradock Hartopp in 1938 and was a member of North Hants from 1949 until his death in 1961. He was a man of many eccentricities. On the golf course he was once described as "sometimes fortified against inclement weather by a mackintosh skirt and an old coat tied about with string". Sometimes he played with a handful of clubs in the tiniest of pencil bags and at other times with a kind of contraption of a golf bag with separate holes for a miscellany of clubs and pockets for suitable refreshment. He regularly took snuff and was a prolific user of the new fruit machine that arrived in the clubhouse in 1951, operated mechanically by hand and spewing out sixpenny coins for the three winning barrels. He was the kind of man around whom stories abound. One concerns a golfing occasion in the 1930s where in a crowded bar his pint tankard was knocked over by an embarrassed member who hurriedly offered to replace it. The member was discreetly advised that it was a pint of sherry.

For keen golfers this was one of the best of all golfing decades. There was a burst of optimism in the country following the return of a Conservative government in 1951 and the end of controls and rationing led to a resurgence enjoyed as much as any by the golfing classes of the day. In particular there was a greater freedom to travel round the country and discover famous golf courses all but deserted and delighted to welcome any visitors at all.

The game was still narrowly based in many private golf clubs, with membership heavily dependent on being born into a golfing family, itself usually drawn from the professional and public school educated classes. This was reflected in the Club's fixture list. In a loose imitation of the Halford Hewitt public schools event there was the Travers-Rountree Cup. It was a match play foursomes held over a weekend for a maximum of sixteen pairs made up of two members or a member and guest, entering from their public school. It attracted a full entry for several years after its introduction in 1947, but gradually faded away until abandoned in 1974.

Of wider public golfing interest in the south of England at the time were annual matches held by leading clubs against the Oxford and Cambridge University teams, which often included some current or prospective amateur internationals. There was added interest at North Hants because three junior members of the Club went on to win golf Blues at Oxford and Cambridge. In opposing teams, but not meeting, were John Churchill, who played for Cambridge in 1956, 1957 and 1958 and your author, who played for Oxford in 1958 and 1959 and was captain in the latter year. We were successive winners of the Gold Medal at North Hants at the time and were followed as Blues by Charles Churchill, younger brother of John, who played for Cambridge in 1961 and was Gold Medal winner in 1963. Other long-standing but later members of the Club to have won Blues are John Parry Jones, who played for Oxford in 1958 and 1959 and in the Home Internationals for Wales in 1959 and 1960, and Tim Hanson who played for Cambridge in 1967.

The Club's fixtures against the universities began in 1951 with a match against the Oxford second team, the Divots, followed in 1952 with a fixture against the full Oxford team. There are no references to how these matches began but they may well have been arranged by Tony Duncan, himself a former Oxford captain. Further annual matches were arranged in 1958 against London University, for which Philip Mitchell then regularly played, and in 1960 against the Cambridge second team, the Stymies. The latter led in 1966 to a match against the full Cambridge team.

This sequence of scratch matches, all in the winter months, created much interest in the Club. The format was usually five foursomes and ten singles and the matches against the two Blues' teams were always well supported both by members of the Club and by the players themselves who, once their match was finished in the afternoon, would walk back to seek out any close matches at the bottom of the draw. In one match against Oxford in November 1959, Philip Mitchell, playing in the last single, found himself all square on the 18th tee and was about to agree a half in the gathering darkness when a rush of players emerged out of the gloom to say that the match was level. Members of both teams scattered to listen out for the drives and the second shots. After finding the second shots, Philip Mitchell remembers "Both of us finished just off the green. By now it was impossible to see where the hole was and Reg Pearce, then Captain, went to the flag and lit up the hole with his cigarette lighter". He chipped to two feet and holed the putt to win the match.

At North Hants the modest number of members in the 1950s meant there was rarely any pressure on the 1st and 10th tees and the condition of the course benefited from far fewer rounds being played in the average week. The typical Cup competition or monthly medal would attract some thirty entrants, nearly all of whom were well known to each other. Rounds were played in two-balls in quick time and mostly in the morning, leaving more time to congregate in the bar and compare scores. There was room on competition days for those members who preferred to play at their leisure, and during the week golfing societies, then few in number, intruded less.

Memories of the 1950s still remain fresh in the minds of some who were members at the time. Robert Alexander was a junior member struggling to keep up with the golfing talents of his younger brother, Neil, who went on to win the Hampshire Boys Championship in 1958, the Club Gold Medal in 1960 and 1961 and the Hampshire Youths Championship in 1961 and 1962. After a brilliant legal career and now Lord Alexander of Weedon, he remembers:

The clubhouse being well laid out, dominated by elegant wall panelling with a discreet but kindly atmosphere. The military, and not least the retired military, were very much in evidence with what seemed to a youngster courtesy but a formal reserve.

Another junior member at the time, Charles Churchill, recalls how the course was so deserted on weekdays during the school holidays that three rounds in a day were often played and "it amazes me now to think how we used to pitch balls from near the ninth green to the 18th and back again for pennies in the evenings". Ann Murch, daughter of the late Mrs. Bobby Slater, now lives in California and remembers how in a frozen winter she and Mary Morrison would endlessly ride their sledges down the slope of the 6th fairway. She recalls how as small children they were allowed in the clubhouse and how in quiet moments they would discreetly use and waste their sixpenny pieces on the one-armed bandit.

The character of the course was very different from today. Frank Deighton recalls his admiration for the course "It had charm, character, a wonderful layout and an endearing privacy". Within the boundaries of the course there were few trees and the fast running fairways and greens were exposed to sun and wind. None of the clumps of silver birches and oaks familiar today were there, as can be seen from the photograph taken from the 12th tee and published in *Golf Illustrated* in January 1951.

There was only a solitary tree by the 10th green. Heather heavily penalised topped drives on many holes and wayward shots, particularly between the 12th/13th and 14th/16th fairways. A tee shot falling short of the 15th green would be in heather deep enough to make recovery to the green difficult. Parts of the 3rd and 11th fairways were mown heather. In a letter written before he died in 1998, Reg Pearce recalled "the skylarks rising and singing on the 11th fairway", no doubt also remembering the distraction they used to cause him.

The greens had the firm and thinly grassed character of the typical seaside green and were larger and faster than today. Many bunkers now often stranded several paces from the edge of the greens today were then literally greenside. The greens were mown right up to a wind blown, drier and therefore flatter front lip of a bunker into which a long putt too firmly struck from one end of a green to the other would occasionally disappear. The greenside bunker at the 17th was smaller than today but within the green itself and, if misjudged, putts of modest distance from below the bank would find their way into it. With only limited hand-watering there were times of the year when golfers were for ever chipping back from behind the green, particularly at the 3rd, 6th and 8th holes, and the danger from over-clubbing was very inhibiting at holes like the 7th, 12th and 14th. In the article by J.S.F. Morrison, he describes how at the 8th, the "tee shot must be really well struck to get sufficient stop to prevent the ball careering over the green".

These comments would, of course, have applied to the playing characteristics of other local golf courses built on Bagshot sand, but one notorious difficulty of North Hants has since been greatly eased. The railway line to the right of the 16th and 17th holes is still out of bounds today but it used to be far more intimidating when it lay in full view from the tee, barely obstructed by trees, particularly from the higher 17th tee. The 16th had the further difficulty that running along the right of the fairway was a deep lateral water hazard into which a drive, avoiding the bunker in the middle of the fairway but with barely a hint of slice, would quickly scamper from a fast running fairway.

Today, the view of the railway line from both tees is obstructed by trees and on the 16th both the ditch and the bunker are filled in. The fear of negotiating these two closing holes used to cast its shadow well before they had been reached whereas today the consequence of a sliced tee shot preys much less on the mind. Although it was frowned upon, some would protect their card at the 17th by driving down the 11th fairway, laying up around the 11th tee and pitching across to the 17th green, an option made impossible by trees today.

Temperaments were tested more in those trickier conditions. Shots to the green had to be fashioned with clubs less forgiving than they are today over distances judged by the eye alone. The bounce of the smaller golf ball and the difficulty in controlling it preyed on the mind as it ran at times uncontrollably through greens and off fairways. These were days when that modern call "be right" would have had about it the flavour of a genuine prayer for a favourable bounce and a ball slowing down in time as a shot threaded its way to the green, rather than its self-congratulatory edge today of exhorting a good shot to pitch close to the flag.

There were very few long hitters, but those who were attracted great attention, as for example when the legendary Ted Dexter occasionally visited the course and comfortably found the first green with a spoon, or a 3-wood as it came to be known. Part of their length was achieved by the greater run of the small ball on firmer fairways and only those few long hitters matched the distances achieved by so many today. In summer conditions in the late 1950s one of the golf ball manufacturers brought along a driving machine. It was installed on the 9th tee and to compete against it, the Club nominated George Gidney, one of those gifted amateurs with the full and powerful whipping swing of the natural games player. He lagged a few yards behind the machine which finished fairly close to the bunker on the left side of the fairway.

There was none of the proliferation today of the many brands of golf balls with their different cores, covers and compressions. It was a question of a Dunlop 65, Penfold Patented, Slazenger or Spalding Top-Flite for the better golfers, with some cheaper versions available such as the Spitfire or the Dunlop Warwick. One way of gaining extra control at a short hole like the 8th would be to take out an old ball with less bounce. All these factors contributed to making the learning process of a young golfer in the 1950s a longer apprenticeship than it is today and as a result the best golfers in any golf club were just as likely to be in their forties and fifties as in their twenties and a teenager playing at county or championship level was a rare genius. It is very different today when an accurate yardage chart is all that is needed for the well-taught teenager to decide which club to use to pitch a balata covered ball close to the flag on a watered green.

On 26th June 1954 the Club celebrated its first fifty years by holding a Jubilee Day. In the morning a mixed foursomes bogey competition was won by Colonel and Mrs. A.A. Duncan and Mrs. Bobby Slater and F.H. Hayward, both returning all square. This was held in advance of a Jubilee Lunch to be followed at 2.45 p.m. by an exhibition match between Henry Cotton and Tony Duncan against Bob Mounce and D.L. Woon, the New Zealand Amateur Champion. It must have been a disappointing moment for a large crowd, and an embarrassment for him, when Henry Cotton limped to a halt with a pulled muscle at the 8th and his place was taken by Tique Lock.

Cotton entertained the members at a buffet supper with a film show and a long question and answer session and promised to return later in the year. This he duly did in November when he played in an exhibition match in front of some seventy-five members with Bob Mounce against Tique Lock and John Cradock Hartopp. The amateurs were given a three up start but lost 4 and 3.

The president of the Club, Sir Fitzroy Anstruther-Gough-Calthorpe, died in 1957 after holding this position for a remarkable forty-six years. He had become the second president of the Club after the death of Lord Calthorpe and was created a Baronet in 1929. He was married to Rachel, daughter of Lord Calthorpe, who inherited the Estate and was honoured as Dame Rachel for services to the Red Cross during the Second World War.

The Club was fortunate to enjoy their understanding, generosity and goodwill over more than forty years. In addition to his presidency, Sir Fitzroy had been captain of the Club in 1925 and 1926 and was throughout his life an enthusiastic golfer playing well into his eighties. Bob Mounce described his weekly Friday afternoon round with Sir Fitzroy which, with the passing years, became matches over twelve, nine and six holes and eventually twice round the putting green.

Dame Rachel died in 1951, when the Estate passed to her son, Brigadier Richard Anstruther-Gough-Calthorpe, who was a regular army officer and member of the Club, although he rarely played. Having succeeded his mother as landlord of the Club in 1951, he now succeeded his father as the third president of the Club in 1957 and he was later to play a critical role in its future.

This chapter closes with an account of a difficult decision faced by the Committee in 1958 about the future of the Club. It is written in some detail because of a common belief that persisted amongst many members that in 1958 the Committee turned down an offer from the Estate to buy the Club for £8,000. No such offer was ever actually made but discussions were held that might have led either to the negotiation of a new and longer lease or to the possible purchase of the Club and the building of a new clubhouse.

The existing lease was for thirty-five years from 1947 to 1982 at an annual rent of £400, with the Club responsible for internal repairs and maintenance and the Estate responsible for external and structural repairs to the clubhouse. This latter liability was bearing heavily on the Estate and a serious dry rot problem had also been identified. In December 1956, the agent suggested a cancellation of the lease and its replacement by a new twenty-five year lease at a reduced annual rental of £200, but with full repairing responsibility assumed by the Club after all existing defects had been put right by the landlord.

Negotiations moved forward very slowly, but eventually the Club accepted strong professional advice to turn down the proposal because of the inevitable long-term burden of repairing a building in a deteriorating condition. Thoughts about a new clubhouse then came to the surface. This could only be achieved either by the landlord building it in return for a higher rental in a new lease or by the Club building it after buying the freehold. A Sub-Committee chaired by the captain, Sir Paul Pechell, was formed in August 1958 to consider the alternatives. Its other members were the vice-captain, George Gidney, and Ron Bellamy, Tique Lock and Charles Neate.

Upon being informed that this was happening, the agent for the Elvetham Estate, H.E. Greening, wrote to the Club advising that "there could be no question of my recommending the Estate to build a new Clubhouse", but with regard to a possible sale "it would depend entirely on the offer which your Committee put forward. Personally I should say that this would have to be of the order of £8,000 … but I have no authority for saying it would be accepted".

In November 1958, the Sub-Committee presented a detailed report written largely by Ron Bellamy, who applied his financial expertise as the investment manager of the Middlesex County Council Pension Fund. He estimated that a new clubhouse would cost £16,000. It could be financed by the landlord in return for an increase in the annual rent from £400 to £1,200, or the Club could offer £8,000 for the freehold and raise total borrowings of £24,000. However, he cautioned that finance may be more difficult to raise than expected against the security of a "down-at-heel golf club" and an interest rate of $7\frac{1}{2}$ per cent might be required. This would cost £1,800 a year plus a provision of, say, £600 a year to amortise the loan. After allowing for savings from rent and from running a more efficient clubhouse, the overall additional cost worked out at an average increase in all subscriptions of around one-third.

The report concluded by saying that if rebuilding is not possible, then the Club has either to continue its lease or negotiate a new lease, with either prospect leading to a rising maintenance burden and increased subscriptions. The report was an excellent analysis of the options but its impact was muted by its opening paragraph that "the Sub-Committee has been unable to agree upon a unanimous recommendation".

This uncertainty must have bedevilled discussion of the report in the Executive Committee. It was decided to approach the Estate to ask the landlords to build a new clubhouse in exchange for a higher rental, but this was rebuffed in a letter from Mr. Greening in December 1958:

> So far as a new Club House is concerned there is no possibility at all of the Estate providing this. On the question of a sale of the freehold I am quite frankly apprehensive that this is not in the best interests of the Estate. Nevertheless if the Club cares to put forward an offer of £8,000 I will submit this to my Board for consideration.

The offer of a new lease made two years earlier was still left open but would be withdrawn at the end of January.

In a further letter he reminded the Club that if it purchased the freehold conditions would be imposed that upon any future sale to a third party the Estate would have first refusal and any development profits would be shared with the Estate. All the efforts of the Committee were frustrated by uncertainty and it all came to naught when the Committee decided by a majority vote at a meeting on 3rd January 1959 to continue with the present lease.

The decision was found to be "extremely disappointing" by the Estate, after so much effort had been made over such a long period, and the relationship could at best only be described as uneasy. In conclusion, careful reading of the correspondence shows that no offer of £8,000 was ever made by the Estate and that an offer from the Club of that amount would almost certainly not have been accepted.

By 1960, the Club was becoming better known, primarily due to the early success of the Hampshire Hog. This was a change from only a few years earlier when one of the finest golf writers of his day, Pat Ward-Thomas, golf correspondent of the *Manchester Guardian*, visited North Hants in December 1956 to report a Guildford Alliance meeting. Quite clearly, he knew nothing of this course which was still hiding its light under a bushel.

He began his report:

At the westernmost edge of the incomparable stretch of golfing country which runs through Surrey and Berkshire, and just before the pastoral meadowlands of Hampshire begin, lies Fleet, home of the North Hants club and as charming a course as one could wish to see.

He continued:

The course played beautifully and is one of unsuspected character, secluded within pine and birch but never too closely confined by them or by heather. It is not severe in length, but neither is it easy, for the fairways are not expansive and the greens must be among the largest on any inland course in the country. The approach shots must be accurate or putting becomes alarming.

Within a few months of this report the course would start to become better known with the inspirational decision of Reg Pearce to create the Hampshire Hog.

*Chapter Six*

# Golfing Peaks
## 1960–1970

THIS WAS a good decade for talented amateur golfers at North Hants. The Hampshire Hog had revealed the Club's existence to golfers of international rank and from within an ever widening radius it became the centre of attraction for good golfers settling in the area.

The first to join in a distinguished list of international golfers was Major D.A. Blair, who became a member in April 1960. He was followed in due course by two other Walker Cup players, S.W.T. Murray and D.W. Frame, and by English international, L.O.M. Smith. To this list of golfing talent should be added the name of T. Koch de Gooreynd.

These golfers brought much distinction to the Club as members during this golden decade. David Blair won the Hampshire Hog in 1966, 1967 and 1970. He played in the Walker Cup in 1955 and 1961, and was a regular Scottish international in the 1940s and 1950s. He was Scottish Amateur champion in 1953. His career was spent in the whisky business where he was a main Board Director of Distillers and he came to live in Finchampstead in 1960. He was of that generation when the top amateur golfers sustained both a career and golf over many years. He won the Hampshire Hog for the third time in 1970 at the age of fifty-two with rounds of 73 and 68.

His golf was unusual. He putted with a 3-iron and could not play bunker shots, but rarely needed to because his long game was so extraordinarily accurate. He played very little, but practised assiduously. His somewhat austere demeanour perhaps reflected a natural shyness and he was a man of few words. On one occasion after a match at the Club against one of the universities he was tentatively asked about his interests other than golf to which came the laconic reply "I hunt, I shoot, I fish, I ski". In 1981, he became the first president of the Club to follow the many decades of the Anstruther-Gough-Calthorpe family, having then returned home to the club of his birthplace, Nairn, in 1979. He died at the age of sixty-seven in 1985.

*David Blair – winner of the Hampshire Hog, 1966, 1967 and 1970*

The next to join the Club in June 1962 at the suggestion of Gerald Micklem was Stuart Murray. His golfing career closely matched that of David Blair. He was a regular Scottish international from 1959 to 1963, Scottish Amateur champion in 1962 and within a year of joining he was selected to play in the Walker Cup in 1963. He became only the second golfer from North Hants to win the Hampshire County Championship in 1963.

His glittering period of membership ended abruptly in October 1963. Murray was a sales representative for John Letters, one of the major golf club manufacturers, and he became a victim of what many at the time believed to be a harsh decision of the Amateur Status Committee of the R&A that his career was so specifically dependent on playing golf that it offended his amateur status. He faced the alternative of finding another job or turning professional. He never regretted his decision to turn professional, enjoying local competitive success in the Midlands in the 1960s and remaining a club professional until recent retirement.

Tim Koch de Gooreynd first joined North Hants in 1953 for a brief spell when he was remembered as a chronic slicer who could never complete the last three holes. When he returned in April 1963 he had blossomed into a formidable amateur golfer and was about to embark on a period of extraordinary golfing success, which began when he won the Hampshire Hog in 1965. In 1966 he achieved a golfing double of match play events by winning the Wentworth Foursomes and the London Amateur Foursomes. He won the Wentworth Foursomes, then an important early spring event for leading professionals and amateurs, in partnership with Robin Davenport, a young assistant at the Club to Bob Mounce and in partnership with Lionel Smith he won the London Amateur Foursomes for North Hants.

In the Hampshire County Championship held at North Hants in 1968 he and fellow member, Lionel Smith, worked their way through the match play stages to meet in the final, and in a close match Koch de Gooreynd became the third member of the Club to win the county title. Together with Mike Blanford, they also won the Club team championship based on aggregate

*Reg Pearce presents the Hampshire Hog to winner, Tim Koch de Gooreynd, 1965, watched by the captain, Dick Ubee*

medal scores in the thirty-six hole qualifying rounds. He won the Gold Medal three times at North Hants in 1965, 1967 and 1969.

He was an outstanding foursomes player. In addition to winning the two tournaments with Robin Davenport and Lionel Smith, he was also a member of the successful Eton team that won the Halford Hewitt Tournament at Deal in 1967 and 1968. He played in the top foursome with Bruce Critchley, winning all four matches in the semi-finals and finals in those two years.

His visible excitement at winning the Hampshire Hog suggested that this was his proudest moment on the golf course. He was an extrovert with a beaming smile, larger than life and a larger than average waistline for a golfer of his modest height. He was an Etonian and a music publisher whose partnership with Lionel Smith, an intrepid Lancastrian working in the chemical industry, was a true example of opposites working successfully together on the golf course. His punchy, powerful three-quarter swing was in complete contrast to the full classic flowing swing of Lionel Smith, but he was highly competitive and an inspirational putter with a magical stroke.

He was a wealthy man who decided in 1969 to emigrate to Portugal to escape the clutches of what then seemed like endless years of Labour governments and high personal taxation. It was ironical that the Conservatives should, within a year, win the 1970 general election, an outcome that seemed

*Robin Davenport and Tim Koch de Gooreynd win the Wentworth Foursomes, 1966*

so unlikely at the time of his move to Portugal. He had generously presented two Dinner Cups in 1963 for that combination of a dinner on an October Friday evening, with betting on the foursomes pairings drawn out of a hat for an eighteen hole stableford on the Saturday morning. After he emigrated his name was warmly toasted in his absence and good wishes were sent to an ebullient, competitive golfer with a laugh that could be heard from one end of the clubhouse to the other.

The Dinner Cups successfully survives, retaining its popularity over many years. It has produced one extraordinary statistical quirk, given that partners are drawn out of a hat. In 1984, Don Waddington and John Shepherd drew each other and went on to win. In 1988 they drew each other again and went on to win for a second time. For Don Waddington the latter win was a most unusual highlight of his year as Club captain. The event thrives, but as each year passes fewer members will know of or remember its donor, Tim Koch de Gooreynd, who died in Penina in 1987.

David Frame played in the Walker Cup in 1961 and was a regular England international from 1958 to 1963. He joined the Club in October 1963 although his membership was always going to be secondary to the role played in his golfing life by Worplesdon. There he holds the extraordinary records of having won the club championship in six successive decades and having his name appearing on the honours boards more times than the standard scratch score of the course. He was a member at North Hants for only two years, but revisited the Club to win the Hampshire Hog in 1971.

The last of the five to join was Lionel Smith in April 1965, when he moved south from his native Manchester to live in Fleet, although for long periods his career took him overseas to live in the Middle East. He played for England in the Home Internationals in 1963 and quickly made his presence felt at North Hants in 1966 when he won the Gold Medal and the London Amateur Foursomes. His battles with and against Tim Koch de Gooreynd are recorded above. Together they formed a highly successful top foursomes partnership for Hampshire and won the County Foursomes Championship in 1967. He won the Gold Medal at North Hants three times in 1966, 1975 and 1976 and won the Courage Trophy, a county stroke play event, in 1973. In recent years he has enjoyed his role as non-playing captain of a very successful Hampshire county team.

The achievements of the young assistant professional, Robin Davenport, should not be overlooked. After winning the Wentworth Foursomes in 1966, he completed a spring double ten days later by winning the Sunningdale Foursomes with another assistant professional, A.N. Walker, from Royal Wimbledon. Davenport enjoyed some modest success on the professional circuit, not least finishing in the top twenty-five in the 1967 Open Championship. He later became a reinstated amateur and has since won the Derbyshire County Championship five times.

These were wonderful golfing years for North Hants. Adding in the victory in 1959 of Tony Duncan, an Honorary Member, the Club laid claim to winning five Hampshire Hogs, two County Championships, the London Amateur Foursomes, the Sunningdale Foursomes and the Wentworth Foursomes. The Club celebrated its sixtieth anniversary with a professional exhibition match on 3rd May 1964 when Dai Rees, then a relatively recent successful Ryder Cup captain, completed the course in 70 together with Peter Alliss, who scored 76.

There was also cause for celebration for the ladies. Heather Clifford, whose father was captain of the Club in 1954, clearly emerged towards the end of the decade as the outstanding lady member with a string of victories. She followed Gwen Morrison to become only the second member of the Club ever to win the Hampshire Ladies County Championship in 1967 and 1969. She won the South Eastern Ladies Championship in 1966, 1971 and 1972, the West Transvaal Ladies Championship in 1968 and 1970 and the Transvaal Championship in 1970. These victories were a reward for the conscious decision she made at the age of twenty-six to play golf seriously.

She went to John Stirling, a professional with a fine coaching reputation at Woking Golf Club, and remained under his tuition throughout her golfing

*Hampshire Ladies reach the County Finals at Little Aston, 1967. Back row: Gwen Morrison (first left), Mary Morrison (centre). Front row: Heather Clifford (left)*

life. She pursued her objective to be a serious golfer with a single-minded determination that was also the strongest feature of her game and her lowest handicap was plus 1. She came close to international selection during these vintage years, but it eluded her, probably because at the highest level, although very straight, she lacked length and was too dependent on a fine short game to achieve necessary success in the national championships. However, her golfing reputation was widely known enough for her to be appointed an England selector in 1977.

She married Geoffrey Glynn-Jones in 1976 and under both her maiden and married names played regularly for Hampshire from 1963 to 1985 and was County captain in 1978 and 1979. She particularly enjoyed the years 1967 and 1973 when Hampshire reached the national County finals. In 1967, the team of eight included three members from North Hants, Heather Clifford, Gwen Morrison, then bringing to a close eighteen years of regular county golf and her daughter, Mary Morrison, then in the early stages of county appearances that would continue through eleven years. In 1973, Heather and Mary were both members of the team. On both occasions the team was outgunned by the winners, Lancashire and Northumberland respectively, but either won or lost the remaining matches by a single point. Gwen and Mary

Morrison twice won the annual tournament for mothers and daughters held at Royal Mid-Surrey.

Meanwhile, there was a golf club to be managed and some of the pressures commonplace today raised their heads for the first time. There was unrest in late 1962 when the emergence of a deficit of more than £2,000 led to proposals that subscriptions should be increased from £14.14s.0d. to £18.18s.0d. for men and from £10.10s.0d. to £12.12s.0d. for ladies. There was a loss of confidence in the Executive Committee and a record number of fourteen candidates stood for seven places in 1963 including only three of the current members standing for re-election. The election marked the return to the Executive Committee of Reg Pearce, frustrated with the apparent loss of control over events.

The proposed subscription increases were eventually agreed after considerable discussion at the Annual General Meeting in March 1963. It was attended by 120 members and many were probably swayed only by a heavy loss of income during the great freeze that had lasted from January to March. Nevertheless, here were the first signs of what was to be a long-standing reluctance on the part of many members to pay a realistic subscription that matched the quality of the golf course they were privileged to play.

It was in 1962 that the first reference was made to a waiting list for new members. Membership ceilings of 300 for men and 120 for ladies were imposed but three years later the ceiling for men was raised to 350, because the course was "never over-crowded". Thought was given to closing the waiting lists and for the first time in its history the Club found itself in a seller's market. In the space of thirteen years the playing membership of the Club had more than doubled from 170 in 1949 to over 400. Golfing ability became a prime consideration for new members, with any golfer with a handicap of 4 or less allowed immediate entry and those with a handicap over 18 allowed only a restricted membership with limited playing rights.

Through the 1960s the Executive Committee took a robust line in pushing up the daily rates for Societies from £1.5s.0d. in 1960 to £3.15s.0d. in 1970, raising green-fees and re-introducing entrance fees, but always found it difficult to keep revenues ahead of rising costs. Inflation was beginning to edge higher and repair costs in the clubhouse were a running sore. Annual subscriptions for men were increased from £18.18s.0d. in 1963 to £25 in 1968 and £30 in 1971, but this last proposal of a twenty per cent increase in the light of an emerging deficit led to another display of heads in the sand by enough members for the proposal to be voted down at the Annual General Meeting on 23rd March 1970.

The minutes record that 160 members attended a fraught meeting and the proposal to increase subscriptions was rejected by forty-seven votes to thirty-four with many abstentions. With a deficit of some £4,000, the absurdity of the situation persuaded the Committee that this rejection was an emotional outburst rather than a vote of no confidence and a Special General Meeting was called for 11th April at which the same proposal was approved, but only for one year.

Quite separately the Executive Committee, as with its predecessor some seven years earlier, had been considering the possibility of altering the thirty-five year lease agreed in 1946. The captain at the time was Air Vice-Marshal Richard Ubee, who had helped Douglas Bader learn to play golf before the war. Dick Ubee had a commanding presence not least because of his rather vivid black eye patch that resulted from having to crash land an aeroplane during his post-war years as a test pilot at Farnborough. The Club wrote to the Elvetham Estate in June 1964 requesting either an extension to the lease or an opportunity for outright purchase. The Estate declined the latter but indicated a willingness to offer a full repairing fifty year lease at an annual rent of £600 for fifteen years, £900 for fifteen years and £1,400 for the last twenty years. Clubhouse repairs were running at such a level that there was a reluctance to accept the responsibility of a full repairing lease and in August 1964 the Executive Committee requested that a new clubhouse be built in exchange for a higher rent.

There was no enthusiasm on the part of the Estate to build a new clubhouse and negotiations made little progress over the next year, until in February 1966 the Estate formally offered the fifty year lease on the original terms. Under the recommendation of Ron Bellamy and Reg Pearce, the offer was rejected by the Executive Committee by six votes to two, the latter being the captain and vice-captain. The landlord, Sir Richard Anstruther-Gough-Calthorpe, made his exasperation known at this stage and, after further negotiations in which Ron Bellamy was much involved, the Estate responded by throwing in an offer to spend £4,000 immediately on some badly needed repairs and donating a further £3,000 to a repair fund. This was accepted by the Executive Committee and in January 1967 the new fifty year lease was signed.

At the same time that these promised structural repairs were being carried out by Rentokil, extensions to the clubhouse were also proposed and agreed. There was a phased programme to extend the men's locker room, build a new bar in the main lounge, improve the kitchen area and create the extended corner in the main lounge. Although the clubhouse had its problems, its character was part of the charm of the Club. Robin Mallinson, later to be captain and president of the Club, joined in 1969. He welcomed its "friendly, old-fashioned" clubhouse and remembers how without central heating "the stone-flagged hall would have been cold and unwelcoming were it not for the hot fire always burning on cold days". Robin Mallinson has over many years been a consistent low handicap golfer who once played to his handicap of 5 by returning a card of eight threes and ten fives. More recently, he has achieved the rare distinction of three times breaking his age on the golf course, one of them with a round of 69.

Close to the golf course the M3 was being constructed in 1969. It cut across the corner behind the 2nd green and 3rd tee, taking away some three acres of land and unfortunately the Club lost an intended screen of trees due to a felling error by the contractors. In return the Club benefited from a two per cent reduction in rent for loss of land and a newly surfaced and marked car park at a bargain price built by the embarrassed contractors. However, nothing would ever compensate for the loss of the heavenly silence in what had been a heavily wooded corner of the course.

There were other changes on the golf course during the 1960s. The 2nd hole was lengthened by thirty-five yards in 1963 and the 17th by twenty yards in 1968, but this additional length was more than nullified when the Army School of Survey measured the course later in 1968 and found it to be 207 yards shorter than shown on the card. As a result the par and the standard scratch score were both reduced by one stroke to 69 and 70 respectively. In smaller detail, rakes were provided in the bunkers in 1963 and a refreshment hut was built behind the 10th tee in 1964. Perhaps of more surprise is that winter rules were generally the exception rather than the rule, even with the use of the smaller ball.

As the number of members grew, the number of competitions began to proliferate. "A" and "B" Divisions were introduced for monthly medals, bogeys and stablefords in 1963 and time sheets on competition days quickly followed. By this time the number of entrants to competitions had on occasions exceeded 100. Midweek medals began in 1970. A welcome new competition was introduced by Brian Foot, a local farmer and popular member, who in 1969 presented pheasants for a dinner and as prizes for a stableford foursomes, with pairings drawn out of a hat. After he died in 1977, a trophy was presented by many of his friends for what became known as the Phoots Pheasant Phoursomes and for many years Mary Foot continued to provide pheasants for the winners.

There were changes in the greenstaff and in the clubhouse. Bill Brown was appointed head greenkeeper in 1966, a position he was to hold for twenty-one years. Charles Neate stepped down as honorary secretary in November 1962 and was succeeded by Major Tom Pratt, one of the nicest and gentlest members in the Club, but within a matter of months the golfing adage that existing members rarely succeed as secretaries in their own club proved to be all too true. He stood down as secretary but remained a popular and stalwart member of the Club, captain in 1969 and 1970 and for many a year the hard-working starter of the principal Club events.

DAILY MAIL, Friday, November 11, 1966

# Oh NO sir
## We don't tuck our trousers in our socks to play golf

**LANDLORD** Jack Harding has banned members of the local golf club from his public house-because they did not like him playing with his trousers tucked into his socks.

He played a round like that at North Hampshire Golf Club at Fleet.

Mr Harding, of the Cambridge Hotel, Aldershot, said yesterday: "My partner and I were just packing up our trolleys when we were approached by a tubby fellow with glasses.

"He said to us: 'This club is

### By Daily Mail Reporter

rather select and the committee does not like people playing our course with their trousers stuck in their socks.'"

Mr Harding added: I think this is typical of the sort of thing which is keeping British golf back. I play golf every day, and have been on every course between here and London without complaint.

"If this is their attitude, I don't

want any members of this club on my premises."

The Secretary of the 18gn.-a-year club, Mr.Maxwell Holles, said: "It was probably me. We don't approve of people with trousers tucked in their socks, and I do tell visitors quite politely of the club rule.

"This is a gentleman's club. We have ten knights and quite a number of senior Army officers including 14 major-generals as members. They are very keen on keeping up traditions.

"A players should wear trousers or plus-fours. To tuck trousers into socks is simply not golf."

Daily Mail *press cutting – November 1966*

Daily Mail *cartoon by Emwood of Harold Wilson following trousers in socks episode with Max Holles at North Hants*

Max Holles was appointed secretary in July 1963. His cheerful extrovert manner made him popular within the Club and he achieved national fame in November 1966 when his challenge to a visitor being improperly dressed with trousers tucked in socks and his somewhat pompous justification was reported in the *Daily Mail.* An original cartoon by Emmwood reflecting this incident hangs in the clubhouse. He resigned as secretary in February 1968, possibly because of the rejection by the Executive Committee of his staff report which outlined serious understaffing in the clubhouse and recommended an increase in permanent staff.

He was succeeded in April 1968 by George Dickinson, who had previously been secretary of three well-known clubs, Royal Cinque Ports, Stoke Poges and Formby. He had a fraught introduction. In his first year he dismissed Ernest Fordham, the extremely popular steward who had then recently completed twenty-one years service. It was a decision that was never properly explained. Charles Churchill, one of several junior members in the early 1950s, writes movingly of Ernie Fordham that "He had a great memory for names and many a member and visitor was delighted to be welcomed with a greeting using his correct name. To me and to many others he was North Hants Golf Club". Many members shared that affection and in the absence of an official appeal for a leaving present Charles Churchill circularised all members to seek donations. There was a gratifying response, including contributions from several members of the Executive Committee. Concerns about the apparent harshness of his dismissal were not eased when the next two new stewards and their wives handed in their resignations after six months and three months.

Finally, it was a decade when some distinguished members were elected to Life Membership in recognition of their services to the Club. These included Sandy Sellors, Sir Paul Pechell, John Nelson, Sir Richard Anstruther-Gough-Calthorpe and Gwen Morrison. It was also a decade that ended on a lighter note. Cyril Wain was a popular member of the Club, a diminutive figure with a mischievous smile and never short of an irreverent word. On 24th August 1969, at the age of eighty-eight, he holed in one at the 15th hole, then measuring 143 yards, so being listed in the *Golfer's Handbook* at the time as the second oldest golfer to record a hole-in-one. When asked whether it was his first hole-in-one, he replied that he thought it was his fifth or sixth, but it was certainly the first one with a driver.

In so doing he brought about a notable double for the Club. He became the second member of the Club to be mentioned in the Feats section of the *Golfer's Handbook*, with his name joining that of Lieutenant Colonel Farquahar who had been recorded since 1929 as the second earliest incidence of a hole-in-one by a one-armed golfer. Their names continued to be recorded in the Feats section until it was shortened in the early 1980s.

*Chapter Seven*

# Special General Meetings
## 1970–1979

CHANGES IN the history of North Hants Golf Club closely mirror the changing history of golf. There was another example of this in the 1970s when the spectacular victories of Tony Jacklin in the 1969 Open Championship and the 1970 US Open dramatically widened golfing horizons across the country. If the son of a lorry driver from Scunthorpe could achieve overnight sporting fame and riches playing golf, then here was a game that anybody could try. Jacklin's success and his chirpy, confident personality prompted an upsurge of interest in golf, particularly amongst the young. This was reflected at North Hants with the emergence of some outstanding junior golfers.

But this new and widening interest in golf was not just confined to juniors. Many first generation golfers were drawn to the game from people of all ages and classes. At one extreme were the humblest of workers whose unsocial working hours allowed free time during the day and they sought out the pay and play municipal and public courses. At the other extreme were business men and professionals who discovered a game they could learn to play at a relatively mature age which also offered, to use a modern phrase, valuable networking opportunities. In ever increasing numbers they sought membership of private golf clubs or they joined golfing societies as a means of gaining access to golf courses. Last, but not least, many a golfing widow decided it was time for change, and not a few husbands purported, through clenched teeth, to welcome this new found interest.

These changes made themselves felt at North Hants, which was a prime attraction for aspiring golfers. By the end of the 1970s candidates for membership for both ordinary and ladies joined a waiting list that stretched three to four years into the future, despite the ceilings for ordinary men members having been increased from 325 to 400 since 1970. The image of the game of golf began to change from that of an upper and middle class activity largely handed down through the generations to the classless game it has now become.

A consequence of the arrival of so many first generation golfers has been a decline in etiquette. Each year the Club diary spells out the first official rule of etiquette of the game of golf concerning Behaviour During Play "No one should move, talk or stand close to or directly behind the ball or the hole when a player is addressing the ball or making a stroke". This is intended to mean that on the tee, the other players, in cricketing parlance, should stand at point or square leg and not as first slip or wicketkeeper and it means standing still on the fairway as each player plays their shot to the green rather than trundling on regardless. Philip Mitchell, who joined the Club in 1952, believes the decline in etiquette is one of the single biggest changes over his golfing lifetime.

*Hugh Clifford, donor of the Hampshire Rose, with Jenny Pool*

It was during the early 1970s that an important if unintended change took place in the playing character of the course. Large areas of fairway were being literally stripped of their turf by crows and other birds feeding on cock chafers and leatherjackets. The turf was particularly vulnerable because it was thin and sparsely grassed and the recommended solution was to encourage stronger root growth by the application of agricultural lime over a three to five year programme, beginning in the spring of 1971. This achieved its purpose and left behind grassier fairways that took away some of the bounce and tight lies that had been such a feature. Ever since, the fairways have been given occasional applications of fertiliser and their condition in some years has been as fine as any to be found. The stronger growth of the grass combined with more protection from drying winds given by the steady growth of trees has led to the character of the course becoming less heath-like.

In 1973, Hugh Clifford, a former captain and long-standing member of the Club, and his daughter, Heather, whose considerable success in women's golf was set out in the last chapter, jointly presented a trophy for a new

*Junior Trio, 1976. Richard Johnson, Ashley Sharpe, Nick Green*

competition, the Hampshire Rose. It is a thirty-six hole scratch competition for women amateur golfers, mirrored along the lines of the highly successful Hampshire Hog, and played annually in October until 2002 when it was moved to follow the Hampshire Hog in April. It has attracted strong entries and its list of winners recorded in the appendix includes many internationals. The ladies seem to prefer ties to sudden death play-offs and Heather Clifford was a tied winner in 1976 and again in 1978 under her married name of Heather Glynn-Jones.

On the golf course, the 1970s was probably the strongest decade of any for the depth of golfing talent at North Hants. Tim Koch de Gooreynd had now emigrated but David Blair and Lionel Smith remained. Some quality golfers joined the Club in the 1970s including Martin Farmer, Tim Hanson, who was Derbyshire County champion in 1970, Geoff Henney and John O'Dowd Booth, all of whom played for the Hampshire County team. At a different level, the Club enjoyed in 1972 a victory in the inaugural Marston's Over-50s Trophy, a team matchplay event for Hampshire golf clubs. This would be followed by a second victory in 1974, strangely on both occasions for the "B" team.

As the decade moved on, some talented junior members emerged. Richard Johnson, Ashley Sharpe and Nick Green all became Category One golfers at the age of sixteen in 1976, but under the existing rules were not allowed to play in the Gold Medal. The rule was changed in the following year whereupon it was promptly won by Ashley Sharpe in 1977 and 1978 and Richard Johnson in 1979. Both became regular members of the Hampshire County team. In his Captain's Newsletter in November 1979, Freddie Parsons was able to refer to six members representing the county and "some twenty members" with Category One handicaps (plus 2 to plus 4).

These three talented boy golfers were matched by an equally talented girl, Jennifer Pool, who joined in 1975 as a junior at the age of eleven and, along with her two elder brothers and her parents, Graham and Pam Pool, became

## SPECIAL GENERAL MEETINGS 1970–1979

*North Hants win the Over-50s Marston's Cup, 1972. Left to right: Bob Mounce, Reg Pearce, John Davey, George Dickinson, John Littlejohns, Paddy Byrne, Barry Armstrong, Forrest Falconer (holding cup), Tony Noble, –, Robert Briscoe, –, Leslie Goodey, Peter Goswell*

*North Hants win the over-50s Marston's Cup, 1974. Left to right: Alex Stembridge, Charlie Moss, George Parr, Bryn Williams, Rocky Knight, Leslie Goodey (holding cup), Ian Bull, Bill Middleton, Leslie Moore, Ossie Williams*

*North Hants Golf Club vs. Hampshire County, 1979. Back row, left to right: Martin Farmer, Ashley Sharpe, Tim Hanson, Richard Johnson, Gordon Shakespear, John O'Dowd Booth, Geoff Henney. Front row: John Littlewood, David Blair, Freddie Parsons, Reg Pearce, Danny Daniels*

the fifth member of the family at the Club. It is a family that has played a large part in the fortunes of the Club. Both Graham and Pam Pool later became Club and Lady captains and together they ran the Junior Section of the Club for eight years in the 1990s. Meanwhile, Jenny progressed rapidly to win the Junior Calthorpe Cup in 1977 and 1978. A Golf Foundation award enabled her to have coaching from Bernard Gallacher at Wentworth and she developed the rhythm and timing of a full swing, essential for one of slim build. Her golf flourished and in 1981 she won the Hampshire Girls Junior Championship and reached the last eight of the English Girls Championship where she was defeated by a certain Laura Davies at the 20th hole. She was selected in that most frustrating of all positions as reserve for the England Girls team, so near and yet so far from international selection.

It was in the middle of this decade of ever emerging talent that your author was privileged to captain the Club team in the annual scratch matches against the university teams from Oxford, Cambridge and London, albeit from somewhere near the bottom of the singles order. Over a ten year period the Club was rarely defeated, as befitted a team whose singles order began Blair, Sharpe, Johnson, Farmer, Henney, Hanson, Green and O'Dowd Booth.

## SPECIAL GENERAL MEETINGS 1970–1979

The high point came in 1979 when Freddie Parsons convened a match against the Hampshire county team to celebrate the anniversary of the Club's seventy-five years. The result was a remarkable victory for the Club team led by David Blair. A narrow three points to two lead after the morning foursomes was converted into a twelve and a half points to two and a half victory, with North Hants winning the first nine singles. However, it should be remembered that at the time the regular county team was deprived of at least half its usual members as they were playing for the home club. It was a closer match than the overall result might suggest because eleven of the fifteen matches went to either the 17th or 18th green.

| North Hants Golf Club | | | Hampshire County | | |
|---|---|---|---|---|---|
| *Foursomes* | | | *Foursomes* | | |
| D.A. Blair & A.P. Sharpe | 2/1 | 1 | K. Weeks & N. Rogers | | 0 |
| M.J. Farmer & G.B. Henney | 1 up | 1 | A. Wells & I. Tilbrook | | 0 |
| R.W. Johnson & J.N. Littlewood | | ½ | I. Summers & P. Lane | | ½ |
| T.J. Hanson & J.A. O'Dowd-Booth | | 0 | T. Gray & T. Smith | 3/2 | 1 |
| H.G. Shakespear & T.F. Daniels | | ½ | D. Warr & J. McCracken | | ½ |
| | | 3 | | | 2 |
| *Singles* | | | *Singles* | | |
| Sharpe | 2/1 | 1 | Weeks | | 0 |
| Farmer | 3/1 | 1 | Rogers | | 0 |
| Henney | 4/3 | 1 | Summers | | 0 |
| Hanson | 2/1 | 1 | Wells | | 0 |
| Johnson | 3/2 | 1 | Warr | | 0 |
| O'Dowd-Booth | 1 up | 1 | Gray | | 0 |
| Littlewood | 2/1 | 1 | Tilbrook | | 0 |
| Shakespear | 4/3 | 1 | Lane | | 0 |
| Daniels | 1 up | 1 | Smith | | 0 |
| Blair | | ½ | McCracken | | ½ |
| | | 9½ | | | ½ |
| | Total | 12½ | | | 2½ |

It was not only on the golf course that North Hants mirrored changes in golfing history. The 1970s were an unhappy decade for the country and there were some unhappy moments at the Club when discontented members forced difficult Special General Meetings upon hapless Executive Committees in 1970 and 1973, and in 1979 rejected the advice of the Committee at the fateful Special General Meeting convened to consider the proposal to buy the Club.

The Special General Meeting in 1970 was largely to do with unhappiness about higher subscriptions and was described in the last chapter. The problems raised at the Special General Meeting held on 24th November 1973 were of a different character and concerned a general feeling of lack of communication and drift in the running of the Club. Ironically, the origins of the problem lay partly in some initiatives taken just one year earlier, by the then captain, Lieutenant Colonel W.B.J. Armstrong.

Throughout his years of membership from 1956 until his death in 1998 at the age of eighty-six, Barry Armstrong was one of the most popular and respected members in the Club. He arrived at the Club with an outstanding golfing record. He reached the semi-final of the Irish Open Amateur Championship in 1934, 1948 and 1952. In the latter two he twice defeated in the quarter-finals the legendary Joe Carr, then widely recognised along with Ronnie White as one of the two greatest amateur golfers of the immediate post-war era. He qualified for the Open Championship at Royal Portrush in 1951 and, although he failed to make the cut for the final two rounds, he much enjoyed the experience of playing on the first two days with Harry Bradshaw, the famous Irish Ryder Cup professional.

Perhaps his finest moment was in 1947 when he reached the last sixteen in the British Amateur Championship at Carnoustie, by heroically defeating the famous French Amateur champion, Henri de Lamaze. For many years he was a pillar of the Uppingham team in the Halford Hewitt, regularly playing in the top foursome with another member of the Club, Sir John Cradock Hartopp, and he represented the Army during his career in the Royal Engineers. One achievement that can never be taken away from him is that he set up the amateur course record of 69 at the ill-fated Bramshot Golf Club in 1938. At North Hants he won the Gold Medal in 1958.

Barry Armstrong was born in Malaya and took up golf seriously at Trinity College, Dublin, after his parents retired from Malaya and came to live in Ireland. He married Margaret McKay, an Irish hockey international, who then applied her sporting ability to golf with such success that she reduced her handicap to 3. Together they twice won the scratch Open Mixed Foursomes at North Hants in the 1950s. His son, Michael, has been a long-standing member of the Club since 1956.

After his death in 1998 he was accorded by the Club the unique honour of having a tree planted in honour of his memory, a robinia to the right of the path to the 10th tee. He was always a friendly, kind and humorous man with a ready smile who took more interest in other people's golf than his own. In particular he encouraged young golfers and was secretary of the Golf Foundation. He was a deceptively good golfer with one of those individual swings possessed by so many golfers brought up in Ireland. With its

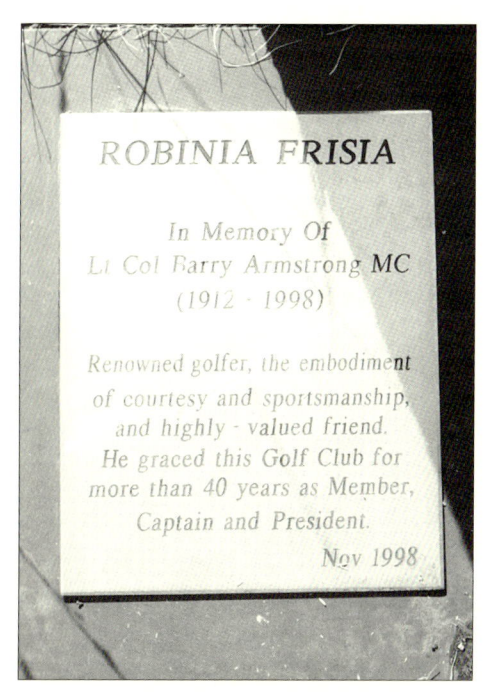

*Barry Armstrong, captain (1970) and president (1987-90)*

*Barry Armstrong – Memorial Plaque*

complicated loops on the way up and the way down, his swing was something of a collector's item, difficult to describe, easy to recognise and unfailingly repetitive.

As captain in 1972, he made a determined attempt to make improvements to the facilities of the Club. Automatic watering systems had been successfully introduced by many local golf clubs and he openly raised this issue, challenging the reluctance of members to face the cost and the opposition of the head greenkeeper, Bill Brown. He proposed and investigated the possibility of building a nine hole pitch and putt course in the wooded triangle between the practice ground and the 1st and 2nd holes. He rightly believed that the clubhouse should be made more comfortable and welcoming with new carpeting, furniture and decoration.

The cost of these projects was estimated at £10,000 for watering, £6,000 for a pitch and putt course and £4,000 for clubhouse improvements, but the Club had neither surpluses nor reserves to cover expenditure of anywhere near this amount. Nothing daunted, Barry Armstrong took the issue to the members. In a circular in November 1972, he sought reactions to each project and boldly proposed the creation of a Capital Loan Fund to raise £20,000. It would be made up of £100 Bonds which would entitle the owner to a £5 reduction in subscription.

Members responded enthusiastically. There was a strong margin in favour for automatic watering of 154 to 83 and clubhouse improvements of 146 to 92, but less so for the pitch and putt course at 131 to 108. More remarkable was the response of 122 members willing to subscribe a total of £20,200. However, by the time of the Annual General Meeting in March 1973, doubts had begun to surface. There was insufficient support to justify the pitch and putt course, but, more seriously, the Executive Committee gave way to opposition to automatic watering, which served only to delay the inevitable by several years. The outcome was a proposal put to members at the Annual General Meeting to limit the Capital Loan scheme to £10,000 and this was only narrowly passed by forty-two votes to thirty-eight.

Barry Armstrong was succeeded as captain by Henry Quinlan, but the momentum was lost and in October the Capital Loan scheme was quietly allowed to lapse. Perhaps expectations had been raised too much but within a matter of days unrest developed amongst the membership and following a letter from Reg Pearce, a Special General Meeting was convened. Its attendance by 146 members suggested that concerns were real, although difficult to define. The meeting cleared the air and the Committee acknowledged that communication had been lacking and too many rumours had been allowed to spread.

One consequence of this episode was that Barry Armstrong's letter to members in November 1972 would thereafter set the pattern of an annual Captain's Letter. Meanwhile, this episode coincided with changing secretaries. George Dickinson resigned in December 1972 and was succeeded by Wing Commander James Marshall, recently retired from the R.A.F. and embarking on a new career. His was not a happy tenure and he resigned after barely a year in December 1973. He was succeeded by Neil Brown, who enjoyed a popular five years in office before returning home to Scotland in November 1978 to become secretary of Bruntsfield Golf Club. He was a big man with a personality and presence to match and he carried out his secretarial duties very effectively by being both friendly and obstinate at one and the same time. He was much liked by the junior members whom he so strongly supported.

It was also a time of change in the professional's shop. After the completion of thirty years as Club professional, Bob Mounce retired in January 1976 and later died in 2000 at the age of eighty-seven. He had grown up in a golfing family and began his career in 1928 at the age of sixteen as apprentice club maker to his father, the club professional at Camberley Heath. He never really grew out of those roots put down in the pre-war years when the club professional had to judge carefully the boundaries of courtesy, formality and deference that separated him from the members. There were moments when the Executive Committee wished he had more of a "can do" approach, but he was a good teacher, never seen out of plus-fours and very much a gentleman in a professional's world. Over the years he played regularly with many of the members. His golf was a creature of his time, when greater emphasis was placed upon playing to ninety per cent of your strength by swinging through the ball rather than hitting it. He was succeeded by Tim Gowdy in a leap to an altogether younger generation.

When Neil Brown retired in November 1978, he was succeeded by the affable Nigel Lockyer, previously secretary of Highgate Golf Club. He joined at a moment when the Club was about to celebrate its anniversary of seventy-five years and then was heavily preoccupied with the distracting episode of deciding whether or not to accept an offer from the landlord to sell the Club and course. The responsibility for this fell on the sturdy shoulders of Lieutenant Colonel F.A. Parsons, who had already volunteered to mastermind the anniversary celebrations when he suddenly found himself elected captain in March 1979, a position he held for two years.

Freddie Parsons enjoyed a long and varied army career and after retiring in 1966 he enjoyed an equally long involvement with the Army Benevolent Fund. His date of birth is the rare combination of 1.1.11 and he was one of those keen cricketers who turn to golf in their forties only to find it a more difficult game than they had expected. After occasional moments of service membership, he joined the Club in 1967. He is a born enthusiast and natural administrator, qualities that he has given both to the Club and to the Hampshire County Golf Union, of which he became president from 1988 to 1994. He was only the second member of the Club after Sir Paul Pechell to achieve that honour and like Sir Paul was elected a Life Member in recognition.

His first decision upon taking office as captain was to abandon the format of the Captain's Prize, the handicap match play knockout event played over six rounds over the Easter holiday. It was a favourite competition for me in which over the years I reached the final eight times, winning four and losing four. My enthusiasm was fired by a first appearance in 1955 when, just out of the junior ranks, I reached the final to meet George Gidney, whose golfing prowess has already been described. In those days the final on Easter Monday afternoon was something of a Club occasion when the captain and some twenty or so members would follow round. They proceeded to watch George Gidney play the first eight holes in an impeccable 27 strokes and to my considerable embarrassment he was 8 up. He spoiled his card with a 6 at the 9th and lost a solitary stroke hole and two others before inevitable victory.

The format was first questioned by Robin Mallinson, captain in 1974, who held two rounds over Easter with the remaining four rounds as a running knockout, but it was not until 1979 that the links with Easter and match play were finally broken. Freddie Parsons was right to make the change from a format which meant that the incoming captain had no influence over his own prize which was over and done within two or three weeks of taking office and although the event was always well supported, its format of playing six rounds over the four days of Easter was by no means universally popular. Instead he launched what has become a very popular Captain's Weekend in the summer, which initially took the form of a thirty-six hole stableford over two days, before eventually settling down as an eighteen hole stableford and a Texas scramble open to the ladies. Freddie Parsons quickly filled the match play gap by creating the Parsons Putter in 1981.

In this busy year, he also arranged the principal events to celebrate seventy-five years since the foundation of the Club. On 8th June 1979 an exhibition match was arranged, including Brian Barnes, Neil Coles and Max Faulkner. Their respective scores of 71, 70 and 70 were modest, but a large gathering enjoyed the long hitting of Brian Barnes and his attempts to drive the 3rd green where his ball was still running fast when it found the bunker before the green and the 14th where he finished some twenty yards short on the left. Another event was a buffet supper attended by some 200 members and guests, including many representatives from other clubs and there was the match against Hampshire already described.

It was against this busy background that the question of the possible purchase of the Club came before the Executive Committee. The process had begun earlier in the year when towards the end of his captaincy the late Philip Ricketts found himself in conversation with the president, Sir Richard Anstruther-Gough-Calthorpe, who expressed the wish to do something for the Club. With one of those chance spontaneous replies the captain suggested he might let us buy the Club. In March 1979 a letter was received from the Estate concerning the possibility of outright purchase or an extension of the lease to sixty years. The agents managing the Estate were unenthusiastic about selling, but Sir Richard insisted that an offer be made. He was sensitive to the close relationship that had long existed between his family and the Club and he was aware that following the tragic death of his son and heir in a car accident there was no immediate successor to continue the unbroken family line of presidents of the Club.

The formal offer to sell the freehold for £160,000 was received from the Estate in a letter of 12th June with a deadline of 31st October for acceptance. The Executive Committee immediately decided that it did not have the power to take a final decision which must rest with the membership at a Special General Meeting. A Sub-Committee was set up under the chairmanship of the captain to examine the offer and make proposals. The

Aerial view of North Hants Golf Club, 2001

Scenes on the golf course taken by Paul Seivers, 2003

*1st green*

*3rd hole*

*8th hole*

*10th hole*

*12th hole*

*14th hole*

facts were simple. The Club could buy a golf course of 152 acres, a clubhouse, two cottages and various outbuildings for £160,000. Alternatively, it could leave in place a lease with thirty-seven years to expiry in September 2016, based on what amounted to peppercorn annual rentals of £650, rising to £900 in 1982 and £1,400 in 1996.

There were two immediate issues to be addressed. A scheme would have to be proposed to raise capital from the membership because the Club had no reserves and, secondly, the price would have to be justified. A position paper was presented to the Executive Committee in August, setting out the advantages and disadvantages of the purchase. It proposed that the sum be raised by a combination of a compulsory returnable deposit from all members and the offer of voluntary debentures carrying a subscription rebate. At this stage the valuation was measured against the current insured value of the clubhouse and buildings of £175,000 and a current agricultural value of 152 acres of £300,000. The principle of purchase was endorsed by the Executive Committee and it was agreed that, after some fine tuning of the financial proposals, a letter be sent to all members seeking their approval of the purchase by a simple majority at a Special General Meeting. The Committee would also seek from the Estate an extension of the deadline, which was agreed to 31st December, and a reduction in the price which was refused.

It was widely known amongst the members that the offer was under consideration and reactions to it were believed to be positive. On 4th October a detailed letter was sent to all members from the captain, Freddie Parsons. Comments were specifically invited on the financial proposals. The position paper originally presented to the Executive Committee had been written in an enthusiastic tone, setting out the advantages followed by the disadvantages and including some helpful valuations.

In contrast, and members were not aware of this, the letter sent to them was written in an altogether more negative tone. For example, the only reference to valuation comes early in the second paragraph that "an independent firm of valuers recommended by the National Golf Clubs Advisory Association consider that this figure is a little high". A summary of the negative factors "The arguments against purchase are clear enough" preceded a rather weaker summary of the positive factors "The arguments in favour of purchase are based, of necessity, much more on judgement and opinion".

It did not read as a ringing endorsement of the merits of purchase on the part of the Executive Committee and the comment that "… your Committee is unanimously in favour of purchase in principle …" was hedged with qualifications and rather lost in the middle of a long letter. With hindsight, Freddie Parsons acknowledged that the letter should have led with the positives, but he wanted all the arguments to be given to the members for their decision and at the time of writing the letter he was convinced that the purchase would be widely supported.

The task was also made more difficult by a Committee decision that this was such an important decision that it should be subject to achieving a two-thirds majority, rather than the simple majority that the Club rules would allow. Given this stricter requirement and the fundamental importance of the proposal to the future of the Club, it was probably unfortunate, with hindsight, that no consideration appears to have been given to allowing those members unable to attend to apply for a postal vote.

In the event 364 members replied to the letter and a summary of their comments and the detail of some amendments to the financing proposals was sent to all members in a further letter from the captain on 22nd November, which also included a formal agenda for the meeting on 13th December. The financing of the purchase would be achieved by compulsory deposits levied on all members on a sliding scale to a maximum of £190 for ordinary members to raise a total of £94,360 and the issue of voluntary £250 Preferred Loan Units to a maximum total of £80,000. Individuals could own a maximum of eight units, each of which would entitle the holder to a $12^1/_2$ per cent reduction in subscription. Indications from replies suggested that the issue would be fully subscribed. This was not surprising as the rebate of a percentage of the subscription amounted to a generous index linking against inflation. On the other hand twenty-three members said they would either choose, or be forced, to resign if the scheme went ahead.

The meeting was the most momentous of any in the history of the Club. It was held in the Civic Assembly Hall in Fleet at 8.00 p.m. on Thursday 13th December and attended by 329 members. Feelings within the membership were running high from the extremes of "blindingly obvious" to "over my dead body" and as the meeting began there was tension in the air and great uncertainty about the outcome.

The first resolution to amend the Club rule to require a two-thirds rather than simple majority was readily approved before the main debate. Opposition speakers from the floor quickly seized the initiative and, with a strength of feeling and vehemence that took the meeting by surprise, they swamped a rather lacklustre series of statements from each of the members of the Executive Committee. Freddie Parsons had decided that as chairman of the meeting he should hold the ring rather than join the debate and, in effect, nobody led the case for purchase with the necessary conviction to carry the audience. The proposal was lost long before the debate ended.

The Committee had already identified two of the principal arguments against purchase, but failed to find any counter to them. The first argument was the simple fact that a lease with thirty-seven years to run would comfortably see out the golfing aspirations of anybody over the age of fifty. Buying the Club would be irrelevant to many of the older retired members, many of whom feared the consequences of having to finance the cost of purchase and pay higher subscriptions.

The second argument was the risk of a financial crisis prompted by loss of membership and rising costs. Inflation was running at 17 per cent and rising and there were rumours of financial problems at Woking Golf Club and West Hill Golf Club after they were bought by their members. Members of Woking were believed to have been forced to put up £500 each to keep the club afloat and West Hill was believed to have suffered serious loss of membership.

These arguments were persuasively put by Ian Bull, a well-known member and recently retired City insurance underwriter, whose fluency on his feet was a powerful factor. Equally persuasive if less fluent was Bert Osborne. He was another well-known member with a high reputation as a successful local industrialist who happened also to be a member of West Hill Golf Club and his blunt words of warning about the risks involved carried much weight. John Littlejohns, a recent captain, asserted that there was no possibility whatever of the Estate refusing to renew the lease in 2016, although no such guarantee was present in the lease.

They were joined in opposition by Ron Bellamy, a much respected former honorary secretary and captain, who spoke clearly against the proposal. Having been involved with the negotiation of the existing lease, he believed that its terms imposed a healthy discipline on the Club to manage itself sensibly. He also admitted after the meeting to a real concern that a purchase might lead to control of the Club falling undesirably into the hands of a small number of members, a moment of foresight that was to become all too true many years later at Camberley Heath Golf Club. These were the speakers whose contributions stood out amidst many others from the floor but once the debate had begun it was soon apparent that a two-thirds majority would not be achieved.

The discussion was eventually called to a halt and a secret ballot convened. The result was announced, 145 in favour and 167 against and the meeting closed at 9.45 p.m. Nobody was proud of the result and it was not very long before an uneasy feeling developed within the Club that the wrong decision had been made.

Many of the opposing votes had been cast by members who put short-term interest ahead of long-term advantage. Furthermore, it became apparent that active campaigning against the purchase had for some time been pursued by a number of the more senior members of the Club, including some former captains and the treasurer, Peter Hammond. The impression remains of a

Committee unaware of the extent and seniority of the opposition. It was not matched by campaigning in favour which, with hindsight, could only have been mounted by the captain and his Committee.

Philip Ricketts, a well-known local surveyor and valuer, who had been so successfully involved in many stages of the negotiation with the Estate, estimated at the meeting that the marriage value of unlocking the lease would create a freehold with a value of £400,000. This could have been highlighted long before the meeting. Greater emphasis could have been placed on the three to four year waiting list to offset any fears of resignations. The problems of West Hill and Woking were not really comparable. Woking was a town encircled by five competing golf clubs. North Hants was a golf club encircled by five expanding towns.

It is commonplace now to look back and criticise the membership for rejecting the offer, but it is easy to judge the past by the standards of today. In 1979, the country had suffered a depressing decade of its highest ever peacetime inflation, slow growth, high taxation, strikes and very high interest rates. Confidence in the economy was at a low ebb and against that background people were simply not willing or accustomed or able to take financial risks with the alacrity with which they would later take them. Nevertheless, it was a lost opportunity and the Estate was bewildered by the rejection of the offer.

*Chapter Eight*

# Railroad Heath
## 1980–1995

THE CONSEQUENCES of failing to purchase the freehold were to hang like a threatening cloud over the Club throughout the 1980s. Feelings of regret, and even some bitterness, quickly began to surface after the decision and successive captains lamented a lost opportunity. These were years of alarming uncertainty at simply not knowing whether the development of the land known as Railroad Heath would take the Club out of existence. It would not be until 1993 that it would become apparent that negotiations to save the Club were likely to succeed and on 27th January 1995, the captain, Len Woods, signed the 999 year lease that secured the future of the Club.

For many years the Club became piggy in the middle. On one side stood our landlord, the Elvetham Estate, at first dismayed by our rejection of a reasonable offer but later unable to resist the attractions presented by a development opportunity. On the other side stood a local authority, pursuing its own housing agenda and apparently indifferent to our cause. They would come to work together to bring about an enormous development in Railroad Heath. It was an atmosphere in which rumours thrived and the confidentiality forced upon the negotiations of the Environment Committee, which so admirably and successfully represented the interest of the Club throughout, made it difficult for members to know exactly what was happening for much of the time.

However, enough of this uneasy background for the moment. The early 1980s were outstanding golfing years and the decade began on a triumphant note. At the age of nineteen, Richard Johnson won the County Championship at Liphook in May 1980 with a blistering display of golf. In the match play final he was five under par for eleven holes when he overwhelmed Brian Winteridge of Stoneham by 8 and 7, producing the round of his life in a final against an intimidating opponent who had previously been County champion twice and would later win twice more. At the same event he formed the team with Martin Farmer and Ashley Sharpe that won the Club Team Championship for North Hants for only the fourth time.

Richard Johnson had emerged as the most successful of that triumvirate of junior members described in the last chapter. Behind a diffident presence here was a complete golfer with a lovely rhythm and superb short game, and he joined Tique Lock, Stuart Murray and Tim Koch de Gooreynd as the only Club winners of the County Championship either then or since. He was later to be a finalist for a second time in 1986 when he was defeated in a close match at North Hants by prospective Walker Cup player Bobby Eggo, after beating English International, Kevin Weeks, in the semi-final. Perhaps sadly, he could not be persuaded to put himself really to the test at a national level.

As well as winning the County Championship in 1980, Richard Johnson went on to win the Gold Medal for the second successive year and in 1981 won the Courage Trophy, the unofficial county stroke play championship. It was at this time that he led a strong Club representation in the county team along with Martin Farmer, Geoff Henney and Ashley Sharpe. The latter had earlier achieved success in 1978 by reaching the semi-final of the County Championship.

These were good years whilst they lasted and they had been much enhanced by the frequent presence at the Golf Club of Greg Norman who arrived in England early in 1977 to play the European Tour. His reputation as a highly promising and glamorous young Australian golfer already preceded him and upon his arrival he made a fast start by winning only his second tournament on the tour, the Martini International at Blairgowrie, at the age of twenty-two. His newly appointed manager was James Marshall, who lived at Heckfield and was a temporary member on the waiting list at North Hants.

Greg Norman used Heckfield as his home base when he was in the country and James Marshall arranged for him to use North Hants for play and practice mid-week. He quickly achieved folk hero status amongst the cluster of outstanding juniors at the Club, whose midweek company he happily enjoyed and tales of his legendary length and power began to spread. His brief association with the Club over these few years was a cheerful talking point for the members.

He paid a warm tribute to the Club in a recent letter:

In the late 1970s, shortly after I turned professional and moved to Europe to further my playing career, the membership at North Hants Golf Club provided me the privilege of playing and practising there, a tremendous gesture that I will not soon forget. These privileges were instrumental in my development as a player, and to this day I can't thank the members of North Hants enough for what they did for me.

I owe a lot to North Hants Golf Club as well as its members, and both will always have a special place in my mind and heart. I congratulate the Club on its centenary in 2004 and I wish the Club and all its members the very best.

This particular cycle of golfing excellence gradually faded after Geoff Henney moved to Suffolk in 1982, Ashley Sharpe to Kent in 1982 and Richard Johnson emigrated to the United States in 1987, the latter leaving behind an outstanding record on a wider golfing stage that would not be matched until the emergence of Justin Rose in the mid-1990s.

Meanwhile, after her successes as a junior, Jenny Pool had also been furthering her golfing reputation. In 1983, at the age of nineteen, she won the Hampshire Rose with scores of 73 and 69, setting the lowest winning total and breaking the ladies' course record in the afternoon round. This was probably her outstanding individual achievement and she joined Heather Glynn-Jones as the only lady members of the Club to win the Hampshire Rose. She was also a fine foursomes player. In 1985, she partnered the then recent British Amateur champion, Philip Parkin, to reach the last sixteen of the Sunningdale Foursomes, before being defeated by Sam Torrance and John O'Leary. Encouraged by Torrance she decided to test her golfing skills with a two year golf scholarship in the United States where she reduced her handicap to scratch. She played at her university with Catrin Nilsmark, who turned professional, played five times in the Solheim Cup and was captain of the successful European team in 2003. Upon her return from the States, Jenny considered but resisted the temptation of women's professional golf.

*Jenny Pool wins the Hampshire Rose, 1983*

She preferred the attractions of amateur golf and with her husband to be, Michael Kershaw, won the Hoylake Open Mixed foursomes in 1987, and, after marriage, the Worplesdon Foursomes in 1989. She has played county golf for Hampshire many times and has been Ladies' Club champion at North Hants twelve times between 1981 and 2001. With an ever ready smile and an outgoing personality, Jenny is a popular member of the Club.

Events were also happening within the Club hierarchy. Sir Richard Anstruther-Gough-Calthorpe, who had been president of the Club since 1957 and was now aged seventy-two, expressed the wish to retire from that office. His wishes were accepted with some sadness because he had been a good friend of the Club and his retirement would end a family link stretching back to the foundation of the Club. The Executive Committee amended the Club rules to allow for the election of a president and a vice-president each to hold office for a maximum of three years.

The first president to be elected under the new rule at the Annual General Meeting in March 1981 was David Blair, winner of the Hampshire Hog three times and a recent past captain of The Royal and Ancient Golf Club of St Andrews. Although David Blair's distinction made him an obvious candidate for the non-executive role of president, it did seem to be a slightly strange decision because he had left the district to live in Scotland some two years earlier. In view of his contribution to the Club, Reg Pearce, who was elected vice-president at the same meeting, could reasonably have expected to have been nominated as the first president to follow the ending of the long Calthorpe family tradition.

It was greatly to the credit of successive Executive Committees in the 1970s that they were able to keep the Club on sound financial lines through that inflationary decade. These same pressures continued in the early 1980s and the Committee was obliged to raise annual subscriptions by twenty per cent in both 1981 and 1982. Both were accepted with unusual aplomb by a membership perhaps still chastened by memories of that fateful decision not to purchase the Club.

As a reminder of that decision, Alec Walkling explained in his Captain's Newsletter in November 1981 that part of the 20 per cent subscription increase for 1982 was due to the burden of the lease and the need to spend £12,000 on repairing the leaking roof of the clubhouse. In July 1982, the captain, Charles Donovan, was encouraged to reopen the question of a possible purchase and he wrote to Sir Richard, only to receive a reply from the Estate that they were not prepared to reopen negotiations. In his Newsletter in November he drew attention to the insured values of the clubhouse and buildings of £325,000 and 150 acres of land worth £150,000 and wrote that "I am not a financial expert but I can only conclude that we got our sums drastically wrong in 1979".

In October 1983, Eric Carpenter, as a member of the Executive Committee, proposed the formation of an Advisory Committee to be drawn from different talents within the Club. Its objective would be to bring about the purchase of the freehold. It was fated to meet only once when it agreed that a discreet approach should again be made to Sir Richard. This approach was comprehensively rebuffed in a letter from the Elvetham Estate which stated that "The Estate has not altered its decision to retain the freehold in this local amenity and it is extremely unlikely that this position will change in the foreseeable future".

Perhaps it was out of frustration that at the following Annual General Meeting in March 1984, the captain, the late Harry Lewis, controversially gave vent to his feelings when he stated that younger and future members "may have cause to revile our memory due to the decision made in 1979".

There the matter lay and in the mean time, although regret would soon turn suddenly to alarm, there were some big changes taking place on the golf course. The Club had prevaricated for many years over the question of automatic watering, due partly to cost and partly to a reluctance towards it by the head greenkeeper, Bill Brown. It had been investigated and rejected in 1972 at a cost of £10,000 and again in 1976 at a cost of £15,000. By 1984 the Club was in a small minority of leading clubs not having automatic watering and with the imminent retirement of two of the greenkeepers, including Bill Brown, its absence was likely to make recruiting their successors more difficult. Moreover, the overtime costs for hand watering were becoming an increasing financial burden.

The moment was seized by the Executive Committee, led by the captain, Eric Carpenter, who simply went ahead without reference to the members and installed it a cost of £34,000. It was financed retrospectively by a graded one-off levy on all members at the next renewal in January, £69 for ordinary members and £55 for ladies and, apart from some lone muttering, the reality of the decision was readily accepted.

Eric Carpenter joined the Club in 1969. The Club has been fortunate to benefit from both his business skills displayed in getting things done and from his creative skills that enabled him to build a successful design company. In particular his masterly head and shoulder portraits of the captain of the year advertising the Captain's Weekend in June are an annual clubhouse feature and his drawing skills are evident from the treetop view of the pre-war tennis courts and the occasional sketches that appear through this book. An enthusiast with many a ready smile and friendly chuckle, his golfing achievements may well be described as modest. Indeed he is best remembered for a thin drive at the first hole which hit one of those old concrete tee boxes on the ladies tee and rebounded to shatter the main window in the lounge where the incident was suitably marked with a plaque.

Whilst taking the initiative to install automatic watering during his captaincy Eric Carpenter also proposed that consideration be given to incorporating the lake at the 3rd hole and extending it to a par 5. The golf course architect, Donald Steel, was invited to advise and in due course in the spring of 1985 members were invited to comment on a model of the proposed new hole which was displayed in the clubhouse. Its estimated cost was £10,300. Ironically, it was at this moment that the Club was invited to send representatives to a meeting of the Hart District Planning Office in May 1985.

*Concorde pilot, John Cook, Club captain (1985) with Open champion Greg Norman and the claret jug*

The vice-captain, Pat Kay, attended and was informed that the Planning Officer wished to explain the implications of a project involving the development of up to 2,600 houses on Railroad Heath. This scheme would require road access through land on the golf course, probably across the 2nd green and 3rd tee, and it was disturbing to discover at the meeting that discussions had already taken place with the Elvetham Estate without our knowledge, although the Estate maintained that these had been of only a general nature. An immediate consequence was to put any plans to extend the 3rd hole into abeyance and when in September the Club was formally asked to supply Hart District Council with plans of the course layout, the Executive Committee, under the captaincy of John Cook, formed a Sub-Committee whose brief was to monitor and advise all matters concerning development on an ongoing basis. John Cook was one of the earliest Concorde pilots for British Airways and in 1985 he donated the Concorde Trophy for a somewhat unusual annual match against the Army Golf Club in which the morning round is played on one course and the afternoon round on the other.

The creation of this Sub-Committee was a crucially important decision because in January 1990 it would become established as the Environment Committee which was to play a long and vital role for the Club. The new

*A quartet of Club captains: Charles Donovan (1982), Eric Carpenter (1984), Ian Johnston (1990) and Philip Ricketts (1977-78)*

Sub-Committee was chaired by the captain and was made up of some annually co-opted and, in effect, permanent members, together with the captain and vice-captain of the day as ex-officio members. It had to deal with bewildering changes of policy and the sheer length of time it takes to agree major developments and in the early stages there were periods of inactivity with shifting moods of optimism and pessimism. In fact little happened after the meeting with Hart District Council in 1985 apart from an expectation that a North-East Hampshire Structure Plan would be ready for implementation from 1990 and that it would probably include Railroad Heath. Pat Kay, now captain of the Club, established links with the Estate in June 1986 with John Anstruther-Gough-Calthorpe. He was an uncle of Sir Euan Anstruther-Gough-Calthorpe who had recently inherited the baronetcy at the age of nineteen following the death of his grandfather, Sir Richard, in 1985. He was also an enthusiastic golfer and was immediately made an Honorary Member to maintain the family connection.

At a subsequent meeting with John Calthorpe it was made clear to Pat Kay that there was no possibility whatever that the Club would be offered the opportunity to purchase the freehold during the interim period of five years or so before Sir Euan reached his majority at the age of twenty-five when he would inherit ownership of the Estate. However, at this early stage the impression was also given that the Estate was opposed to any development on Railroad Heath for environmental reasons.

By the time of the 1987 Annual General Meeting events had moved forward. Hampshire County Council now proposed that of its housing requirement in the Hart District 1,700 dwellings should be built on Railroad Heath, starting in 1992, and this would require an access road running across the course close to the 2nd green and 3rd tee. The apparent inevitability of development now persuaded the Elvetham Estate to inform the Club in October 1987 that it was applying for planning permission to develop both Railroad Heath and North Hants Golf Club, whilst openly admitting that whereas the former was probable, the latter was only possible. However, if permission were to be given to develop the golf course then the Estate would be obliged to provide alternative golfing facilities of equivalent merit for relocation. Nevertheless, the possibility of the Club disappearing under a sea of houses induced a sombre mood and in his November Newsletter, the captain, Bruce Squirrell, wrote that "the future of North Hants Golf Club beyond the expiry of our present lease in 2016 is now in great doubt".

In the event the Estate decided only to apply for planning permission for the parts of the course needed for access rather than for the whole course. Railroad Heath now became subject to the slow-moving processes of planning applications and an Inspector's Report and the next news was altogether more favourable. The Estate's planning application was refused on the grounds that it was premature. There was major criticism of the Railroad Heath proposals by the Inspector and the Council had released sufficient land elsewhere to meet its housing targets for the next five years from 1989. As a result at the 1989 Annual General Meeting, the captain, Don Waddington, was able to report in optimistic mood that "any threat to the golf club has receded for the foreseeable future".

Would it be so easy. The Club now became victim of an unexpected ministerial decision to reprieve Foxley Wood near Bramshill from being developed into a new town in an intended large and controversial new development. The consequence was to remove a major element of Hampshire's planned housing supply. The captain, Peter Breedon, reported at the 1990 Annual General Meeting that "Alas, the foreseeable future has proved to be very short indeed because the unexpected reprieve of Foxley Wood has resulted in immediate pressure to resurrect, and indeed expand, the Railroad Heath proposals".

Even more alarmingly, the Head of Planning at Hart District Council appeared to be promoting a strong personal view that in the context of a Railroad Heath development, the golf course should become a landscaped business park. The proposed development would be 1,700 houses with supporting community buildings and "More particularly, the proposed development would include the 150 acres currently occupied by the golf course". It did not help the Club's peace of mind to receive letters in late 1989 from housing developers Wimpey and Trencherwood, both alert to development potential and seeking active cooperation with the Club.

Development of some kind had now become inevitable and to deal with it the former Sub-Committee was reconstituted as a permanent Environment Committee in January 1990. Its terms of reference were strengthened to allow it not only to monitor all development matters but also to undertake negotiations on behalf of the Club with relevant third parties. The chairman was to be Pat Kay, whose robust and driving organisational skills as a Major General in the Royal Marines made him an ideal choice. There were three other permanent members. Peter Breedon brought to the table the skill and acumen of a business man with a successful career in advertising and marketing in Masius and Distillers. As secretary to the Committee he kept an impeccable and invaluable record of the more than 100 meetings held by the Committee during its eight year existence. Philip Ricketts, the senior partner of Poulters, was a highly knowledgeable surveyor and valuer with an acute understanding of the property world. John Pothecary provided legal input as a local solicitor and was able to view the proceedings from the perspective of a low handicap golfer. They were joined throughout by the captain and vice-captain of the day and this was to prove to be a successful combination that provided continuity over a long time-scale together with clear links to the Executive Committee. Serving on the Environment Committee in these roles were Gerry Cooke, John Lidstone, John Bermingham, Len Woods, David Best, Peter Stanbrook, Graham Pool, Brian Gallagher and Derek Skillin.

Sadly, Philip Ricketts died in 1998 at the age of sixty-seven and Peter Breedon died in 2003 at the age of seventy-six but both had at least seen the

*Pat Kay, captain (1986), president (1990-93) and chairman of the Environment Committee*

*Freddie Parsons, captain (1979, 1980), president (1997-2000)*

*Peter Breedon, captain (1989)*

successful outcome of their hard work. Possessed of charm and good humour, they were two convivial members who enjoyed to the full the camaraderie and banter of the Golf Club.

Despite the underlying uncertainty, the Club had prospered through the 1980s with some subtle changes taking place in its day to day life. The Club was inundated with golfers wishing to become members and the waiting list, fluctuating throughout the decade at between 80 and 100 men, was suspended in 1981, reopened and then closed again in 1987. The initial response of the Executive Committee in January 1981 to this surfeit of demand was to propose a phased reduction in the membership ceilings of 400 men and 105 ladies to 375 and 100 respectively. This policy of exclusivity was never implemented and indeed was reversed in May 1986 when the ceilings were raised to 412 and 108. Over the decade the number of temporary members was quietly allowed to rise from sixteen to thirty-two.

It is a matter for debate whether subsequent Committees were right to reverse the original intention and allow increasing numbers to put playing pressure on the golf course. There were problems at both ends of the age spectrum. At one end members were living longer and the concession to those over seventy of paying a reduced subscription of one-half the full rate had become an expensive gesture. By 1989, this concession had become available to 83 out of 520 playing members and the Executive Committee took the bold but correct decision that a subsidy on this scale was too generous and should be abandoned. The captain, Peter Breedon, had to endure personal hostility from a small number of highly aggrieved members. At the other end, a policy of encouraging good juniors to join the Club was leading to their filling a large number of available places when they reached the 18/22 category and later full membership. These pressures combined to make it more difficult for the Club membership to evolve.

Another illustration of an active but ageing membership has been the emergence and expansion of Club matches between teams aged over fifty-five. It was in October 1983, that Ronnie Nightingale proposed that North Hants should join an elder league of ten clubs by forming the Stoics who would initially play five matches home and away, usually a fourball between teams of twelve on a Friday morning. This was duly agreed and Ronnie Nightingale organised it with impeccable efficiency. With a national trend towards earlier retirement and living longer, the number of Stoics quickly mushroomed, as did the number of clubs forming veteran teams. Within four years of its formation, the original request for five home matches had turned into twelve and twelve-a-side had become fourteen.

Any thought that the Stoics might have been entering a competitive league that was hinted at in the original proposal was quickly forgotten. Their matches are extremely popular social occasions involving reciprocal opportunities for visiting other clubs. At the same time, the many traditional matches against other clubs that had long been a feature of the annual fixture list were also beginning to change their character. The format of foursomes in the morning and singles in the afternoon with a good lunch in between fell victim to slower play, crowded tees and a fading interest in foursomes. In 1989 the Club proposed to some of its traditional opponents that these matches be converted into afternoon fourballs with an evening meal.

These matches have also become largely social occasions. However, at the same time there has been an increase in competitive matches that appeal to many of the lower handicap golfers who are more interested in the result than the quality of the wine. The Border League, a competitive competition involving Farnham, Hankley Common, Hindhead, North Hants, Liphook and West Surrey, is a prime example and the Club was delighted to win it in 1982 and 1986.

It was also at this time that a somewhat impulsive decision was made in 1987 to cancel the annual matches against Oxford, Cambridge and London Universities which had long been a feature of the fixture list. The decision was not helped by Cambridge University cancelling the match in 1986 and then reinstating it. A rather harsh judgement was taken of the standard of university golf at the time, which stood at one of its low points in its golfing cycle and, in fact, was just about to produce in the early 1990s some of the finest university teams of the post-war period.

The North Hants team was especially strong and the decision was made to replace the university matches with scratch matches against other local clubs. Much of the strength of the team was due to the policy of encouraging good juniors to become members and the team included highly focused teenagers who were not on the same wavelength as the more outgoing and older university golfer. He, in turn, having been demolished by an intense teenager, was more likely to retreat to the bar than to the practice ground and, as a result, attract the comment made unfairly at the time that university golfers treated the matches as "jollies".

The disparity was shown in that same year, when four of these teenagers left the Club to join the professional ranks, where one of them, Scott Watson, later obtained his card for a number of years on the European Tour. As an alternative to the university matches some scratch matches were arranged and won in the following year against Beaconsfield, Brokenhurst Manor and Ealing, the latter then fielding one of the strongest club teams in the country. These matches have been played somewhat fitfully over the years, but without ever becoming permanent annual fixtures. They tend to be arranged at the busier times of the golfing season, whereas a particular advantage of the university matches was that they were played out of season between November and February.

There were other golfing features in this decade. Two successful new competitions were introduced, the Parson's Putter in 1981 and the Lewis Shields in 1984, both donated by Club captains, Freddie Parsons and Harry Lewis. The first was a running match play knockout to replace the previous Captain's Prize. It has been highly successful and in its first year attracted some 200 entries. The Lewis Shields are separate winter knockouts for the "A" and "B" divisions.

In 1988, Martin Farmer, playing with his father, won the Fathers and Sons Tournament at West Hill. In the same year Tim Hanson finished third in the new English mid-Amateur Tournament at Little Aston. He was a Cambridge Blue and former Derbyshire County champion who moved south and joined the Club in 1976. An immensely powerful golfer, he sometimes gave the impression that the green is something to be carried and that his idea of a course record would be to list the shortest iron with which he had reached each green. He is a practising accountant who has served the Club with great dedication as honorary treasurer since 1987, when he succeeded Trevor Morgan who had occupied the role since it had been resurrected in 1981.

In 1986 and 1987, the Club convened Pro-Am tournaments in aid of charity. In the first year it had been an inherited responsibility after the Rotary Club had planned the idea but then dropped out. It was a successful event, raising some £4,300 for the Douglas Bader Foundation and sufficiently encouraging for it to be repeated in the following year. However, a Pro-Am requires much hard work both to attract sponsors and good professionals and it was decided, not unreasonably, that the idea should be laid to rest before it became a burdensome annual commitment.

Apart from the introduction of automatic watering, some modest changes were taking place on the golf course. Bunker rakes were introduced in 1980 and shorts were allowed to be worn from 1982, but with full length stockings. Ball washers carrying advertisements in 1982 and refreshments at the 10th tee in 1986 were new features. In October 1986, a tree planting programme was started under the guidance of Gordon Shakespear who must have had a premonition that precisely a year later a hurricane would topple some 200 trees on the course. His great love for trees was founded from an army posting to Nepal in the 1960s where he transformed a nine hole golf course by planting colourful flowering trees. Upon return home, he turned his attention first to Tidworth Golf Club and then to North Hants where his many plantings are now growing in maturity. A powerful cricketer turned golfer, he was runner-up in the Army Championship in 1971 at the age of fifty-one.

An interesting experiment was tried in the closing months of 1986 to start the second nine holes from the 13th tee, largely through dislike or inconvenience of starting with a short hole. The proposal was to continue through to the 16th and then play the 12th, 10th and 11th. This was resisted on the grounds that the traditional finish over the last three holes would be interrupted and the experiment was carried out over October and November starting the back nine with the 13th, 12th, 10th and 11th. Traditionalists amongst the membership were thankful to see the experiment fail. They would have been no less thankful on another occasion in 1989 if they had known that the Executive Committee decided at one meeting to change the name of the Club to North Hampshire Golf Club, only to reverse the decision at the following meeting.

The fortunes of the ill-fated Bramshot Golf Club have strayed into these pages from time to time and a postscript to its post-war demise took place in 1992. The National Gas Turbine Establishment, Pyestock, was built on the course after the war and within its grounds the former 10th tee had been roped off, mown regularly and preserved for posterity. A nostalgic return visit was organised by the captain, John Lidstone, for two members of North

*10th tee, Bramshot Golf Club. Barry Armstrong, course record holder in 1938, drives off watched by D'Arcy Mander and John Lidstone, captain (1992)*

Hants who had played at Bramshot in the 1930s. One was Barry Armstrong, who, as has already been mentioned, held the amateur course record at Bramshot when it closed down in 1939. The other was D'Arcy Mander who had been a Mess member of both Bramshot and North Hants in the 1930s and after retirement from the army joined North Hants in 1963.

D'Arcy Mander was a great survivor. During the war, he made a remarkable escape from capture in North Italy and worked his way to Rome, where he lived for six months whilst the city was still under German occupation. He was as sprightly a nonagenarian golfer as the Club may ever know before he died at the age of ninety-one and earlier he had been instrumental in setting up the octogenarian meetings which are now firmly established in the Club calendar. On their return visit to the 10th tee, which is still there to this day, all three dutifully drove plastic golf balls to an imaginary fairway and the occasion was recorded in the local golfing press. Intriguingly, it was my father, George Littlewood, a member of North Hants in the 1950s and personnel manager at the N.G.T.E., who originally roped off the tee in 1950. He was well aware of the club's history as the venue of the Daily Mail Professional Tournament. He took up golf in 1929 after losing the sight of his right eye in an accident and a year later turned professional in a career that continued until the outbreak of the war.

However, back in the clubhouse it was a decade of musical chairs for the positions of professional, secretary, head greenkeeper and steward. Tim Gowdy had succeeded Bob Mounce as professional in 1976, but he never really settled and left in 1982. From fifty-six applicants for the position the Club was delighted to select the former Ryder Cup player and genial Irishman, Hugh Boyle. Unfortunately, within a few weeks of arriving in January 1983 he abruptly resigned to accept an offer from Royal Wimbledon, leaving behind, it has to be said, a sour taste in the Club.

The Club immediately approached Steve Porter, the professional at Hartley Wintney, who had been short-listed in second place amongst the original applicants, and he was appointed professional in May 1983. He has been a model professional, a fine teacher and a popular member of the Club in a position which he holds to this day.

Steve Porter was a talented junior tennis player and it was a fine choice for him whether to pursue a golfing or tennis career. He played golf at Sunningdale and when still at school at the age of fifteen and a half he was offered a position as an assistant professional by Arthur Lees, the famous Ryder Cup golfer and Sunningdale professional. He had to wait until he could leave school before he could take up the position on his sixteenth birthday in July 1969. He remained as assistant for nearly four years and then played the European tour for two years with some success in the Northern Ireland PGA tour. After getting married he exchanged the uncertain nomadic life of the tour professional for the greater stability of the club professional, briefly at Lavender Park and then Hartley Wintney.

Over the twenty years that he has been Club professional he has observed a course that has become far busier and, as he puts it, has changed in character from "true heathland" to "friendly heathland". He has witnessed the dramatic changes in technology of both club and ball, but strongly believes that the improvement in golf at the highest level is also due to a third factor, the greater physical fitness and strength of many top golfers today.

Many members have enjoyed the annual series of fourball matches against the captain and the professional. They are played out of season from the white tees and one memorable round played by Steve Porter was with Eric Carpenter in November 1984, when he holed out at every hole for a round of 62, a card that is happily framed on display in his shop.

It was a moment of much sadness in the Club when Nigel Lockyer, a popular and affable secretary, died on the golf course in August 1984. He was playing a singles match and after hitting his second shot to the 7th from a good drive, he collapsed with a heart attack, much to the consternation of his opponent who continued walking some way towards the green unaware of what had happened. Nigel Lockyer's ashes were later scattered on the 7th fairway.

Pat Kay, who has served the Club so well in so many ways, immediately volunteered to act as temporary secretary and after the usual processes of sifting through forty-five applications, Keith Symons was appointed to take up the position in November 1984. He, too, was a popular secretary but he only remained for two years after applying for and accepting the position of manager and secretary of Moortown Golf Club, one of the most famous of all Yorkshire golf clubs. Having given three months notice, Keith Symons allowed an orderly succession and John Gostling was appointed in October 1986. Rather sadly, the responsibilities proved too onerous for him and he departed in June 1987.

Just as Pat Kay stepped into the breach after the death of Nigel Lockyer, so this time "Danny" Daniels, former captain for two years in 1975 and 1976 and now an Honorary Member living in Wales, volunteered to be acting secretary until the Club offered the position to Roy Goodliffe, who had been one of the three short-listed candidates a year earlier. He was secretary at Ashford Manor Golf Club and accepted the position with alacrity, joining the club in October 1987. Roy Goodliffe took the course for golf club secretaries after retiring from a long career in the Royal Air Force, initially gaining experience at Knebworth Golf Club and Fulwell Golf Club. He was attracted to North Hants by the ambience of the Club, a liking for the golf course and a preference to live further away from London. He was a very enthusiastic cricketer and able golfer, attaining briefly in his younger days a handicap of 4. He was to serve the Club as a quite outstanding secretary for fourteen years.

Bill Brown retired as head greenkeeper in March 1987 after twenty-one years of loyal service to the Club. His final years were clouded by deteriorating health following the death of his wife and, sadly, he died within months of his retirement. He enjoyed much popularity within the Club and a tulip tree was planted in his memory on the first hole, just beyond the practice putting green. He was succeeded by his deputy, Allan Sharp, who had been recruited little more than a year earlier, but he departed in October 1988.

He in turn was succeeded by Nigel Stainer, whose knowledge and experience of golf had embraced fifteen years as a professional golfer and twelve years as a head greenkeeper. As a talented schoolboy he represented Dorset at junior level at cricket, rugby and athletics, but then found himself joining Percy Alliss in 1960 as an assistant at Ferndown despite then having done little more than caddying for the members. He started with a handicap of 7 which quickly fell to scratch and in 1970 became the professional at Knighton Heath Golf Club. Throughout his professional career his greater interest was in greenkeeping and in 1976 he was appointed head greenkeeper at Ashley Wood Golf Club, later moving to Three Rivers in Essex.

The course he now inherited had been declining in condition and attracting criticism from the members. This followed some particularly difficult years of extreme weather conditions and something of a drift during the closing years under Bill Brown and the failed appointment of Allan Sharp. Nigel Stainer was to prove to be an outstanding greenkeeper with a personal motto of never being satisfied. His instincts are to treat the course in as natural a way as possible. He emphasises the use of organic fertilisers, regularly on the greens and every three years or so lightly on the fairways, clearing trees where needed to allow access of light to tees and greens and keeping the course tidy. His preparation of the course for the Hampshire Hog regularly draws praise from the competitors and during the six year cycle of Open Championship regional qualifying in the 1990s, the course looked magnificent in July, when the rough in view from the clubhouse became a shimmering field of the wispy brown heads of freely growing fescue grass.

The role of steward was no less fluctuating. Claude Denton had been appointed to the position in October 1975. He was a many talented character, possessing a quite extraordinary range of interests and hobbies – musician, linguist, sailor, clock repairer, crossword solver and osteopath. He was able to turn his hand to practical tasks of almost any kind and was publicly thanked by Philip Ricketts in his Captain's Report in 1978 "for the many other little duties, ranging from first aid to drain cleaning which Claude took in his stride".

His natural enthusiasm led him from time to time to cross the invisible barrier that in a golf club exists between the members and the staff at the point where exuberance turns into familiarity. The result was the occasional yellow card for behaviour and he did not always help his cause by a tendency to express publicly some strong personal opinions. He left the Club in February 1985 to the regret of many members.

The post of steward was redefined as house manager and after two appointments of short duration, Gerry Halliwell was promoted to this position in May 1989. He had joined the Club two years earlier as deputy house manager after working for eight years at the Mendips Golf Club in Somerset, where before that he had worked for twenty years in Showerings, the cider and Babycham company. He, too, served the Club efficiently and well for fifteen years before retiring in 2002.

Whereas the 1980s was an unsettled decade that found the Club with four secretaries, three professionals, three greenkeepers and four house

*Together through the 1990s – professional, head greenkeeper, secretary and club steward – Steve Porter, Nigel Stainer, Roy Goodliffe and Gerry Halliwell*

managers, there was now to follow in the 1990s a happy and welcome contrast. With Roy Goodliffe, Steve Porter, Nigel Stainer and Gerry Halliwell in place, the Club is able to make the rare claim that the positions of secretary, professional, head greenkeeper and house manager were occupied unchanged through a calendar decade. It is a tribute to all of them.

Spirits were low in the early 1990s. The existence of the Club was in doubt and years of negotiation were about to begin. However, before returning to this aspect of the Club's history, other happenings are worth recording. The waiting list for membership might already have seemed stretched at 100 men and 48 ladies in January 1990, but it simply went on rising. It rose to 140 men and 43 ladies in 1993, suggesting an eight to ten year wait and the ceilings were raised from 412 to 425 for men and 108 to 112 for ladies. By the end of 1995 it had reached 164 for men, at which point the list for ordinary members was again closed. At the same time, the number of temporary members had been allowed to rise to around ninety with one-third of them having playing rights on a rotating quarterly basis.

For the golf course, the decade began with a then rare architectural change. In March 1990 a new bunker was opened for play on the 17th hole on the left of the fairway some 220 yards from the back tee, as recommended by golf architect David Thomas as a means of tightening up the lone par 5. The Executive Committee fretted over the introduction of fairway yardage markers. In October 1990, the white concrete squares to mark 150 yards to the centre of the green were voted in by four votes to three, but the red 200 yard markers were voted out, only to be voted in two years later. However, this was a mere trifle compared with the highly controversial affair of the bunker in the middle of the fairway on the 16th hole. This bunker had been introduced by Tom Simpson as part of his structural review of all the bunkers on the course in 1929. An earlier chapter described his theory that bunkers should be strategic rather than punitive and that they should be designed to make the better golfer think very carefully about his drive or shot to the green.

It was a classic example. Here was a bunker in the middle of the fairway at 200 yards from the tee, forcing a choice between the dangerous line to the right to give an easier shot to the green or a safer line to the left leaving a more difficult second shot. In the Club brochure published in 1948, Bernard Darwin described it as a "venomous" bunker but continued "If we keep bravely between the bunker and the railway, we shall get the open shot at the green". This bunker achieved its strategic purpose for the best part of fifty years until overtaken by advances in the technology of club and ball. A redundant test for the better golfer had now become a nuisance for too many other golfers. It was for precisely this reason that in November 1992, the captain, John Lidstone, reported in his Newsletter a proposal, subject to consultation with the membership, to move the bunker forward by some twenty to twenty-five yards, where it would continue to bemuse the better golfer.

Unfortunately, in a fit of democracy, this and other options were put to a referendum of the membership and the result in January 1993 was a two-thirds majority for the soft option of a new bunker on the left edge of the fairway. A feature which, long before the phrase was invented, had created a reputation in the outside golfing world for the 16th as a signature hole, was destroyed. In a recent letter, Frank Deighton, the Walker Cup player, made an Honorary Member during a brief interlude here in the early 1950s, wrote of his memories of the course that the "bunker in the middle of the 16th hole was a masterpiece of golf course architecture". The incoming captain, John Bermingham, inherited the decision of the members and rightly observed in his Newsletter that "I realise that some will feel that they have lost an old friend".

Prior to the removal of this supposedly obsolete bunker, the 16th hole regularly featured amongst the three or four most difficult holes on the course in analyses of the Hampshire Hog or Regional Open Qualifying scores. Its teeth have now been drawn and all that removing the bunker has served to do is to diminish the finish of those once fearsome last three holes.

It was in the same year that another old friend was forcibly removed from the club. Surviving from the original building had been a fine sweeping staircase rising from the entrance hall to the first floor. This no longer satisfied the fire regulations and at considerable expense it was removed and replaced by an enclosed back staircase of no architectural merit.

North Hants was invited by the R&A to be a Regional Qualifying course for the Open Championship in 1992, an annual event that lasted through a six year cycle until 1997. It was a compliment to the Club and the first Monday in July was an occasion much enjoyed by the many members who helped the event to take place. It was a good test of the Club's organisational abilities, a great incentive for the greenstaff to show off their skills and the weather was unfailingly kind. Many a compliment was paid to the Club and there was something missing when the cycle came to an end.

However, the story now returns to the future of the Club as it appeared to be in 1990. Although not known at the time, the Club was about to enjoy the unusual stability already mentioned in its principal offices of secretary, professional, head greenkeeper and house manager and so also was the Club fortunate to benefit from the same continuity of the members of the Environment Committee. Its membership remained unchanged from January 1990 until the loss due to serious illness of Philip Ricketts in 1997. It entered the new decade of the 1990s with many years work ahead of it. The trigger that had led to its formation had been a meeting in December 1989 with the Elvetham Estate at which they had alerted the Club to their clear intention to develop Railroad Heath whether or not it included the golf course and, furthermore, advised that a renewal of the lease in 2016 could not be guaranteed.

In February 1990, the Director of Planning of Hart District Council confirmed his intention to seek the development of the area of the golf course as a "high-class employment campus" and to provide a main access road to the housing development. The next few months were probably the time of greatest unrest and speculation amongst the members about the future of the Club, although it was partly quelled at the Annual General Meeting in March, when the captain, Peter Breedon, reported that the Estate had provided a written undertaking to relocate the Golf Club in the event of its development. He presented two options facing the Club, either resist the development and hang on until 2016 or cooperate with the Estate to secure a relocation.

The Environment Committee was comforted by a preliminary professional valuation suggesting that compensation for relocation would be considerable and this information was revealed to members by the late Ian Johnston in his Captain's Newsletter of November 1990 when he wrote that "the club's entitlement in money terms would be more than enough to cover the costs of providing a high quality replacement for the present course and associated buildings".

However comforting this assurance might have been, the background to gloomy speculation amongst the membership was that relocation seemed to be the best that could be expected. Many members were appalled at the thought of a historical gem being built over and dismayed by the prospect of having to adapt to a new course on a greenfield site.

The closing months of 1990 probably represented the lowest point in the fortunes of the Club. Proposals for developments of the size and scale of Railroad Heath move ahead at a slow pace and most of 1991 was spent in waiting for a Public Inquiry to begin on 19th November. It would last for some two months and the Inspector would hear representations from circles far wider than just the Golf Club. On the advice of Philip Ricketts, the club engaged Mr. J. C. Woolf from Chartered Town Planning Consultants, Chancellors, based in Odiham, to register formal objections on our behalf and to represent us at the Inquiry. Jerry Woolf, who was then on the waiting list and later became a member in 1995, was to make an invaluable contribution to the Club's fortunes over several years of representing us and negotiating on our behalf. He played a vital role in helping to steer the Environment Committee through the intricacies and obscure language of the planning world.

It gradually became apparent through 1991 that the Estate had reservations about developing the golf course land as a business and leisure area and that opinion at Hart District Council was divided, but it was also clearly apparent that both sides were intent upon developing the remainder of Railroad Heath. The consequence of this outcome for the Club would be the need for a northern perimeter access road that would cut across the practice ground, the 2nd green and 3rd tee. At the same time, the Estate formally reiterated the point that there was "little prospect" of the lease being renewed in 2016 and that contingency planning should continue for relocation.

The Inspector's Report was published in September 1992 and at face value it was encouraging for the future of the Club. He recommended against the business campus proposal. Furthermore, he recommended that the golf course should be excluded from the Plan except to the extent that it would be affected by a northern perimeter access road which he supported. In a significant passage in his Report, the Inspector observed that the Golf Club "holds the key to Railroad Heath, if the development is to be carried out in a properly planned and comprehensive manner". Out of this emerged a strong mutual interest on the part of the Club and the Estate to come to an agreement which would suit both sides.

The access road had become the key to the Estate obtaining maximum financial advantage from the development of Railroad Heath. The preference for the Club between a slow death in 2016, a relocation to a new site or a modification to the 2nd, 3rd and 4th holes was quickly resolved in favour of the latter. The particular interest of the Club was to obtain long-term security of tenure and a share of the considerable development benefit that the Estate would gain from obtaining access. This latter point was strongly emphasised by Philip Ricketts.

*Len Woods, Club captain, signs the 999 year lease in January 1995*

The Environment Committee took the initiative and in December 1992 authorised Jerry Woolf to pursue active discussions with the Estate. There followed six months of lengthy correspondence, frequent meetings and watchful negotiation as the two sides worked their way to a basis for agreement on Heads of Terms. These negotiations were concluded successfully at the end of June 1993 and the Environment Committee owed much to the guidance of Jerry Woolf and of John Ratcliffe, the senior partner of local solicitors, Neale Turk, who had been appointed as legal adviser. His excellent advice and calm presence were important factors in the negotiations.

In outline summary, the Heads of Terms agreed a 999 year lease at a peppercorn rent, staged capital payments amounting to some £4 million and reimbursement of £200,000 for a broadly estimated cost of redesigning the 2nd, 3rd and 4th holes. These details were highly confidential and would probably have surprised many of the members, but they still had to be negotiated into the detail of signed legal agreements. This did indeed prove to be a protracted and frustrating period of some eighteen months of legal and taxation niceties, until on 27th January 1995, the captain, Len Woods, enjoyed the privilege of signing the Lease and Financial Agreement.

In a letter to all members he wrote that he was "delighted to tell you that the lengthy negotiations with the Elvetham Estate have been brought to a satisfactory conclusion and I have today signed the new Lease and Agreement". The letter summarised the terms, but specifically added that details of the financial arrangement must remain confidential.

In the final paragraph of his letter, Len Woods paid a warm and generous tribute to the Environment Committee:

> None of the arrangements I have outlined could have been achieved without the outstanding work of the Environment Committee. I am most grateful and appreciative to this co-opted committee – Pat Kay, Peter Breedon, John Pothecary and Philip Ricketts together with the Captain and Vice-Captain of the day – for their diligent and conscientious work over the past five years. They undertook what turned out to be an enormous, demanding and time-consuming task and their efforts have now been aptly rewarded. I am certain that all members will join with me in thanking them for the long hours and tremendous work they have performed in the interests of North Hants Golf Club. We are most fortunate to have members with such devotion and dedication in our Club and we owe to each of them a great debt of gratitude.

It was a well-deserved tribute, but they were about to discover that their task was not yet over and would continue for a further three years. As will be seen in the final chapter, some complications would arise. They would not be to the disadvantage of the Club, but they would delay the implementation of the agreement.

This chapter closes with the removal of the threat of a famous golf course being developed out of existence. It had been hanging over the membership for the best part of ten years and in January 1995 it was a time of relief and celebration. In April 1995, the membership was to have further cause for celebration. The occasion was the Hampshire Hog. The achievement was a stunning victory. The name was Justin Rose.

# Chapter Nine

# Justin Rose

THERE CAN be few golfers who have given as much pleasure to the members of a golf club as has Justin Rose given to the members of North Hants Golf Club. He displayed a remarkable golfing talent from the moment he became a junior member in 1992 at the age of twelve and combined with that talent an open friendliness and modesty that charmed all who met him.

His golfing feats made members proud of him and proud of North Hants Golf Club. After his astonishing performance of finishing fourth in the 1998 Open Championship at the age of seventeen, many a member would find that a chance reference to North Hants Golf Club would elicit the comment "Isn't that where Justin Rose plays?" Since turning professional his career has sparked enormous interest at the Club. Many members have been prompted to install Sky television to follow his fortunes in routine tour events, only for their attention quickly to evaporate if Justin has completed his round or is not playing. Live hole by hole scores on tour websites are regularly surfed on the internet. The Justin Rose website is accessed and e-mailed by more than fifty members. Some might even claim to be Justin Rose "groupies", not least Ann and George Jackson and Malcolm and Margaret Roberts, who have taken holidays abroad to follow him round over every single hole of a seventy-two hole tournament and whose round by round support at the European Tour School was deeply appreciated.

Justin was born in Johannesburg on 30th July 1980. His parents, Ken and Annie, were first generation South Africans, who in 1985 decided to return to Britain, the homeland of their parents. Their elder son, Brandon, has remained in South Africa, where he played for one year on the professional tour. They chose to settle in Hook and there began a remarkable partnership between father and son that was to take Justin to the very highest levels of amateur golf. At the age of five he played initially at Hartley Wintney and one of his earliest golfing memories is of breaking 90 for nine holes and being

# The 1998 Open – Royal Birkdale Golf Club

During the four days of the 1998 Open from 16-19 July, golfing history was made by Justin Rose, a junior member of North Hants Golf Club. As a Walker Cup player – the youngest ever – he was exempt from the pre-qualifying rounds. Qualifying rounds of 75 and 72 at Hillside enabled him to tee off at Royal Birkdale in The Open, where he had an opening round of 72.

His 66, in the second round, equalled the lowest score ever by an amateur in The Open. During the third round, for a few magical moments, he was top of the leader board. Justin, however, left the highlight of his four days until his last shot, when he holed his approach of 45 yards to the 18th to tie for fourth place on 282 and to become the youngest amateur ever to win the Silver Medal.

That holed approach was the last shot he ever played as an amateur, because on 20th July 1998 – ten days before his 18th birthday – he turned professional.

In recognition of his outstanding amateur golfing achievements, Justin was appointed an Honorary Member of North Hants Golf Club on 8th August 1998.

*The sequence of photographs shown below was taken from live coverage on BBC Television.*

*1998 Open Championship. Montage by Philip Mitchell*

141

*The Captains – Drawing by Eric Carpenter, 1996*

*Hampshire Rose – Twentieth Anniversary – Previous winners*
*Back row, left to right: Carole Caldwell (1973, 1984), Pru Riddiford (1974), Heather Glynn-Jones (1976, 1978), Angela Uzielli (1992), Jill Thornhill (1982, 1987, 1988), Carol Larkin (1979)*
*Front row: Claire Hourihane (1986, 1990), Alison MacDonald (1989), Kate Egford (1991)*

*New Clubhouse – trophies*

*The spike bar in the old clubhouse. Much of the furniture in the old clubhouse was auctioned for charity and the square table in the spike bar was a long-standing feature. Ann Murch successfully bid for the table to have it restored and presented to the Club where it now resides in the new spike bar. In a letter to the club she wrote that "This table has held the glasses of champions and nurtured the dreams of young at heart golfers." Her understanding was that "the table was actually a gift from my mother and father and I suspect it came originally from the old Bramshot club after the war." Her father, Major P.H. Slater, was a vice-president of the Club from 1951 to 1958. Her mother, Bobby Slater, was an Honorary Member who joined the Club in 1946. She died at the age of eighty-five on the day following the auction*

*Sir Euan Anstruther-Gough-Calthorpe opens the new Clubhouse, 20th September 2003*

rewarded with a Scalextric set as part of a carrot and stick approach. At the age of eight he joined Tylney Park.

It was when he played in the Hampshire Boys Championship at Royal Winchester Golf Club in 1990 that he came to the notice of Freddie Parsons, then the County president. Justin had been squeezed in as a diminutive late entrant just after his tenth birthday and he astonished everybody by returning a gross score of 86, for which he received a special prize.

He now needed the challenge of a more testing golf course and in August 1992, with the active encouragement of Freddie Parsons, he joined North Hants where the availability of a good practice ground was a particular attraction. Adjusting to a longer course took a few months and he started slowly over the closing months of 1992 when his handicap hovered between 9 and 10, but he suddenly became a talking point in the Club when at the age of twelve he returned a gross 74 in the monthly medal on 23rd January 1993, whereupon his handicap was reduced from 10 to 8. From this point onwards his golf developed at an astonishing speed.

This round of 74 was to prove to be merely the impetus for the way forward as it was quickly followed by a gross 72 in the April medal and a further reduction in handicap to 6. In the course of a year of extraordinary consistency he produced another half-dozen competitive rounds of 73 or 74 and by June 1993 his handicap was 5 at only the age of twelve. In October he won the Lloyd Cup with 38 points and his handicap was reduced further to 4. He was equally successful away from the Club, winning the first of three successive County Junior Under-15 Championships, various Junior Open events and, on a wider stage, the Weetabix Golf Foundation Under-14 Championship at Patshall Park Golf Club.

It was in 1994 that awareness of his talent, already well known at club and county level, was drawn to national notice when he won the McGregor Salver for Under-15 boys at Ratcliffe-on-Trent. This was a serious national event that stood out amidst a handful of local junior titles, but back home at the Club even this paled beside the open-mouthed astonishment of his round of 65 in a junior medal on 22nd July, just days before his fourteenth birthday. Some precocious boy golfers achieve early success by being big, strong and heavy for their age group, but Justin was only of modest build. His success was based on a beautifully balanced and rhythmical swing that was so pin-splittingly square through the ball that he would attack the flag wherever it was placed. This was combined with a short game that fearlessly attacked the back of the hole with every chip and putt. By the end of 1994, his handicap was reduced to 2.

It was another year of quantum leaps in 1995. He reached the quarter-finals of the English Amateur Championship and the last sixteen of the

*Justin Rose, aged 14, wins the Hampshire Hog with a record score of 134*

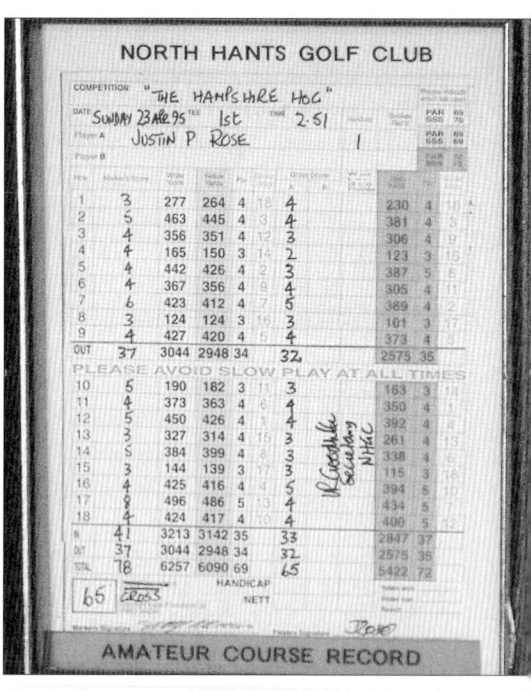

*Justin Rose sets a new course record of 65 to win the Hampshire Hog*

Amateur Championship. However, winning the Hampshire Hog with scores of 69 and 65 must rank as one of the finest achievements by any fourteen year old golfer. To establish a new course record to win the event and in the presence of many excited Club members was an extraordinary feat and from that afternoon round Justin attained a scratch handicap at the age of fourteen. Through that summer he proceeded to win the Currie Cup with a round of 70, the Gold Medal with 70 and 71 and to lead the regional qualifiers for the Open Championship with a 67. At national level he won the McGregor Trophy Under-16 Championship at Ratcliffe-on-Trent and, most remarkably of all, the Carris Trophy, the Under-18 stroke play championship for boys, at Burnham and Berrow. This he won three days before his fifteenth birthday, to become the youngest ever winner and selection for England Boys in the Home Internationals naturally followed.

By the end of 1995 his handicap was plus 1 and at the age of fifteen he was believed to be the youngest British golfer to have achieved this. The claims on his golfing calendar were now becoming almost impossible. He was an established boy international with another two seasons to run at that level, a serious competitor in national championships and a county regular for both seniors and colts. So it was that in 1996 at the under-18 level he represented

England in the World Championships in Tokyo and the European Team Championships in Austria, and Great Britain & Northern Ireland against the Continent of Europe. He finished runner-up in both the Carris Trophy and the McGregor Trophy and at the age of fifteen he was selected as first reserve for the full England team in the Home Internationals.

At the same time he played for the Hampshire County team that won the national County Championship finals for the first time in its history and he won the County Boys and Youth Championships. Within the county he particularly enjoyed winning the Mike Smith Memorial Trophy at Brokenhurst Manor with rounds of 67 and 63, the latter a course record. With priorities stretching from club to county to country and from boys to youths to full internationals, it was not surprising that he played fewer rounds at North Hants in 1996. However, he managed to win the Gold Medal with two rounds of 70 and to equal his course record of 65 in the Silver Medal, by which time his handicap was plus 2.

In 1996 Justin faced an entirely different decision. With the enormous amount of golf that he was playing it is easy to forget that he was still at school, where he actively enjoyed both soccer and basketball. He took his G.C.S.E. exams at Robert Mays School in Odiham and passed with six Bs and two Cs, despite being plunged into them immediately upon returning from playing for England Under-18s in Tokyo and in fact too late to take his favourite subject. He could clearly have successfully stayed for another two years to take "A" levels, but golf was not only taking up a quite extraordinary part of the time of a fifteen/sixteen year old schoolboy, he was also loving every minute of it. The decision to leave school was easy to take and never regretted. By this time Justin was intent upon a professional career as quickly as possible and the alternative of two more years at school possibly followed by a golf scholarship to an American university held little or no appeal for him.

He now entered 1997 as a full-time golfer on the amateur circuit and his father, Ken, gave up his work to give him full-time support. Ken Rose had been a competent golfer with at best a modest handicap of 8, but as Justin progressed he studied the various coaching methods and the mechanics of the game. His knowledge of the golf swing and the magnificent swing that he helped Justin to build is a quite remarkable tribute to his self-taught coaching skills, although at times it was almost as if they were teaching each other.

The ultimate reward and highlight of 1997 was the selection of Justin as the youngest ever golfer to play for Great Britain and Ireland in the Walker Cup against the United States at the age of seventeen years and ten days. Before that there had been some frustration. At North Hants, he began the year with a sparkling 65 in the April Junior Open which qualified him for the finals of

*1988 Open Championship, Justin Rose finishes 4th and wins the Silver Medal*

The Daily Telegraph Junior Championship in the United States in Georgia, which he duly won later in the year.

This was just before the Hampshire Hog where a second victory had seemed to be there for the taking when, with three holes to play, Justin held a two stroke lead over Gary Wolstenholme, who then smothered his second shot into the bunker well short of the 16th green. Justin played a towering iron shot to the heart of the green, whereupon Wolstenholme made his 4 from the distant bunker, followed by 4, 3 to tie. With the honour, he drove to the middle of the 1st green to win with a 3 and Justin's rounds of 67 and 68 had been to no avail.

In the County Championship in Guernsey, Justin closely defeated Matthew Blackey in the semi-final in a match of the highest quality between the two best players in the field. It should have been the final and it left him unable to raise his game in the afternoon. There was further disappointment in the Amateur Championship at Royal St George's where his play in difficult conditions in the qualifying rounds had been the talking point of the second day, but he then lost in the early stages of the match play. However, much was redeemed by victory in the St Andrews Links Trophy, one of the leading seventy-two hole amateur tournaments, with three of the rounds over the Old Course.

Meanwhile, he had been performing well at international level. Although still eligible for selection for England Boys, he had earlier in the year made his senior international debut against Spain at the age of sixteen. He was unbeaten, winning three and halving one of his four matches, including appearances in the top foursome and top single on the second day. There followed selection for the England team in the Bolivar Cup and the European Team Championships. His performance in these internationals and his victory in the St Andrews Links Trophy clinched his place in the Walker Cup, so realising a long held ambition. Later in the year he also made his first appearance in the Home Internationals at Burnham & Berrow.

The Walker Cup was played in the August heat of Quaker Ridge in New York State. The Americans led from start to finish but Justin acquitted himself well, winning his single on the first day and his foursome with Gary Wolstenholme on the second morning. A small group of supporters flew over to watch. Bob Wyatt recalls his pleasure in following Justin through his four matches "there were no ropes and you could walk along the fairways with the players. Typically, Justin always had a word and a smile for his gallery" which for much of the time also included Michael Bonallack, then secretary of the R&A.

Two of Justin's friends from his earliest days, George Porter, assistant professional to his father at the Club, and John McGlashan also flew over for the match. George Porter believes Justin would have probably been more at ease with his regular England foursomes partner, Gary Wolstenholme, when he put his opening drive in the morning foursome out of bounds and "For the rest of the competition, Justin paired up with Gary Wolstenholme putting points on the board and in the singles he took on the highly rated and much fancied Joel Kribel, beating him one up".

For Justin 1998 was, of course, the annus mirabilis of the Open Championship at Royal Birkdale. Before that he played for England against France and for Europe against Asia Pacific in Australia and, briefly dropping back into boys golf, he won the Peter McEvoy Trophy, so completing a clean sweep of the three principal 72 hole championships for boys, along with the Carris and McGregor Trophies. In yet another packed and hectic schedule he only played competitively once at North Hants, when he convincingly won the Gold Medal for the third time in four years with rounds of 68 and 65. The afternoon round completed a remarkable sequence. He had now returned a competitive medal card of 65 at North Hants in each of five consecutive years from the ages of thirteen to seventeen. His handicap was now plus 3.

And so he arrived at Royal Birkdale where he was so dramatically to impress his name upon tens of thousands of the golfing public. His second round of 66 was probably the finest by any recent amateur in the Open Championship and after nine holes in the third round there on the screen for all to see was the name of this seventeen year old amateur at the top of the leader board. He finished fourth, easily winning the Silver Medal for leading amateur, and when he holed his pitch from some eighty yards at the seventy-second hole it was received with a spontaneous roar from the multitude around the green that many believe was the loudest ever heard in the history of the Open Championship.

The next day he turned professional. His amateur career for England had extended to seventeen matches in singles and foursomes of which he won thirteen, halved two and lost two. For six years he had given the members of

North Hants a rare and privileged opportunity to share the fame and fortune of an outstanding boy golfer who was still only a junior member when he turned professional. In early August an evening reception was given by the Club to celebrate his achievement and the captain, Brian Gallagher, announced with great pleasure to a large gathering that Justin was to be an Honorary Member.

The clubhouse walls bear tribute to Justin. Eric Carpenter presented one of his inimitable portraits and Philip Mitchell devised and presented a montage of text and photographs of still moments from television coverage showing the story of those famous four rounds in the 1998 Open Championship. Another display by Rosemary McMillan shows his career record in the beautifully scrolled text of a certificate of honour. The notice boards regularly display items of press coverage and details of his tour schedule.

His professional career has taken both him and his many supporters through a wide range of emotions. The week after the Open he played his first professional tournament in the Dutch Open amidst a wave of supercharged publicity in both press and television. He began with a distracted 77 followed by an impeccable 65, only to miss the cut by one stroke. The next week in the Scandinavian Open he three putted the last green from no sort of distance to miss the cut by one stroke. So near and yet so far. As he himself put it "the momentum was lost" and the pressure to make the cut intensified. Over the next twelve months he now suffered the agonies of a sequence of twenty-one missed cuts, interspersed with a disappointing visit to the 1998 PGA Tour School, and all made worse by unrelenting press coverage.

Despite setback after setback over many months, his fortitude and self-belief never failed him and he was widely praised for the patience with which he dealt with endless questions about his lack of progress. Criticism that he had turned professional too young was deflected by the much repeated conviction of his father that "the best place to learn about the professional tour is the professional tour".

The eventual turning point was a fine display in the 1999 Tour School when he finished in third place to secure his tour card. However, the next year was still to prove to be a struggle. He made two top twenty finishes but frustratingly ended the year in 122nd place in the Order of Merit, just outside the spot to retain his card. It was back to the Tour School. Another fine performance over this six round marathon led to him finishing in ninth place. After the turning point came the breakthrough. He began 2001 with successive second places in the Alfred Dunhill and the South African Open, the latter being especially cruel when Mark McNulty holed a ten yard putt

*Justin Rose playing with Tiger Woods in the 2002 Open Championship*

across the last green to deprive Justin of at least a play-off. Over a much more consistent year, he followed with two top ten and four top twenty finishes and thirty-third place in the Order of Merit.

After the breakthrough in 2001 came the triumphs of 2002. It began excitingly with his first European tour victory in the Alfred Dunhill in South Africa at the age of twenty-one and he followed this with a second victory in the Nashua Masters on the South African tour. This was an emotional victory for Justin, because his father was unable to share his triumph, being at home and about to undertake a serious operation for leukaemia. In May came his third victory on a visit to an important event on the Japanese tour, the Chunichi Crowns Tournament. After running Tiger Woods and Colin Montgomerie to within a stroke in third place in the Deutsche Bank Open, he achieved his first professional victory on home soil at the British Masters at Woburn. He won this in style, finishing with two successive rounds of 65 to win by one stroke from his close friend, Ian Poulter. Sixty-five was his favourite score from his amateur days at North Hants.

A significance of this fourth victory of the year was to take him to forty-fourth position in the world rankings, the top fifty being the springboard for eligibility to play in world events. He was to prove entirely at ease on this larger stage. In the Open Championship at Muirfield he opened with an unabashed 68, two strokes ahead of his playing partner, Tiger Woods. He was now eligible to play in his first major in the United States, the USPGA, immediately followed by a select World Golf Championship event. He finished a creditable twenty-third in the USPGA and in a remarkable fifth place in the WGC Invitational, easily the best placed European. This took him to thirty-fourth place in the official world rankings and he finished the year in ninth place in the Order of Merit of the European Tour.

In 2003, Justin broadened his golfing horizons by competing in ten tournaments in the United States, including three majors and three World Golf Championship events. His outstanding achievement was to finish in fifth equal place in the US Open, followed by third place in the Deutsche Bank US Championship. He lacked consistency on the European tour, but clearly showed his ability to rise to the big occasions at the end of the year in November when he contributed three and a half points out of five for GB and Ireland in the Seve Trophy and, playing with Paul Casey, took England into second place in the World Cup.

His father, Ken Rose, had been fighting leukaemia for nearly two years and it was with great sadness that he died at the age of fifty-seven in September 2002, some three weeks after he had been able to follow Justin round the USPGA. It was at least a comfort to them both that he had lived to see his belief in Justin so wonderfully rewarded, but for Justin it was the loss of not only his father, but also in the truest sense, his guide, philosopher and friend. It is greatly to the credit of Ken and his mother, Annie, that Justin should have the determination and ambition to play this highly competitive game at the highest level and yet at the same time display such friendliness and modesty to all who meet him. He will enjoy lifelong support and every good wish from many, many members of North Hants Golf Club.

## Chapter Ten

# The Hampshire Hog
## 1957–2003

THE HAMPSHIRE HOG is a magnificent silver trophy, oval-shaped with extensive design detail, twin handles and mounted with a wild hog, the emblem of Hampshire golf. It was presented by Reg Pearce in 1957 for a new thirty-six hole scratch amateur event and was a welcome April addition to a then modest calendar of amateur golfing events. It is a fascinating subject for golfing history because from 1957 to 1999 the course was little changed in length and, apart from playing in three-balls from both tees from 1976 onwards, its format has remained unchanged.

The Hog quickly attracted entries of international quality and it was fitting that the inaugural event should have been won by Michael Bonallack, then a twenty-two year old former Boys champion, but about to begin a glittering career as probably the finest British amateur golfer of all time, winning five British Amateur Championships and five English Amateurs.

Indeed, it could be argued that this victory was for him the platform of a marvellous opening year in which he later won the Berkshire Trophy and won selection for England in the Home Internationals and for Great Britain in the Walker Cup. He won the opening event with two rounds of 71, one shot ahead of fellow Walker Cup player that year, Doug Sewell.

There followed a stream of top names amongst the winners. In the first fifteen years from 1957 to 1971 it was won on eight occasions by six actual or prospective Walker Cup players. Five were English, Michael Bonallack, Philip Scrutton, Michael Attenborough, Bruce Critchley and David Frame and one Scotsman, David Blair, who won it three times. On a further five occasions it was won by actual or prospective internationals, neatly doing the rounds of the home countries with Tony Duncan and Hew Squirrell for Wales, David Wilkie for Scotland, Bill McCrea for Ireland and Michael Burgess for England.

The two exceptions to this list were the late David Physick in 1962 and Tim Koch de Gooreynd in 1965, who each in their own way probably gained greater satisfaction from their victories than any of the other winners. Physick won in appalling conditions of wind and driving rain with the highest ever winning score of 150. It was a remarkable victory for a tenacious, diminutive, left-handed golfer from Worplesdon, who compensated for lack of height with a set of many wooden clubs of fishing rod length. A master of repartee and irreverent humour, he quite rightly relished the irony that on such an awful day he had defeated so many international golfers.

The victory of Tim Koch de Gooreynd was rather different. He was a home member already making his mark in Hampshire golf and his winning score of 142 was only two strokes more than the then lowest winning score. It was a popular victory for the Club and winning gave him the confidence to embark on those highly successful few years described in an earlier chapter.

A common theme linking most of the winners, and indeed most of the competitors, in this first phase of the history of the Hampshire Hog is their maturity. They belonged to that era when amateurs were amateurs, enjoying golf as pastime from work and the top golfers enjoyed long golfing careers. David Blair won the Hog three times at the ages of forty-eight, forty-nine and fifty-two and three others were in their forties. Only three younger golfers were successful, Michael Bonallack at the age of twenty-two, Michael Attenborough at twenty and Bruce Critchley at twenty-five.

At this point the theme suddenly changes. Younger golfers emerge from a variety of backgrounds and, inspired in part by the Open Championship successes of Tony Jacklin, begin to dominate the game. The age of the teenage champion arrives in amateur golf, just as teenage influence was reflecting itself in golfing success for junior members at North Hants.

The list of winners of the Hog comes to be dominated by young golfers for whom amateur golf is but a stepping stone to a professional career and from 1972, five of the next six winners, Roger Revell, Carl Mason, Tim Giles, Hogan Stott and Sandy Lyle, were aged respectively 20, 19, 18, 16 and 19 when they won. Two of these, Mason and Lyle, were about to embark upon long professional careers.

In 1979, Michael Bonallack returned and remarkably repeated his inaugural victory twenty-two years earlier. He had not played the course since defending the trophy in 1958 but he followed a morning 67 with a 74, making 141, one stroke lower than when he first won.

Winners in the 1980s included Gordon Brand Jr. and Steven Richardson, who together with Sandy Lyle are the three winners of the Hampshire Hog later to become Ryder Cup players. By this time the Hampshire Hog was to some extent being crowded out of an ever expanding amateur golfing calendar and, in 1979, the Club was somewhat reluctantly persuaded to combine the event with the more recent Selborne Salver held on the preceding day at Blackmoor. The Hampshire County Golf Union presented the Hampshire Salver for the best seventy-two hole aggregate over the weekend.

The standard of entry remained very high through the 1980s and 1990s, attracting many current internationals, but the typical amateur international today is a transient teenager for whom amateur golf is but the briefest of stepping stones to an attempted professional career. There are so many young amateur golfers of a high standard that some of the recent winners of the Hampshire Hog have been less well known than in the past and some of them will spend years struggling in the lesser tours of professional golf.

Nevertheless, the winners from 1979 onwards have included another nine golfers who went on to achieve Walker Cup status, making fifteen in total since the competition began. In welcome contrast to many a teenager they include the only two long-term career international amateurs of recent decades, Peter McEvoy and Gary Wolstenholme, who together have broken all records for the number of international appearances. McEvoy won in 1989 at the age of thirty-six and Wolstenholme won in 1997 at the age of thirty-seven and again in 2002. Another popular victory was that in 1986 of Bobby Eggo, Walker Cup player and long-standing Hampshire County golfer. The list of winners includes the previous or prospective international status of each individual winner.

A review of the Hampshire Hog must conclude with the finest victory of all in 1995. Justin Rose won at the age of fourteen with rounds of 69 and 65, setting a new course record in the afternoon and a new record winning score of 134. It was all the more remarkable because he broke the course record in the presence of dozens of members all willing him to win.

The Hampshire Salver, awarded for the seventy-two hole aggregate with the Selborne Salver, is a somewhat artificial trophy because it has no resident home or list of winners. In its twenty-two years, it has, perhaps surprisingly, only been won by the winner of the Hog on four occasions, of which the most remarkable was in 1990 when John Metcalfe won both individual events and set a record score of 272, which was later equalled by John Knight in 1996. David Gilford, later to be a Ryder Cup player, won it in 1986 and our only home winner has been Justin Rose in 1997, when he was defeated for the Hog by Gary Wolstenholme at the first extra hole.

The results of the Hampshire Hog have usually been close and particularly in the last fifteen years when the overall standard of the entry has been so high. In its history over forty-five years there have been six ties and seventeen wins by a single shot. Sudden death has only once extended beyond the first two holes, in 1996 when four extra holes were required.

# NORTH HANTS GOLF CLUB

*Reg Pearce presents the Hampshire Hog to Michael Bonallack, 1979*

*Freddie Parsons, Club captain, presents the Hampshire Salver to Peter McEvoy, 1979*

*International foursomes partners – Gary Wolstenholme, winner of the Hampshire Hog and Justin Rose, winner of the Hampshire Salver, 1997*

*Lionel Smith presents the Hampshire Salver to Martin Sell, 2003*

Runaway victories have been rare, but include two of the finest golfing performances. The victory by Michael Attenborough by nine strokes in 1960 on a day of gale force winds was outstanding when he returned 69 and 71 to become the only winner in the first ten years of the event to break 70. The victory of Sandy Lyle in 1977 was another fine achievement when on a very cold day he returned two rounds of 70 to win by five strokes. Apart from these two years there have been winning margins of six strokes in 1959 and of five strokes on two other occasions.

The event is usually held on the third Sunday in April and the weather can be unpredictable. The worst ever conditions were in 1962 when David Physick won in driving wind and rain, but the most extraordinary year was 1981 when competitors arrived to find an inch or more of snow lying on the course. Fortunately, the temperature was rising and the snow had all but disappeared by lunchtime, allowing the event to be decided over eighteen holes. Gordon Brand Jr. won with a round of 68.

The list of winning scores below reflect the rising standards apparent everywhere in competitive golf. The course was little changed in length and design from 1957 until 1999, when for one year the 2nd and 3rd holes were significantly shortened to enable redesign to take place. Just as in the early years a winning round under 70 was rare, so in the latter years a round higher than 69 was equally rare. Average winning scores over the decades show how the course has become vulnerable to the evolving technology of clubs and balls:

1957–1969    143.1
1970–1979    140.6
1980–1989    139.6
1990–1999    136.4

Record winning scores on the original course from 1957 to 1999 have followed the same pattern:

142  Michael Bonallack      1957
140  Michael Attenborough   1960
137  Michael Burgess        1968 (later equalled by Andy Clapp in 1985)
136  Steven Richardson      1988 (later equalled by John Metcalfe in 1990)
134  Justin Rose            1995 (later equalled by Philip Rowe in 1998)

Similarly, the amateur course record has been gradually lowered through the years in the Hampshire Hog. The sequence has been:

68  David Blair        1967 (later equalled three times)
67  Carl Mason         1972
66  Mike Hughesdon     1976 (later equalled three times)
65  Justin Rose        1995 (later equalled by Chris Rogers in 1999)

# THE HAMPSHIRE HOG 1957–2003

*Three winners of the Hampshire Hog who later became Ryder Cup Golfers*

*Sandy Lyle (1977)*

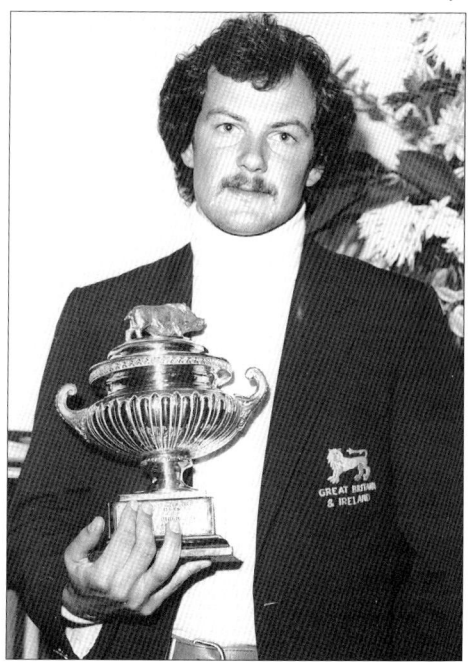

*Gordon Brand Jr. (1981)*

*Steven Richardson (1988)*

The records of Rose and Rogers will be frozen in the record book for the course as it was from its inception until 1999. For the event in 2000, the existing 2nd and 3rd holes were shortened as work proceeded on the new holes, which were opened in time for the following year. In 2001 and 2002 the Hog was played under winter rules, but in the latter year Gary Wolstenholme won for the second time with two magnificent rounds of 66, creating a new aggregate record and amazingly playing inside his handicap of plus 5.

## The Hampshire Hog

| Year | Winner | Club | Score | Status |
|---|---|---|---|---|
| 1957 | M.F. Bonallack | Thorpe Hall | 71 + 71 = 142 | Walker Cup/England |
| 1958 | P.F. Scrutton | Sunningdale | 72 + 74 = 146 | Walker Cup/England |
| 1959 | A.A. Duncan | North Hants | 72 + 73 = 145 | Wales |
| 1960 | M.F. Attenborough | Chislehurst | 69 + 71 = 140 | Walker Cup/England |
| 1961 | H.C. Squirrell | Moor Park | 74 + 70 = 144* | Wales |
| 1962 | F.D. Physick | Worplesdon | 74 + 76 = 150 | |
| 1963 | W.E. McCrea | Walton Heath | 74 + 72 = 146 | Ireland |
| 1964 | D.F. Wilkie | Falkirk Tryst | 73 + 72 = 145 | Scotland |
| 1965 | T. Koch de Gooreynd | North Hants | 72 + 70 = 142 | |
| 1966 | D.A. Blair | North Hants | 74 + 71 = 145* | Walker Cup/Scotland |
| 1967 | D.A. Blair | North Hants | 73 + 68 = 141 | "          " |
| 1968 | M.J. Burgess | West Sussex | 68 + 69 = 137 | England |
| 1969 | B. Critchley | Sunningdale | 70 + 72 = 142 | Walker Cup/England |
| 1970 | D.A. Blair | North Hants | 71 + 68 = 139 | Walker Cup/Scotland |
| 1971 | D.W. Frame | Worplesdon | 70 + 72 = 142 | Walker Cup/England |
| 1972 | R. Revell | Farnham | 70 + 68 = 138 | England |
| 1973 | S.C. Mason | Goring and Streatley | 72 + 70 = 142 | England |
| 1974 | T.J. Giles | Northants County | 73 + 68 = 141 | |
| 1975 | H.A.N. Stott | Nelson | 71 + 70 = 141 | England |
| 1976 | M.J. Hughesdon | Sunningdale | 75 + 66 = 141 | |
| 1977 | A.W.B. Lyle | Hawkstone Park | 70 + 70 = 140 | Walker/Ryder/England |
| 1978 | G.F. Godwin | Thorndon Park | 72 + 69 = 141 | Walker Cup/England |
| 1979 | M.F. Bonallack | Thorpe Hall | 67 + 74 = 141 | Walker Cup/England |
| 1980 | R.A. Durrant | Moor Park | 72 + 68 = 140 | England |
| 1981 | G. Brand Jr. | Knowle | 68 = 68 | Walker/Ryder/England |
| 1982 | A. Sherborne | Long Ashton | 71 + 72 = 143* | England |
| 1983 | I. Gray | Army | 72 + 68 = 140 | |
| 1984 | J. Hawksworth | Royal Lytham | 69 + 71 = 140 | Walker Cup/England |
| 1985 | A. Clapp | Harpenden | 67 + 70 = 137 | |
| 1986 | R. Eggo | L'Ancresse | 70 + 72 = 142 | Walker Cup/England |
| 1987 | A. Rogers | Ealing | 69 + 73 = 142 | England |
| 1988 | S. Richardson | Lee-on-the-Solent | 69 + 67 = 136 | Ryder Cup/England |
| 1989 | P. McEvoy | Copt Heath | 68 + 72 = 140 | Walker Cup/England |

THE HAMPSHIRE HOG 1957–2003

| 1990 | J. Metcalfe | Arcot Hall | 69 + 67 = 136 | England |
| 1991 | M.L. Welch | Hill Valley | 69 + 68 = 137 | England |
| 1992 | S. Graham | Ham Manor | 71 + 66 = 137 | |
| 1993 | D.J. Hamilton | East Herts | 71 + 70 = 141* | |
| 1994 | B.S. Ingleby | Royal Cinque Ports | 69 + 67 = 136 | |
| 1995 | J.P. Rose | North Hants | 69 + 65 = 134 | Walker Cup/England |
| 1996 | R.C. Tate | Meon Valley | 68 + 69 = 137* | |
| 1997 | G.P. Wolstenholme | Kilworth Springs | 68 + 67 = 137* | Walker Cup/England |
| 1998 | P.J. Rowe | West Cornwall | 67 + 67 = 134 | Walker Cup/England |
| 1999 | C. Rogers | Royal Mid-Surrey | 70 + 65 = 135 | England |
| 2000 | M.A. B.Booker | Royal Mid-Surrey | 66 + 67 = 133 | (shortened course) |
| 2001 | J.W. Lupton | Middlesbrough | 69 + 67 = 136 | (new course) England |
| 2002 | G.P. Wolstenholme | Kilworth Springs | 66 + 66 = 132 | Walker Cup/England |
| 2003 | M. Sell | Wrag Barn | 71 + 67 = 138 | England |
| | E. Vernon | Burton-on-Trent | 69 + 69 = 138 | |

* After play-off

In 1981 the morning round was cancelled because of an overnight fall of snow.
In 2003 the result was a tie due to lack of light for extra holes.

*Hampshire Hog – Bonallack to Bonallack – Winners 1957-1979*

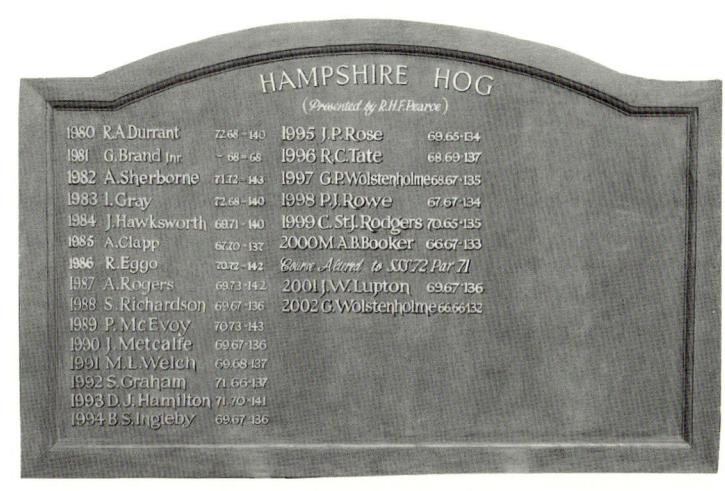

*Hampshire Hog – Winners 1980-2002*

161

*Chapter Eleven*

# New Holes, New Clubhouse
## 1995–2004

For most golf clubs a centenary is but a celebratory pause in their affairs. For North Hants Golf Club its timing has coincided with dramatic change. Three new holes were opened for play in April 2001 and the magnificent new clubhouse was formally opened by Sir Euan Anstruther-Gough-Calthorpe on 20th September 2003. This final chapter of the history of the Club marks the end of one century and the beginning of the next in more ways than just a neat coincidence of dates.

The new lease that guaranteed the future of the Club and course may have been signed by Len Woods in January 1995, but its full implementation was to face some frustrating delays. In particular, within six months of its signature, the Estate discovered to its dismay that insufficient land had been acquired to meet the detailed specification of the access road at the point where it crossed behind the 2nd green and 3rd tee. The shortfall was ten metres and to rectify this the Club was asked to agree to a modest variation in the boundary.

This unexpected request presented the Environment Committee with a number of options including a complete renegotiation of the compensation provisions. After due consideration the Committee sensibly decided to seek an accommodation by negotiating a number of improvements in the terms of the existing lease and agreement in return for accepting the necessary variation in the boundary. The sum of £200,000 allowed in the original agreement for the cost of building the new holes was proving to be seriously underestimated and a more realistic figure of £340,000 was agreed. Secondly, some irksome provisions in the new lease were removed and, thirdly, all professional fees incurred during the renegotiation were recovered in full.

These improvements were eventually agreed but for a number of reasons mainly concerned with planning requirements, the negotiations proved to be protracted and it was not until three years later in January 1998 that the captain, Graham Pool, signed the variation documents, so concluding a process that had taken eight years to complete. Lucky chance had finally put right the failure to buy the Club in 1979.

Just as the signing of the revised lease and agreement was delayed, so as a consequence was the rebuilding of the three new holes. The Estate was paying for the cost of course alterations, but was not able to authorise work to begin until planning approval for the Railroad Heath project as a whole had been granted.

Some clearance of the densely overgrown and wooded areas around the lake had begun in 1994 to enable Donald Steel, the appointed golf course architect, to produce some provisional plans for the new holes. Once the variation documents had been signed in January 1998, the first stage was to build a new and temporary green for the shortened 2nd hole, a par four of 335 yards, which would serve for some two years from May 1999 to April 2001. Together with the shortening of the 3rd hole at the same time the course was briefly reduced to 6,129 yards and for many members the round started with little more than three drive and pitch holes. Meanwhile the outlines of the new 3rd and 4th fairways and 2nd and 3rd greens were beginning to emerge after they were seeded in the spring of 1999.

The feature of the redesigned holes was the new par five 3rd hole, with its new green tucked beyond the lake which had for so long sat largely unseen behind the old 3rd green. It had taken almost one hundred years to make golfing use of this shallow, picturesque lake which had probably been originally constructed for ice-skating.

The particular attraction of this new hole was that it added a second and much-needed par five to the card and created the signature hole that is so fashionable amongst golf architects today. The new and shorter 2nd hole replaced what had previously been the most difficult hole on the course and the extended length of the new 3rd hole allowed the par three 4th hole to be restored to the drive and pitch hole that it once had been. Since the opening of these holes, the course has been further lengthened with new back tees at the 15th and 17th holes.

The new holes were opened for play on 1st April 2001 with a teams of four competition spread throughout the day with two scores to count, attracting a huge entry, followed by a celebration party in the evening. As the captain, John Drake-Lee, put it in his Newsletter "the competition was fittingly won by the Greenkeepers' team". Perhaps more strangely, on the basis that the older you are the less you like change, the prize for the aggregate scores of all four members of a team over the three new holes was won by a veteran group of your author, Philip Mitchell, Michael Armstrong and Neil Jones, who joined the Club in 1951, 1952, 1956 and 1967 respectively.

*Opening of the new holes, April 2001. Winners, holes 2, 3 and 4 competition: Philip Mitchell, Michael Armstrong, Neil Jones and John Littlewood*

The new 3rd and 4th holes have undoubtedly added great visual attraction to the course, not only when playing them but also from the lovely views of them opened up from the 7th fairway. The new par five would have been a magnificent challenge before the days of metal woods and modern golf balls. The pity is that today it is little more than a five or six-iron to the green for so many of today's long-hitting golfers. As is the way with modern design, deeply undulating greens, sometimes referred to as "buried elephants", have been provided for the new 2nd and 3rd greens although they are somewhat out of character with the existing greens.

With the completion of the three new holes, the Club lays claim to the input of a proud list of famous golf architects. James Braid laid out the course in 1904, Harry Colt substantially redesigned it in 1913, Tom Simpson made alterations in 1929 and Donald Steel added new holes in 2001.

Meanwhile, two new Sub-Committees were formed to deal with future planning. In September 1996, a Centenary Committee was formed to consider all aspects of the Centenary celebrations in 2004. Its membership was Eric Carpenter as chairman with Gillian Hawkins and Graeme Ricketts, together with the captain and vice-captain each year as ex-officio members. Designing a new clubhouse to satisfy the wishes of a membership of some 750 is by any stretch of the imagination a daunting task. The responsibility was given to a

*Portrait for the Captain's weekend by Eric Carpenter – John Bermingham (1993)*

*Portrait for the Captain's weekend by Eric Carpenter – David Wheeler (2000)*

Development Committee in September 1998. Its membership was initially the captain and vice-captain, ex-officio, then respectively Brian Gallagher and Derek Skillin, the chairman of the House Committee, the late Ed Horgan, and two co-opted members. These were Vic Kite, a career architect who made a tremendous contribution to the project, and Graeme Ricketts, who continued to offer the property expertise of his late father. The Development Committee continued its work throughout the whole project to completion and other members who served on it included as successive chairmen the Club captains, David Wheeler, John Drake-Lee, Alan Hathaway and Alan Ryder together with Robin Hudson and Harry Row and the Ladies' captain of the year.

To deal with the complicated financial and taxation issues arising from the compensation and its negotiation, the Development Committee formed a separate Financial Sub-Committee. This was chaired by Derek Skillin and its members were Chris Bull, Roy Goodliffe, Tim Hanson and Bob Wyatt. These two Committees were to spend many hours in meetings of all kinds and the Club owes so much to the dedication of those who served on them.

The first task of the Development Committee was to consider the alternatives of either a major refurbishment and extension of the existing clubhouse or the construction of an entirely new clubhouse. The instinct of the majority of the members was that the existing clubhouse had served its purpose and it was time for a larger and more modern building with bigger and better facilities. This history of the Club has already reported several campaigns for a new clubhouse, stretching as far back as 1931 and 1938, but the old clubhouse had been a tenacious survivor and even with the capital available to finance a new building, there were many long-standing members who strongly preferred to refurbish, extend and retain its particular character.

The Development Committee canvassed the views of six firms of architects in the selection process which eventually led to the appointment of Norman and Dawbarn and their advice came firmly down in favour of a new building. At the Annual General Meeting on 27th March 1999, the first to be held in the much bigger arena of the Harlington Centre in Fleet, the captain, Brian Gallagher, explained the decision:

Having taken plenty of advice from various good sources.....it had been concluded that the old building that we all knew and loved would, most regretfully, have to go. However emotionally attached members were to it, however much its character and its atmosphere was admired, it had little intrinsic architectural merit and had been altered and tinkered with over the years. It was a maintenance headache which was already disproportionately expensive and could only become more so.

He further emphasised that its close location to the main road presented a serious practical problem for security, for ease of entrance and exit routes and in particular for the much needed expansion of both changing rooms and catering facilities.

After time given to members to raise many points, Brian Gallagher closed the debate by concluding that "he felt from the tone of the meeting that there was general support for the Executive Committee's move to provide a new clubhouse". Responsibility for taking matters forward now passed to the new captain, Derek Skillin, whose career background in property and finance was particularly relevant for the task ahead.

At this stage the amount of compensation remained strictly confidential and it was not until July 1999 that Derek Skillin was able to write to all members to bring them fully up to date. In that letter he revealed for the first time that compensation would be payable in two instalments – £1.9m in the spring of 2001 and £1.76m within a further seven years. The Executive Committee believed that only a tiny minority of the members had any interest in a distribution of the compensation and recommended in the letter that a new clubhouse should be built, particularly after receiving a recently commissioned structural survey which supported the abandonment of the existing clubhouse. Members were invited to write with comments and suggestions which would be considered in a series of architectural briefs being developed and in due course a presentation of the architect's initial design proposals would be made to all members.

This presentation was made to some 250 members at a well-attended and disciplined meeting in the Harlington Centre on 8th March 2000. At this meeting Derek Skillin was able to announce that the Club was in hopeful negotiations for the compensation to be in the form of a more practical single payment of £4.452m on 31st January 2001, agreement of which was quickly achieved literally over the next few days. The architect's plans had been on display in the clubhouse and the proposal was for a long, low building with a preference for its location to be pitched at an angle across the corner formed by the visual outer boundaries of the 1st and 18th holes. It was an enthusiastic meeting with a long and constructive question and answer session. With regard to the detailed design of the clubhouse, there was debate about a snooker room, the size of the basement and the extent of staff accommodation. It was no surprise that only two weeks later in his report to the Annual General Meeting Derek Skillin was able to say that "It had been a well-attended event and a show of hands had overwhelmingly supported the further progressing of the scheme".

Would it be so easy. The much-loved 1st hole was to prove to be the grain of sand in the oyster. In the detail of the preferred location of the new clubhouse across the angle of the 1st and 18th holes it would be shortened to a par three and a vociferous groundswell of opinion built up through the summer months in favour of saving the 1st hole. Indeed, for some members it is their first choice as the signature hole of the course. The tee is probably in as close proximity to the main entrance of the clubhouse and full gaze of the members as any to be found. At a mere 277 yards in length, it has always been a friendly prelude to a sterner task ahead, well bunkered, but offering the chance of a birdie and, for long handicapped golfers, the rare opportunity to be one under par. On the other hand with modern equipment it had become somewhat out-dated and reducing it to a par three would restore the balance of four short holes.

These strong feelings gathered enough pace for the Executive Committee to decide in September 2000 to consult the entire membership with an opinion survey on this and other questions relating to the new clubhouse because, as the new captain, David Wheeler, put it in his letter to all members "The location of the new clubhouse and the future of the 1st hole are issues which are arousing passionate and opposing views".

The survey elicited a remarkable response from more than 70 per cent of the men members and 75 per cent of the lady members. In particular the answer to the question relating to the retention of the 1st hole showed opinion to be hopelessly divided. To help resolve the matter the proposed location was staked out and from this it became gradually apparent that it encroached too near to the 18th green to be a practical proposition. In November 2000, the captain, David Wheeler, reported that, as a result of the survey, the preferred location would not be pursued and that the Executive and Development Committees were now reassessing both the position and the design of the new clubhouse.

That well attended and encouraging meeting in March 2000 now seemed to be a rather distant event. A new location to the right of the 1st tee was agreed in March 2001, but this required a new design for the clubhouse on a smaller footprint and a longer planning process with the authorities because of greater tree losses. At least the new accommodation area for the greenkeepers and their machinery was able to proceed unhindered and this was completed early in 2002. The 1st tee had apparently been saved, but the interruption undoubtedly put back the whole process by some twelve to eighteen months and, with building rates rising annually at around eight per cent, added some £250,000 to the eventual cost.

Planning permission was eventually obtained, the design put out to tender and the contract awarded in June to Collier & Catley, a Reading firm of contractors with experience of clubhouse building. As the building began it again became apparent that the location of the existing 1st tee would cause problems of safety and also of circulation to and from the course. The hole was reduced to a par three with consideration to be given to extending it to a par four at a future date. The overall result is that the course has been lengthened from 6,257 to 6,432 yards, the par increased from 69 to 70 and the standard scratch score from 70 to 72.

Work began on the new clubhouse in July 2002 and was completed in fourteen months. It is a magnificent building with grey slate tiles and a distinctive architectural feature of the turret above the domed roof to the dining room. It has a magnificent setting which offers a sweeping panoramic view of the golf course from the practice putting green across to the 1st green. However, the course and the clubhouse have not been the only changes occurring as the Centenary approached.

The Ladies' section of the Golf Club has come to play a much more influential role in the Club, reflecting a wider social change. For many decades the Club was ahead of events in giving lady members the right to vote at General Meetings, but in the last few years the widespread golf club tradition of ladies paying a reduced subscription in exchange for limitations on playing rights has come under legislative attack. The Club has been well aware of this and discussions on equal rights began with the Ladies' section in 1998. At North Hants the ladies paid a subscription set at eighty per cent of the rate for ordinary members and in return agreed not to play on Saturdays and Sundays before 11.30 a.m.

The first stage was to extend ex-officio representation to the ladies on the official Sub-Committees and at the 2000 Annual General Meeting the rules were changed to allow the Lady captain to be an ex-officio member of the Executive Committee. On the question of equal rights and subscriptions the ladies carried out an opinion poll in 2000 which showed forty-nine to be in favour and thirty-two for the status quo. Partly as a result of this but primarily to pre-empt inevitable legislation, the Executive Committee introduced equal subscriptions and playing rights for lady members from January 2001. The Ladies' section continues to run their own administration for handicaps, competitions, matches and membership and although all are now ordinary members, the current ratio of gentlemen and lady members of approximately four to one will be maintained. The long-standing contribution played by the ladies in providing constant and beautiful flower arrangements will happily continue.

Another factor influencing change in the Club and in golf generally has been the much greater mutual interest of both husbands and wives in playing golf. Two-thirds of the lady members have husbands who are also members and this has filtered through to competitions and matches. The mixed foursome competition on the Monday afternoon of a Bank Holiday is now a regular feature four times a year, but none appeared in the 1975 diary. The ladies were invited to play for the first time in the Captain's Weekend in 1981. A mixed invitation meeting has been introduced and the traditional matches against other clubs are now as likely as not to be played with mixed teams. On a wider front the Ladies' section inaugurated the North Hants Trophy in 1981 for scratch three-a-side match play knockout for Hampshire golf clubs. North Hants has never won its own trophy but has been runner-up three times, the closest of which was in the inaugural year when Heather Glynn-Jones lost the deciding single at the twenty-sixth hole.

A feature of the Ladies' section over the last fifty years has been the golfing domination of a small number of individual golfers. Judged by the number of times their names appear on the honours boards, the early post-war years were dominated by Gwen Morrison with 62 appearances, then followed by her daughter Mary Morrison with 58 and Heather Glynn-Jones with a record 67. There is currently a close race between Jenny Kershaw with 33 and Dianne Morgans with 32 and they between them have won the Ladies' Club Championship in fifteen of the last sixteen years. Dianne Morgans joined the Club in 1988 after moving from her native Wales, where as Dianne Taylor, she played golf at Newport Golf Club. In 1977 she was runner-up in the Welsh Girls Championship, twice playing for the Welsh Girls team. In 1984, after reaching the semi-finals of the Welsh Ladies Championship, she was selected

*Robin Mallinson, captain (1974), president (1993-96) presents the 1993 Hampshire Rose trophy to joint winners, Angela Uzielli and Claire Hourihane*

*Gerry Cooke, captain (1991)*

to play for Wales in the Home Internationals, but had to withdraw because of her pregnancy.

The lone other winner of the Ladies' Club Championship in 1994 was Di Stock who played off a handicap of 5 and has played for the Hampshire Ladies' second team. Di Stock has been a committed servant to ladies' golf at club, county and national level. She joined the Club in 1978, was Lady captain in 1984 and has been secretary of the Ladies' section since 1986. Within the Club she is well known for the skill of her calligraphy when entering names and scores on the information boards that feature outside the clubhouse in major events. At county level she was president of the Hampshire Ladies' County Golf Association from 1995 to 1997, at the same time that Freddie Parsons was president of the County Golf Union. In 1998 she became a member of the English Ladies Golf Association Executive Committee and chairman of the Rules and Regulations Committee before being elected chairman of the ELGA Executive Committee for the year 2001. Quite apart from these distinctions Di Stock qualified as a referee at the R&A school and has since served at the Curtis Cup and at national championships. This dedication to the cause of ladies' golf was acknowledged by the Club when Di Stock was made an Honorary Member in 2002.

Di Stock now organises the Hampshire Rose which celebrated its thirtieth anniversary in 2003 and continues to thrive. Over the years it has been won by eleven different Curtis Cup golfers and Clare Hourihane, Jill Thornhill and the late Angela Uzielli each won it three times. Pride of place goes to Angela Uzielli who was one of its greatest and most regular supporters. She set a course record of 67 when she won in 1985 and in addition to her three victories was also runner-up three times and in third place five times.

We live in a world today where whatever the game, interest or hobby, there are more people pursuing it and the faster are the changes happening within it. Golf is no exception. In the space of a few years competitions added to the fixture list have included Texas scrambles, Shotgun Foursomes in the summer evenings and Early Bird team competitions at 6.00 a.m. That challenging form of golf, the foursome, has sadly lost some appeal and has been widely replaced in competitions and matches by four-balls, greensomes and fensomes. However, it survives in two important and popular long-standing match play competitions, the Founders Foursomes for men and the Stronach Cups for mixed foursomes. There are now two Octogenarian meetings each year which attract some fifteen entries. Another new feature are the unofficial roll-up competitions, which began on a Saturday morning, but have now spread their net to different groups of supporters on Mondays, Wednesdays and Fridays.

*Pat Kay with Heather Glynn-Jones, donor of the trophy, presents the Hampshire Rose to Kate Egford in 1991*

The numbers of matches played has grown dramatically. The Stoics, which began as a league of home and away matches with five clubs in 1983 have, despite frequent minutes to the effect that no further matches would be allowed, now expanded their fixture list to twenty home matches, mostly on a Friday. The number of visiting societies remains at very high levels, although almost entirely confined to Tuesdays and Wednesdays. The result of this expansion in matches and competitions is a fixture calendar that rarely has a day free of a reserved tee time and a golf course now subject to levels of wear and tear from daily play that were never once envisaged.

The Stoics, the Octogenarians and the weekday roll-ups reflect one of the biggest recent changes in the life of the Golf Club which is that earlier retirement and longer living have now often made the typical weekday busier than those Saturdays and Sundays when there is no competition. It has also combined to make the average age of the membership gradually older and almost one-quarter of the men are eligible to play in the Stoics, even after its age qualification has been raised from fifty-five to sixty.

This expansion of golfing activity can be illustrated by reference to the number of days marked down for a golfing event in the Club fixture cards. The following table compares the Club diaries of the fiftieth and seventy-fifth Jubilee years of 1954 and 1979 together with 2003.

|  | 1954 | 1979 | 2003 |
|---|---|---|---|
| Competitions – Men/Junior | 33 | 30 | 62 |
| Competitions – Ladies | 30 | 32 | 52 |
| Competitions – Mixed | 1 | 5 | 13 |
| Total | 64 | 67 | 127 |
| Home Matches – Men | 12 | 17 | 19 |
| Home Matches – Stoics | – | – | 20 |
| Home Matches – Ladies | 10 | 7 | 18 |
| Home Matches – Mixed | 1 | – | 2 |
| Total | 23 | 24 | 59 |
| Society Matches | 17 | 7 | 5 |
| Society Days | 19 | 65 | 81 |
| Total | 123 | 163 | 272 |

The entry sheets for many of the men's competitions today are completely filled with 144 competitors. The Society matches which featured strongly in 1954 were mostly inter-regimental matches of eight-a-side played on a Saturday or Sunday at a time when the weekend was the prime time for playing golf and the course was fairly deserted midweek. These weekend matches began to intrude too frequently and were gradually discouraged.

Their place has been taken by the growing post-war phenomenon of the Golfing Society playing midweek, some bringing together like-minded members with a golfing pedigree, but many providing little more than a day out for corporate guests and employees of very mixed ability. Societies have always been a bone of contention for the members of any golf club and particularly at North Hants where the facilities of the old clubhouse were liable to be swamped. However, they have been generally limited to Tuesdays and Wednesdays since 1975, they generate revenue that would otherwise

## HAMPSHIRE ROSE
*(Presented by the Clifford Family)*

| Year | Name | Score | Year | Name | Score | Year | Name | Score |
|---|---|---|---|---|---|---|---|---|
| 1973 | Miss C. Redford | 146 | 1987 | Mrs. J. Thornhill | 143 | 2000 | Miss K. Fisher | 138 |
| 1974 | Mrs. P. Riddiford | 153 | 1988 | Mrs. J. Thornhill | 144 | | *Course Altered to SSS73 Par 73* | |
| 1975 | Miss V. Marvin | 151 | 1989 | Miss A. MacDonald | 135 | 2001 | Miss K. Smith | 146 |
| 1976 | Miss H. Clifford | 149 | 1990 | Miss C. Hourihane | 144 | 2002 | Miss K. Smith | 138 |
| " " | Miss W. Pithers | 149 | " " | Miss S. Keogh | 144 | | | |
| 1977 | Miss J. Greenhalgh | 144 | 1991 | Mrs. K. H. Egford | 146 | | | |
| 1978 | Mrs. H. Glynn-Jones | 148 | 1992 | Mrs. A. Uzielli | 139 | | | |
| " " | Miss V. Marvin | 148 | 1993 | Miss C. Hourihane | 142 | | | |
| 1979 | Mrs. C. Larkin | 147 | " " | Mrs. A. Uzielli | 142 | | | |
| 1980 | Miss B. New | 146 | 1994 | Mrs. K. H. Egford | 141 | | | |
| 1981 | Mrs. J. Nicolson | 144 | " " | Miss K. Shepherd | 141 | | | |
| 1982 | Mrs. J. Thornhill | 145 | 1995 | Miss J. Oliver | 141 | | | |
| 1983 | Miss J. Pool | 142 | 1996 | Miss K. L. Stupples | 141 | | | |
| 1984 | Mrs. C. Caldwell | 143 | 1997 | Mrs. S.B.F. Sanderson | 142 | | | |
| 1985 | Mrs. A. Uzielli | 140 | 1998 | Miss C.J. Court | 141 | | | |
| 1986 | Miss C. Hourihane | 141 | 1999 | Miss C.J. Court | 69 | | | |

*Hampshire Rose honours board*

require higher subscriptions and they help make catering a viable operation. The scale of the increase from 1979 to 2003 is understated because in 2003 there were many more occasions when two smaller societies were accommodated on the same day.

Social events have also emerged in new and different forms. The annual events combining golf and dinner have generally prospered, in particular the Dinner Cups and the Captain's v. Vice-Captain's match and a more recent change has been to change the Pheasant Phoursomes into an England v. The Rest match. The Twelfth Night Dance was for many years the only purely social fixture in the calendar. There is now a thriving annual Burns Supper, the Captain's Weekend, numerous quiz and bridge evenings, themed suppers and racing evenings. The better facilities of the new clubhouse should encourage a further widening of these evening events.

The pressure of demand for membership has continued unabated for the last thirty-five years with the waiting lists often remaining closed for years at a time. The lists were last closed in 1996 when they were completely swamped with 164 applicants and were not re-opened until 2001 by which time the list had fallen to around 60. One factor in the equation is that the Club has frequently claimed to have the best golf course in the vicinity and yet at the same time has boasted of having a lower annual subscription than its local

*Recent Gold Medallists – Martin Farmer (2001), Mark Richardson (2002) and Ashley Sharpe (2000)*

rivals. This is a contradiction of the long-standing motto that "you get what you pay for" which has never really applied to playing golf at North Hants.

Subscription increases have often been justified by reference to their still being lower than elsewhere rather than reflecting the quality of the golf course. In the past there may have been a defensiveness about the rather modest clubhouse facilities, but one consequence has been a greater reliance on societies. In the Appendix there is a 100 year record of the basic annual subscription for the full ordinary member.

Demography is playing its part with members now living to much greater ages. The Octogenarians have thriving numbers and the recently introduced tradition of nonagenarians being given honorary status produces a steady trickle of new claimants each year. The average age of the ordinary membership is now a rather alarming sixty-one and it will inevitably continue to rise unless some form of discrimination is applied to the selection process for the election of new members.

The recent golfing achievements of the Club have been wholly dominated by the wonderful career of Justin Rose, highlighted in an earlier chapter. The Club has feasted on his successes, but take these away and the last decade or more has been short of individual success at higher levels. The proudest achievement in fact has been in the non-playing field where Lionel Smith has

## Club Captains

*David Best (1995), Don Waddington (1988) and Charles Donovan (1982)*

*Graham Pool (1997) and Brian Gallagher (1998)*

*Derek Skillin (1999) and chairman of the Development Committee, and Alan Hathaway (2002)*

*Bruce Squirell, (1987)*

*North Hants wins the Border League, 2003. Martyn Griggs (team captain), Neil Johnson, Ashley Sharpe, Alan Ryder (Club captain), Neil Chittenden, John Mathis*

captained Hampshire to win The Daily Telegraph South-Eastern County Leagues in 2000, 2001 and 2002. Even more impressively, Hampshire qualified in 2002 to be one of the four counties competing in the national County final, where they were runners-up to the ever powerful Yorkshire team. In its long history this was Hampshire's sixth appearance in these finals, but only in 1996 had the county won the title and on that occasion Justin Rose had been a member of the winning team.

At team level there have been some recent successes. The Juniors won the County Greenjackets title in 1995 and 1999. Under the captaincy of Martyn Griggs, the Club won the Border League in 1993, 1996 and 2003 and came close in the County Sevens as runner-up in 1994 and in third place in 1995. Martyn Griggs makes two unusual claims. He has an eclectic score of 35 on the old course, consisting of a 1 at the 1st and a 2 at every other hole and, having played with him several times, he placed a bet of £10 at 1000–1 against Justin Rose, then aged thirteen, winning a major before the age of twenty-five.

At Club level, the most successful golfer has been Martin Farmer. He learned to play golf at Bramley Golf Club, beginning at the age of ten with left-handed clubs for the first two years. He joined North Hants in 1978 and between 1983 and 2001 won the Gold Medal a record nine times,

# NEW HOLES, NEW CLUBHOUSE 1995-2004

*Peter Stanbrook, captain (1996) and Martyn Griggs*

*Golfing doctors – Roland Aubrey and John Drake-Lee, captain (2001)*

to which he has added an impressive collection of scratch and handicap match play titles. Ashley Sharpe added two further Gold Medals in 1999 and 2000 to his two teenage victories many years earlier in 1977 and 1978 and his former teenage colleague, Nick Green, won Gold Medals in 1989 and 1991.

There are always some golfing quirks to remember. In his year of captaincy, Derek Skillin enjoyed the pleasure of a hole-in-one at the 8th on 2nd September 1999, only to discover the extraordinary coincidence that on the same day Gillian Staley holed out at the 4th and Lucy Bermingham at the 15th. Holes-in-one recorded at three different holes on the same day must be a rare event.

In an earlier chapter another rare event was highlighted of having the same secretary, professional, head greenkeeper and house manager in place for an entire decade. Time will always tell and this sequence was first broken in September 2001 when Roy Goodliffe decided to retire, followed in October 2002 by Gerry Halliwell.

*Alan Ryder, captain (2003)*

Roy Goodliffe faced the difficult decision of either retiring in 2001 or committing himself to continuing for at least another three years until the completion of the new clubhouse and the Centenary celebrations. Not unreasonably at the age of sixty-three he decided that it was time to settle into retirement in Dawlish and clear the desk for his successor to prepare for a busy three years. He had been a quite outstanding secretary for fourteen years with a fine reputation that spread widely across the secretarial grapevine. He was also a competitive golfer who would represent the Club well in those occasional gatherings involving club secretaries, but his most exciting memory was leading his team of four in a Texas scramble on to the 8th tee, where he took the honour and promptly holed-in-one, leaving his three team members with nothing to do.

The Club was pleased to welcome Gordon Hogg as his successor in September 2001. He hails from Northumberland where he played golf to a high standard at county level before moving south to be secretary at Burhill and briefly at Copt Heath in Birmingham. He carried the responsibilities of the move to the new clubhouse with unruffled aplomb.

Gerry Halliwell retired largely for health reasons in October 2002 after thirteen years as steward and house manager. He has returned to live in Somerset where he spent his earlier career years and he was succeeded by Brian Hassett, his assistant since 1999. He in turn has warmed to the challenge of greater responsibilities.

The Club has been fortunate in its many captains. Over the 100 years from 1904 to 2003 there have been seventy club captains. The longest in office happened to be the six years of Mr.T. Wilks from 1914 to 1919, followed by Reg Pearce with four years and Sir Paul Pechell with three. There have been many examples of captains serving for two years, particularly during the inter-war and immediate post-war years, but since Freddie Parsons in 1979 and 1980, all captains have served for one year, probably reflecting the much greater executive and playing responsibilities that the office involves today.

*Bob Wyatt, vice-captain (2003)*

A glance at the list of captains shows how they have reflected the changing character of the Club. In many of the earlier and middle decades the names were dominated by those drawn from the armed services. There have been twenty-two from the Army, together with Major General Pat Kay from the Royal Marines, the late Air Vice-Marshall Dick Ubee and Group Captain Charles Donovan from the Royal Air Force and Commander Brian Gallagher from the Royal Navy. However, the pattern has changed significantly in recent years with only three captains hailing from the services over the last twenty-one years.

Two notably good golfers to have served as captain in recent years have been Bruce Squirrell in 1987 and Peter Stanbrook in 1996. Bruce Squirrell, a lifelong British Airways pilot, was at his best a prodigious hitter of a golf ball who once drove the 14th green, although he is quick to point out that it was in a following gale. He has obtained a rare albatross at the 17th when he holed his second shot which contributed to his eclectic score on the old course of 40. Peter Stanbrook joined the Club in January 1981 and made an immediate impression by winning the Gold Medal a few months later with a total of 145 that included two 3s at the 16th. He remains a competitive golfer who takes a constructive interest in the activities in the Club.

*Eric Carpenter, captain (1984), president (2003–) and chairman of the Centenary Committee*

The early years within the ranks of the Lady captains were dominated by Elizabeth Wild, who was Lady captain on twelve occasions including eight successive years from 1931 to 1938 and Carrie Stronach for eight years from 1939 to 1946. In the very early years of the Club, Mr. and Mrs. Algernon Nugent and the Honorable and Mrs. Charles White were captains together in 1906 and 1907 respectively and since then five couples have served as captains, but in different years. These are Jack and Carrie Stronach in the 1940s and, more recently, Eric and Pam Carpenter, Gerry and Iris Cooke, Graham and Pam Pool and Bruce and Brenda Squirrell. In a variation of this theme, Roland and Sylvia Aubrey served together as members of the Executive Committee in the early months of 2003.

Within the space of a few months, the Club celebrates both the opening of the new clubhouse in September 2003 and the Centenary in May 2004. The master-minding of these two momentous events has placed additional responsibilities on willing shoulders, not least those of the members of both the recent and current Executive Committees. Alan Ryder as captain in 2003 committed himself whole-heartedly in his year of office, applying his considerable computer skills in many ways and hitting as fine a shot as anybody can remember when driving into office. Bob Wyatt has been his vice-captain and, all things being equal, will be captain for the Centenary year. As a powerful hitter of the golf ball, he will probably be driving in with as short a club as is likely to be seen for many a year. He has brought to the Club his practical experience as a successful banker and his seemingly inexhaustible reservoirs of enthusiasm. Their two names are joined with the president of the Club, Eric Carpenter, who over the last seven years has led the Centenary Committee through the detailed planning of the celebrations in May 2004.

The opening ceremony of the new clubhouse was a splendid occasion blessed by the warmth of a lovely sunny autumnal day. It was attended by some three hundred members and guests who spilled out on to the spacious patio to hear the captain, Alan Ryder, touch upon the earlier days of the Club's history before introducing the principal guest, Sir Euan

Anstruther-Gough-Calthorpe, great-great-grandson of Lord Calthorpe, the first president of the club in 1904. Sir Euan spoke warmly of the strong relationship over the last one hundred years between his family and the Club and at 6.00 p.m. he cut the tape to open the new clubhouse. He then proceeded to unveil a commemorative plaque in the front entrance where, in honour of the occasion, he was presented with an engraved silver trowel.

Members and guests explored and appreciated the spaciousness and quality of the facilities of the new clubhouse, enjoying champagne and canapes, listening through the evening to a traditional jazz band and taking to the new dance floor. The new clubhouse was off to a fine start.

Golf club historians face a particular dilemma as their story unfolds to the present day. It is easy to sing the praises of members past or long retired, but more difficult to write about members present. However, if any current member has epitomised the spirit of the Golf Club as it approaches its Centenary, it could well be Charles Donovan, who has given dedicated service to the Club as captain and president, played golf to a single figure handicap and enjoyed great popularity as an after dinner speaker. After an Oxford education interrupted by the Second World War, there followed a long career rising to Group Captain in the Royal Air Force which culminated in active involvement behind the scenes during the Falklands War as Air Intelligence Chief. He joined North Hants as a service member in 1968 and was a member of the Executive Committee in 1974 and from 1977 to 1980, becoming vice-captain 1981 and captain in 1982. He was elected vice-president from 1997 to 2000 and president from 2000 to 2003.

His lowest golfing handicap was 8 and he has fond memories of Tony Duncan and Barry Armstrong as foursomes partners. All that is enough in its own right, but for a countless number of members he will be best remembered for his friendly smile and for his wit and impeccable timing as speaker and raconteur at many a Club dinner. He has many party pieces but one of the favourites which members never tire of hearing is the simplest of stories about the Accrington Stanley Silver Band.

The scene is a village to the north of Accrington, the Lancashire town, whose ill-fated football team, Accrington Stanley, was always good for a laugh for comedians, particularly those hailing from the north. A small cottage is set on the side of a hill with a gate and path. A young man is collecting and his knock on the door is answered by a little old lady:

> "Good morning, mother, I'm collecting for the Accrington Stanley Silver Band"
> "What did you say young man ? You'll have to speak up. I'm hard of hearing"
>   (louder) "I'm collecting for the Accrington Stanley Silver Band"
> "I can see your lips moving, young man, but I still can't hear you"
>   (shouting) "Have you any money for the Accrington Stanley Silver Band?"

"Nay, lad, it's no use. I can't hear you"
The young man gives up and walks back down the path
"Don't forget to shut the gate, young man"
   (mutters) "To hell with the gate"
"Aye and to hell with the Accrington Stanley Silver Band."

This is a lighter moment but it is a part of the history of this remarkable Golf Club. A theme of this history is that North Hants Golf Club has closely mirrored the history of golf over the last one hundred years. It began as an expression of the interests of the few who played golf in the south of England during the Edwardian era that preceded the First World War. It retained this exclusivity through the inter-war years, but after the Second World War it opened its doors to a much wider membership. Along with many other courses built on open heathland, the golf course has changed in character. Trees have been allowed to grow and the course is less exposed to sun and wind. The greater use of fertilisers and the introduction of automatic watering have encouraged the stronger growth of grass on fairways and greens.

At the same time the Club has developed its own distinctive history. The course is linked with some of the finest names in the history of golf course architecture. In the middle decades its image was closely related to the army and the services. It has played an important part in amateur golf where its name is linked closely with the Hampshire Hog and the Hampshire Rose and with the contribution of individual members to the administration of golf at both county and national level. In the post-war years it attracted a membership that has included as fine a complement of famous amateur golfers as any. It has enjoyed the presence of two English Ladies' Amateur champions and the youngest ever Walker Cup golfer, now an outstanding young talent in professional golf at a world level.

This is the heritage that North Hants Golf Club takes forward into the next one hundred years. It is a heritage of distinction and excellence because the Club has achieved the balance of a thriving, active and cheerful membership within whilst, at the same time, looking outwards to the wider golfing world. Within a couple of decades or so recollections of the original layout of the course and memories of the old clubhouse around which this entire history has been written will, for the large part of the membership, have faded away. They will only know the new holes and the new clubhouse. May these be a springboard for a second century of excellence and distinction.

# Appendices

## Presidents

| | | | |
|---|---|---|---|
| 1904–1910 | The Lord Calthorpe | 1987–1990 | Lt. Col. W.B.J. Armstrong |
| 1911–1957 | Sir F.H. Anstruther-Gough-Calthorpe Bt. | 1990–1993 | Maj. Gen. P.R. Kay |
| | | 1993–1996 | R.J.C. Mallinson |
| 1957–1981 | Brig. Sir R.H. Anstruther-Gough-Calthorpe Bt. | 1996–1997 | P.M.G. Ricketts |
| | | 1997–2000 | Lt. Col. F.A. Parsons |
| 1981–1984 | Major D.A. Blair | 2000–2003 | Gp. Capt. C.P. Donovan |
| 1984–1987 | Air Vice-Marshal S.R. Ubee | 2003– | E.J. Carpenter |

## Club Captains

| | | | |
|---|---|---|---|
| 1904 | Major W.F. Anstey | 1947 | Lt. Col. K.D. Barbour |
| 1905 | Col. F. Darling | 1948 | Lt. Col. K.D. Barbour |
| 1906 | A.J.F. Nugent | 1949 | J.W. Nelson |
| 1907 | Capt. Hon. Charles White | 1950 | E.H. Curling |
| 1908 | F.N. Harvey | 1951 | E.H. Curling |
| 1909 | F.N. Harvey | 1952 | Lt. Col. Sir Paul Pechell Bt. |
| 1910 | J.M. Gibson Carmichael | 1953 | C.W. Neate |
| 1911 | J.M. Gibson Carmichael | 1954 | C.H. Clifford |
| 1912 | C. Armytage Moore | 1955 | R.H.F. Pearce |
| 1913 | W.M. Meredith | 1956 | R.H.F. Pearce |
| 1914-19 | T. Wilks | 1957 | Lt. Col. Sir Paul Pechell Bt. |
| 1920 | S.L. Bullock | 1958 | Lt. Col. Sir Paul Pechell Bt. |
| 1921 | Brig. Gen. O.C. Herbert | 1959 | R.H.F. Pearce |
| 1922 | Brig. Gen. O.C. Herbert | 1960 | R.H.F. Pearce |
| 1923 | Major Sir H.R. Cayzer Bt. MP | 1961 | Col. Sir Harold Smith |
| 1924 | Major Sir H.R. Cayzer Bt. MP | 1962 | Col. Sir Harold Smith |
| 1925 | F.H. Anstruther-Gough-Calthorpe | 1963 | Col. N.C.E. Kenrick |
| 1926 | F.H. Anstruther-Gough-Calthorpe | 1964 | Air Vice-Marshal S.R. Ubee |
| 1927 | Lt. Col. Lord Dorchester | 1965 | Air Vice-Marshal S.R. Ubee |
| 1928 | Lt. Col. Lord Dorchester | 1966 | Lt. Col. A.G.R. Noble |
| 1929 | H.D. Rendall | 1967 | R.W. Bellamy |
| 1930 | H.D. Rendall | 1968 | Major General W.A. Lord |
| 1931 | A. Thomson Clark | 1969 | Major N.H.D. Pratt |
| 1932 | A. Thomson Clark | 1970 | Major N.H.D. Pratt |
| 1933 | A.C.W. Fosbery | 1971 | Lt. Col. J.L.G. Littlejohns |
| 1934 | Maj. Gen. C.L. Gregory | 1972 | Lt. Col. W.B.J. Armstrong |
| 1935 | Maj. Gen. Sir J.R. Longley | 1973 | Major General H. Quinlan |
| 1936 | Maj. Gen. Sir J.R. Longley | 1974 | R.J.C. Mallinson |
| 1937 | F.H. Greig | 1975 | T.F. Daniels |
| 1938 | F.H. Greig | 1976 | T.F. Daniels |
| 1939 | Ian S. Fraser | 1977 | P.M.G. Ricketts |
| 1940 | Ian S. Fraser | 1978 | P.M.G. Ricketts |
| 1941 | J.L. Stronach | 1979 | Lt. Col. F.A. Parsons |
| 1942 | J.L. Stronach | 1980 | Lt. Col. F.A. Parsons |
| 1943 | Col. H.L.F. Grant | 1981 | Major General A.E. Walkling |
| 1944 | Col. H.M. Mackenzie, | 1982 | Gp. Capt. C.P. Donovan |
| 1945 | Col. E.G. Hamilton | 1983 | H.J. Lewis |
| 1946 | Col. E.G. Hamilton | 1984 | E.J. Carpenter |

| | | | | |
|---|---|---|---|---|
| 1985 | J.D. Cook | | 1995 | T.D. Best |
| 1986 | Major General P.R. Kay | | 1996 | P.H. Stanbrook |
| 1987 | B.L.G. Squirrell | | 1997 | G.S. Pool |
| 1988 | Major D.C.K. Waddington | | 1998 | Cdr. B.C. Gallagher |
| 1989 | P. Breedon | | 1999 | D.R. Skillin |
| 1990 | I.H. Johnston | | 2000 | D.R. Wheeler |
| 1991 | A.G. Cooke | | 2001 | J.W. Drake-Lee |
| 1992 | J.B.J. Lidstone | | 2002 | A.J. Hathaway |
| 1993 | J.P. Bermingham | | 2003 | R.A. Ryder |
| 1994 | L.H. Woods | | | |

## Lady Captains

| | | | | |
|---|---|---|---|---|
| 1905 | Mrs. Palmer | | 1965 | Mrs. M. Lang |
| 1906 | Mrs. Nugent | | 1966 | Mrs. M. Trentham |
| 1907 | Hon. Mrs. C. White | | 1967 | Mrs. Marwick |
| 1908 | Mrs. J.G.L. Searight | | 1968 | Mrs. G. Morrison |
| 1909 | Miss Chinnock | | 1969 | Mrs. F.G.M. Bebb |
| 1910 | Miss Bridges | | 1970 | Mrs. N. Orr |
| 1911 | Miss B. Partridge | | 1971 | Miss S.M. Keene |
| 1912 | Mrs. E.M. Hill | | 1972 | Miss E.M. Sellors |
| 1913 | Mrs. Haines | | 1973 | Mrs. K.G. Fraser |
| 1914–18 | Mrs. Porter | | 1974 | Mrs. E.M. Marshall |
| 1919 | Miss B. Partridge | | 1975 | Mrs. E. Carter |
| 1920 | Miss E. Wild | | 1976 | Mrs. J. Yeo |
| 1921–22 | Mrs. Bent | | 1977 | Mrs. M. Jayne |
| 1923 | Miss E. Wild | | 1978 | Mrs. B. Knight |
| 1924 | Mrs. Pilkington | | 1979 | Mrs. P.J. Carpenter |
| 1925 | Miss E. Wild | | 1980 | Mrs. D. Jewell |
| 1926 | Miss B. Partridge | | 1981 | Mrs. E. Byrne |
| 1927 | Miss M.R. Dorman | | 1982 | Miss O. Colthurst |
| 1928 | Mrs. G. Stapledon | | 1983 | Mrs. H. Glynn-Jones |
| 1929 | Miss E. Wild | | 1984 | Mrs. D. Stock |
| 1930 | Miss McCleverly | | 1985 | Miss C. White |
| 1931–38 | Miss E. Wild | | 1986 | Mrs. I. Cooke |
| 1939–46 | Mrs. Stronach | | 1987 | Mrs. M. Smart |
| 1947 | Mrs. D. O'Dwyer | | 1988 | Mrs. P. Pool |
| 1948 | Miss L.M. Nelson | | 1989 | Mrs. M.B. Restall |
| 1949 | Miss O. Colthurst | | 1990 | Mrs. E.P. Kanka |
| 1950 | Mrs. G. Morrison | | 1991 | Mrs. B. Squirrell |
| 1951–52 | Miss E. Sellors | | 1992 | Mrs. M. Lawson |
| 1953 | Mrs. A.D'A. Willis | | 1993 | Mrs. K.M. Cook |
| 1954 | Mrs. C.H. Clifford | | 1994 | Mrs. J. Shakespear |
| 1955 | Mrs. E.G.S. Gray | | 1995 | Mrs. J. Edmonds |
| 1956 | Mrs. R.F. Bateman | | 1996 | Mrs. M.J. Roberts |
| 1957 | Mrs. J. Orr | | 1997 | Mrs. B.E. Fox |
| 1958 | Mrs. Bird | | 1998 | Mrs. C. McGillivray |
| 1959 | Mrs. A.D'A. Willis | | 1999 | Mrs. A. Yates |
| 1960 | Mrs. M. Quicke | | 2000 | Mrs. A. Coombe |
| 1961 | Mrs. Harte | | 2001 | Mrs. G. Hawkins |
| 1962 | Mrs. S. Cowie | | 2002 | Mrs. L.K. King |
| 1963 | Mrs. J.G. Mathewson | | 2003 | Mrs. S.A. Aubrey |
| 1964 | Mrs. L.M. Davidson | | | |

## Secretaries

| | | | |
|---|---|---|---|
| 1904–06 | Capt. J.S. Bridges | 1953–62 | Charles Neate |
| 1906–09 | Lt. Col. J.B. Newbury | 1962–63 | Tom Pratt |
| 1909–23 | W. Bailey | 1963–68 | Max Holles |
| 1923–25 | F. Dunn | 1968–72 | George Dickinson |
| 1925–26 | J. Deakin Yates | 1972–73 | James Marshall |
| 1926–27 | Capt. H.W. Inglis | 1973–78 | Neil Brown |
| 1927–46 | Lt. Col. W.G. Huskisson | 1978–84 | Nigel Lockyer |
| 1946–46 | P. Brailsford | 1984–86 | Keith Symons |
| 1946–47 | Cdr. K.J.T. Southgate | 1986–87 | John Gostling |
| 1947–49 | Col. E.G. le Patourel | 1987–2001 | Roy Goodliffe |
| 1949–51 | Lt. Cdr. H.N. Sheffield | 2001– | Gordon Hogg |
| 1951–53 | Ron Bellamy | | |

## Professionals

| | | | |
|---|---|---|---|
| 1904–06 | J.W. Moore | 1945–45 | Jack Sidey |
| 1906–07 | C. Hope | 1946–76 | Bob Mounce |
| 1907–12 | J. Tickle | 1976–82 | Tim Gowdy |
| 1912–15 | J.H. Oke | 1983–83 | Hugh Boyle |
| 1919–45 | Abe Sibbald | 1983– | Steve Porter |

## Head Greenkeepers

| | | | |
|---|---|---|---|
| 1910–53 | Alf Hindley | 1965–66 | Jack Cranford (acting) |
| 1953–58 | Fred Silver | 1966–87 | Bill Brown |
| 1958–58 | Ern Gregory | 1987–88 | Allan Sharp |
| 1958–65 | Sid Fullbrook | 1988– | Nigel Stainer |

## Ladies Scratch Championship

| | | | |
|---|---|---|---|
| 1981 | Miss J. Pool | 1993 | Mrs. J. Kershaw |
| 1982 | Miss J. Pool | 1994 | Mrs. D. Stock |
| 1983 | Mrs. H. Glynn-Jones | 1995 | Mrs. D. Morgans |
| 1984 | Mrs. H. Glynn-Jones | 1996 | Mrs. J. Kershaw |
| 1985 | Mrs. H. Glynn-Jones | 1997 | Mrs. J. Kershaw |
| 1986 | Mrs. H. Glynn-Jones | 1998 | Mrs. D. Morgans |
| 1987 | Mrs. H. Glynn-Jones | 1999 | Mrs. J. Kershaw |
| 1988 | Mrs. J. Kershaw | 2000 | Mrs. J. Kershaw |
| 1989 | Mrs. D. Morgans | 2001 | Mrs. J. Kershaw |
| 1990 | Mrs. J. Kershaw | 2002 | Mrs. D. Morgans |
| 1991 | Mrs. J. Kershaw | 2003 | Mrs. D. Morgans |
| 1992 | Mrs. J. Kershaw | | |

## Gold Medal

| Year | Name | Score | Year | Name | Score |
|---|---|---|---|---|---|
| 1905 | G.M. Archdale | 78 | 1961 | N.B. Alexander | 71 |
| 1906 | W.K. Whigham | 83 | 1962 | J.F. Burnett | 69 |
| 1907 | Capt. Keller | 85 | 1963 | C.ff. Churchill | 75 |
| 1908 | O.T. Falk | 84 | 1964 | M. Blanford | 75 + 77 = 152 |
| 1909 | F.N. Harvey | 86 | 1965 | T. Koch de Gooreynd | 71 + 78 = 149 |
| 1910 | F.V.H. Hutchings | 76 | 1966 | L.O.M. Smith | 72 + 75 = 147 |
| 1911 | E.J. Dobson | 74 | 1967* | T. Koch de Gooreynd | |
| 1912 | G.M. Melville | 84 | 1968 | M. Blanford | |
| 1913 | C.A. Moore/E.J. Dobson | 80 | 1969 | T. Koch de Gooreynd | |
| 1919 | G.S. Hughes | 82 | 1970 | S.D.R.W. Brewis | |
| 1920 | H.A. Tapsfield | 80 | 1971 | R.H.P. Knott | |
| 1921 | Lt. Col. H.O. Smithers | 87 | 1972 | G.R.H. Pearce | |
| 1922 | F.M. Allen | 86 | 1973 | G.P. Rideout | |
| 1923 | G. Hamilton | 80 | 1974 | J.N. Littlewood | |
| 1924 | Capt. P.E.D. Pank | 82 | 1975 | L.O.M. Smith | |
| 1925 | Col. H.O. Smithers | 83 | 1976 | L.O.M. Smith | |
| 1926 | Brig. Gen. O.C. Herbert | 83 | 1977 | A.P. Sharpe | |
| 1927 | J.M.D. Hunter | 88 | 1978 | A.P. Sharpe | |
| 1928 | L.J. Torrie | 87 | 1979 | R.W. Johnson | |
| 1929 | J.F. Stewart | 81 | 1980 | R.W. Johnson | |
| 1930 | L.J. Torrie | 79 | 1981 | P.H. Stanbrook | |
| 1931 | F. Maxwell Allan | 81 | 1982 | G.B.F. Henney | |
| 1932 | J.F. Stewart | 85 | 1983 | M.I. Farmer | |
| 1933 | J.W. Nelson | 76 | 1984 | M.I. Farmer | |
| 1934 | J.W. Nelson | 75 | 1986 | M. Wild | |
| 1936 | J.W. Nelson | 74 | 1987 | A. O'Neill | |
| 1937 | J.W. Nelson | 74 | 1988 | M.I. Farmer | 68 + 69 = 137 |
| 1938 | C.H. Gidney | 77 | 1989 | N.J. Green | 73 + 72 = 145 |
| 1946 | J.H. Piesse | 85 | 1990 | M.I. Farmer | 71 + 67 = 138 |
| 1947 | J.W. Nelson | 83 | 1991 | N.J. Green | 74 + 74 = 148 |
| 1948 | F.H. Hayward | 73 | 1992 | L. Graves | 79 + 70 = 149 |
| 1949 | R.L. Pearcy | 79 | 1993 | M.I. Farmer | 72 + 71 = 143 |
| 1950 | B.W. Parmenter | 72 | 1994 | M.I. Farmer | 72 + 71 = 143 |
| 1951 | H.P. Lock | 75 | 1995 | J.P. Rose | 70 + 71 = 141 |
| 1952 | H.P. Lock | 72 | 1996 | J.P. Rose | 70 + 70 = 140 |
| 1953 | H.P. Lock | 76 | 1997 | M.I. Farmer | 69 + 71 = 140 |
| 1954 | K.S. Barker | 75 | 1998 | J.P. Rose | 68 + 65 = 133 |
| 1955 | H.P. Lock | 75 | 1999 | A.P. Sharpe | 70 + 71 = 141 |
| 1956 | J.N. Littlewood | 74 | 2000 | A.P. Sharpe | 71 + 71 = 142 |
| 1957 | J.ff. Churchill | 72 | 2001 | M.I. Farmer | 72 + 71 = 143 |
| 1958 | W.B.J. Armstrong | 76 | 2002 | M. Richardson | 70 + 71 = 141 |
| 1959 | G.R. Meier | 73 | 2003 | N.A.G. Robbie | 71 + 69 = 140 |
| 1960 | N.B. Alexander | 73 | | | |

*Note : Detailed competition records from 1967 to 1987 have not been retained.

## The Hampshire Rose

| Year | Winner | Club | Score | Status |
|------|--------|------|-------|--------|
| 1973 | Miss C. Redford | Sunningdale | 148 | Curtis Cup/England |
| 1974 | Miss P. Riddiford | Royal Ashdown Forest | 153 | |
| 1975 | Miss V. Marvin | Easingwold | 151 | Curtis Cup/England |
| 1976 | Miss H. Clifford | North Hants | 149 | |
|      | Miss W. Pithers | Royal Mid-Surrey | 149 | |
| 1977 | Miss J. Greenhalgh | Pleasington | 144 | Curtis Cup/England |
| 1978 | Mrs. H. Glynn-Jones | North Hants | 148 | |
|      | Miss V. Marvin | Easingwold | 148 | Curtis Cup/England |
| 1979 | Mrs. C. Larkin | Royal Ashdown Forest | 147 | Ireland |
| 1980 | Miss B. New | Lansdown | 146 | Curtis Cup/England |
| 1981 | Mrs. J. Nicholson | Worplesdon | 144 | Scotland |
| 1982 | Mrs. J. Thornhill | Walton Heath | 145 | Curtis Cup/England |
| 1983 | Miss J. Pool | North Hants | 142 | |
| 1984 | Mrs. C. Caldwell | Sunningdale | 143 | Curtis Cup/England |
| 1985 | Mrs. A. Uzielli | Berkshire | 140 | Curtis Cup/England |
| 1986 | Miss C. Hourihane | Woodbrook | 141 | Curtis Cup/Ireland |
| 1987 | Mrs. J. Thornhill | Walton Heath | 143 | Curtis Cup/England |
| 1988 | Mrs. J. Thornhill | Walton Heath | 144 | Curtis Cup/England |
| 1989 | Miss A. MacDonald | Andover | 135 | |
| 1990 | Miss C. Hourihane | Stoke Poges | 144 | Curtis Cup/Ireland |
|      | Miss S. Keogh | Wyke Green | 144 | |
| 1991 | Mrs. K.H. Egford | Bramshaw | 146 | England |
| 1992 | Mrs. A. Uzielli | Berkshire | 139 | Curtis Cup/England |
| 1993 | Miss C. Hourihane | Stoke Poges | 142 | Curtis Cup/Ireland |
|      | Mrs. A. Uzielli | Berkshire | 142 | Curtis Cup/England |
| 1994 | Mrs. K.H. Egford | Crane Valley | 141 | England |
|      | Miss K. Shepherd | Worplesdon | 141 | |
| 1995 | Miss J. Oliver | Knebworth | 141 | England |
| 1996 | Miss K.L. Stupples | Royal Cinque Ports | 141 | Curtis Cup/England |
| 1997 | Mrs. S.B.F. Sanderson | Berkshire | 142 | |
| 1998 | Miss C.J. Court | Goodwood | 141 | England |
| 1999 | Miss C.J. Court | Goodwood | 69 | England |
| 2000 | Miss K. Fisher | Royal Lytham | 138 | England |
| 2001 | Miss K. Smith | Waterloo | 146 | Curtis Cup/England |
| 2002 | Miss K. Smith | Waterloo | 138 | Curtis Cup/England |
| 2003 | Miss F. More | Chesterfield | 140 | Curtis Cup/England |

|  | Annual Subscription for Ordinary Members (£ s.d./£) | Annual Income Total (£) | Inflation 1905 = 100 | Playing Membership |
| --- | --- | --- | --- | --- |
| 1905 | 4. 4. 0. | 919 | 100 | 215 |
| 1910 | 5. 5. 0. | 1,470 | 105 | 350 |
| 1920 | 5. 5. 0. | 1,852 | 240 |  |
| 1925 | 7. 7. 0. | 3,380 | 195 |  |
| 1930 | 7. 7. 0. | 4,392 | 175 | 530 |
| 1935 | 7. 7. 0. | 3,623 | 160 |  |
| 1940 | 4. 4. 0. | 1,699 | 205 |  |
| 1945 | 4. 4. 0. | 1,916 | 225 |  |
| 1950 | 8. 8. 0. | 2,979 | 255 | 200 |
| 1955 | 10.10. 0. | 4,878 | 335 | 285 |
| 1960 | 14.14. 0. | 7,315 | 385 |  |
| 1965 | 18.18. 0. | 11,182 | 455 | 440 |
| 1970 | 25.00. | 22,713 | 570 |  |
| 1975 | 50.00. | 42,568 | 1,050 |  |
| 1980 | 90.00. | 85,086 | 2,055 | 580 |
| 1985 | 190.00. | 157,949 | 2,910 | 575 |
| 1990 | 302.00. | 274,443 | 3,880 | 600 |
| 1995 | 420.00. | 387,465 | 4,700 | 640 |
| 2000 | 594.00. | 497,604 | 5,250 | 625 |

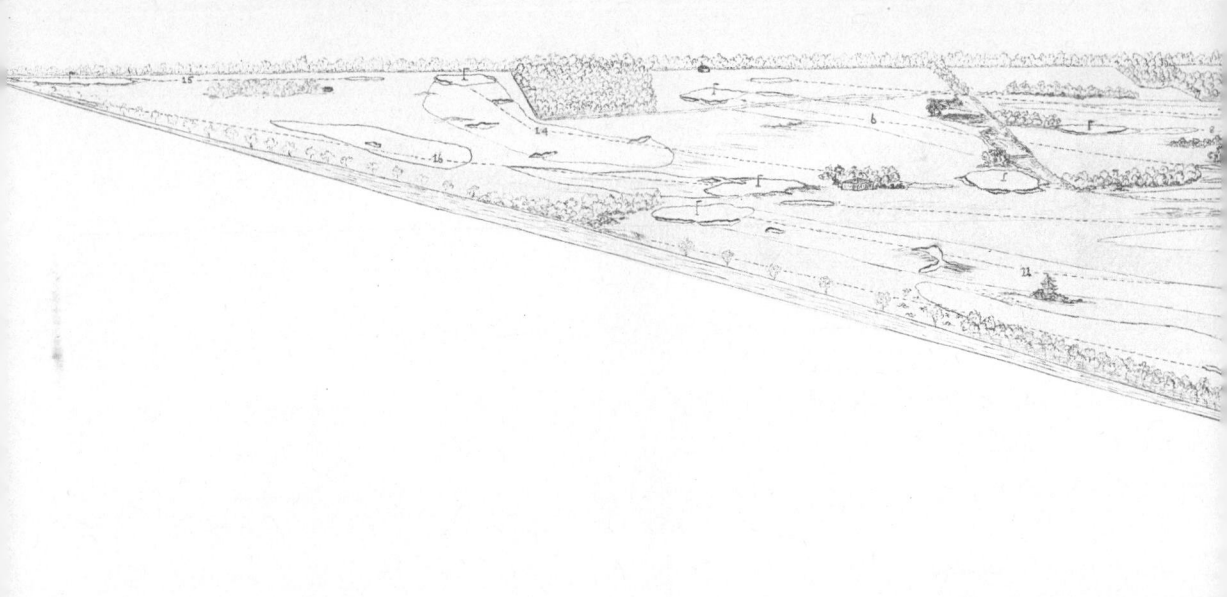

NORTH HANT

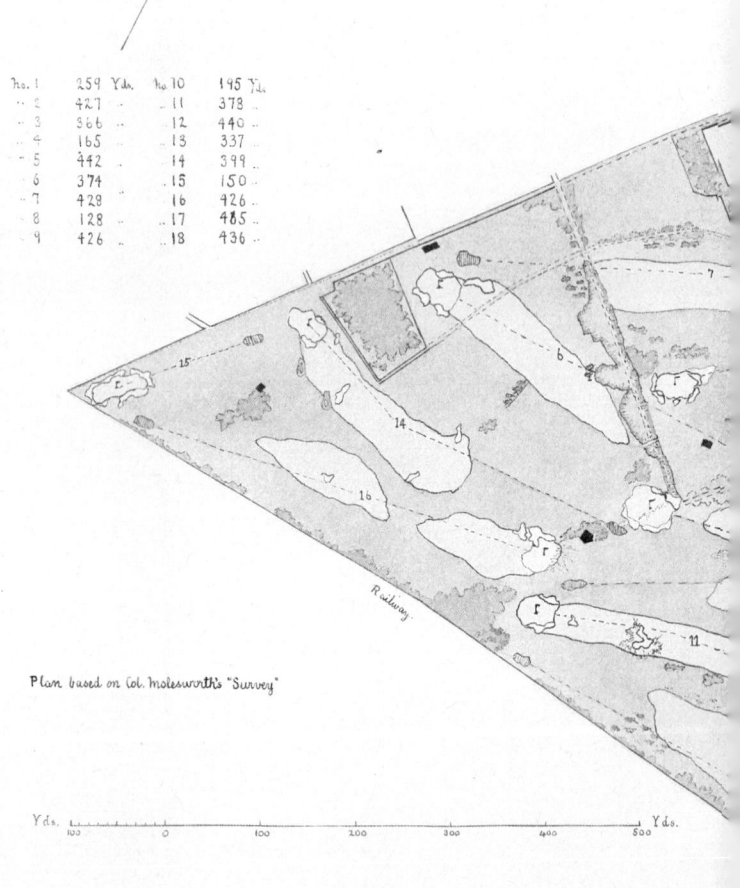

| No. 1 | 259 Yds. | No. 10 | 195 Yds. |
| --- | --- | --- | --- |
| „ 2 | 427 „ | „ 11 | 373 „ |
| „ 3 | 366 „ | „ 12 | 440 „ |
| „ 4 | 165 „ | „ 13 | 337 „ |
| „ 5 | 442 „ | „ 14 | 399 „ |
| „ 6 | 374 „ | „ 15 | 150 „ |
| „ 7 | 429 „ | „ 16 | 426 „ |
| „ 8 | 128 „ | „ 17 | 485 „ |
| „ 9 | 426 „ | „ 18 | 436 „ |

Plan based on Col. Molesworth's "Survey"